Rajesh Lal

Creating Vista® Gadgets

Using HTML, CSS, and JavaScript with
Examples in RSS, Ajax, ActiveX (COM),
and Silverlight™

 800 East 96th Street, Indianapolis, Indiana 46240 USA

Creating Vista® Gadgets: Using HTML, CSS and JavaScript with Examples in RSS, AJAX, ActiveX (COM) and Silverlight™

ISBN-13: 978-0-672-32968-5
ISBN-10: 0-672-32968-9
Library of Congress Cataloging-in-Publication Data

Lal, Rajesh.
  Creating Vista gadgets : using html, css and javascript with examples in rss, ajax, activex (com) and silverlight / Rajesh Lal.
      p. cm.
  ISBN 978-0-672-32968-5 (pbk.)
  1. Microsoft Windows (Computer file) 2. Operating systems (Computers) 3. User interfaces (Computer systems) I. Title.
  QA76.76.O63L3546 2008
  005.4'46--dc22
                              2008016280
Printed in the United States of America
First Printing April 2008

Trademarks

Warning and Disclaimer

Bulk Sales

Sams Publishing offers excellent discounts on this book when ordered in quantity for bulk purchases or special sales. For more information, please contact

    U.S. Corporate and Government Sales
    1-800-382-3419
    corpsales@pearsontechgroup.com
For sales outside of the U.S., please contact
    International Sales
    international@pearson.com

This Book Is Safari Enabled

The Safari® Enabled icon on the cover of your favorite technology book means the book is available through Safari Bookshelf. When you buy this book, you get free access to the online edition for 45 days.

Safari Bookshelf is an electronic reference library that lets you easily search thousands of technical books, find code samples, download chapters, and access technical information whenever and wherever you need it.

To gain 45-day Safari Enabled access to this book:

- Go to http://www.informit.com/onlineedition
- Complete the brief registration form
- Enter the coupon code UWC5-ZPGE-RMIN-P5EG-MSHE

If you have difficulty registering on Safari Bookshelf or accessing the online edition, please email customer-service@safaribooksonline.com.

Associate Publisher
Greg Wiegand

Acquisitions Editor
Loretta Yates

Development Editor
Todd Brakke

Managing Editor
Patrick Kanouse

Project Editor
Jennifer Gallant

Copy Editor
Margo Catts

Indexer
Ken Johnson

Proofreader
Mike Henry

Technical Editor
Marc Clifton

Publishing Coordinator
Cindy Teeters

Book Designer
Anne Jones

Contents at a Glance

Table of Contents

4   Selling Your Gadget   75

Part II   Developing a Gadget

5   Creating a Simple Gadget with RSS/Atom Feed   91

About the Author

Rajesh Lal is an author, technology evangelist, and solutions engineer specializing in web technologies. He has received numerous awards for his articles on Windows Vista and Sidebar Gadgets. He is a frequent contributor to *Windows Vista Magazine* and Code Project websites. With more than a decade of experience in IT industry in progressive roles from graphic designer, software developer, architect, team lead, and project leader to independent consultant, Rajesh enjoys taking an objective and pragmatic approach to developing applications using Microsoft technology. He has a master's degree in computer science and holds MCSD and MCAD titles.

To read his Vista Gadget blog, go to www.innovatewithgadgets.com.

Dedication

Dedicated to Mom & Dad

For Everything I Am

Acknowledgement

Writing is a fascinating journey. I would like to extend my special thanks to Marc Clifton Todd Brakke, and Margo Catts who were along with me on this journey. They corrected, annotated, criticized, and helped me at every step. Thanks also to Joshua Heyer (Shog9) and Rama Krishna for reviewing this book and for their invaluable advice. I also want to add a note of thanks to Dr. Luiji for all the encouragement at the times when I needed it.

I am deeply grateful to Loretta Yates, acquisitions editor at Sams/Que Publishing for her unmatched dedication to quality and progressiveness, without which this book was never possible. Thanks also to Jennifer Gallant, Cindy Teeters, and Rosemary Lewis from Pearson Technology Group.

I would like to extend my appreciation to the folks from Microsoft, for their time and effort to make this book complete in every sense, especially Brian Teutsch, Daniel Moth, and Annuska Perkins. I would also like to thank Rick Kingslan, Karen Wong, and Mark Schmidt.

Last of all, I would like to mention my brothers Rakesh and Rajeev, for all the wonderful things I have learned from them, and Simple and Shilpi for just being so wonderful. And my inspiration and my driving force Neelu.

We Want to Hear from You!

As the reader of this book, *you* are our most important critic and commentator. We value your opinion and want to know what we're doing right, what we could do better, what areas you'd like to see us publish in, and any other words of wisdom you're willing to pass our way.

You can email or write me directly to let me know what you did or didn't like about this book—as well as what we can do to make our books stronger.

Please note that I cannot help you with technical problems related to the topic of this book, and that due to the high volume of mail I receive, I might not be able to reply to every message.

When you write, please be sure to include this book's title and author as well as your name and phone or email address. I will carefully review your comments and share them with the author and editors who worked on the book.

E-mail: consumer@samspublishing.com

Mail: Greg Wiegand
            Associate Publisher
            Sams Publishing
            800 East 96th Street
            Indianapolis, IN 46240 USA

Reader Services

Visit our website and register this book at informit.com/register for convenient access to any updates, downloads, or errata that might be available for this book.

With the broadest ever worldwide release of a PC operating system, in 2007 Windows Vista opened the door to an era of gadget development. Gadgets, which reside on the Windows Vista Sidebar, are small, lightweight, and can be very useful applications. The Sidebar is a brand new platform for innovation and it gives users a unique way to interact with information.

This book is for people who want to create feature-rich and professional-looking Vista Sidebar gadgets. It's a guide for designers, developers, and anyone else who has a basic knowledge of HTML, CSS, and JavaScript and wants to leverage this new and innovative platform. It's for anyone who wants to create a gadget for his company, or for a programmer with a great idea to implement on a Sidebar gadget platform, or even for a hobbyist programmer, who wants to try his hand on a gadget platform. This book is intended to give you ideas for *what* you can do with this new platform and *how* you can do it.

What's in the Book

This book starts with a brief background on gadgets, and then gives a broad and clear view of the architecture of gadget development. Gadget design considerations are an important part of this book and they go side by side with almost all the chapters that deal with gadget development. Once you've read up on the concept and scope of gadget development, the book helps you create a gadget called MyBlog. During this process the text elaborates on the architecture, design constraints, and implementation details for the gadget and then details some standard practices applicable to all gadget development. The last section deals with more advanced gadget examples that utilize .NET, XML, XHTML, CSS, Ajax, and Microsoft Silverlight.

This book is divided into three broad sections.

Section 1: The Foundation

The four chapters in this first section give a thorough background of Sidebar gadgets. The section explains the types of gadgets, the architecture, and the technology behind the gadget development. The "Approach to Design" chapter helps you know the difference between a merely good-looking gadget and a one that is professional, rich, and worth the space it takes up on the user's desktop. The last chapter discusses the revenue model of the gadget: what you need to know to sell your gadgets.

Section 2: Developing a Gadget

This section walks you through the standard development process of a gadget. It details the creation of the basic MyBlog Gadget, which makes use of an RSS/Atom feed. It also goes through best practices with the user interface, design guidelines, and common assumptions. The later chapters improve on the basic gadget based on standard practices and also deal with deploying and distributing a gadget.

Section 3: Advanced Samples

The section deals with advanced samples. You will be able to create advanced gadgets such as a Site Statistics Gadget, a Radio Gadget, and a YouTube Video Gadget. All the samples follow standard patterns, making it easier to switch between the features and functionality you want, when you want. You will also learn how to use ActiveX COM for creating a utility gadget with a sample .Net Most Recent Used (MRU) Gadget. The final chapter shows you how to create a gadget with Microsoft Silverlight. You will also see how, in just a few minutes, to create a Sidebar gadget with Microsoft Popfly.

If you are a relatively new gadget developer, I would suggest you to start with the first section. If you have basic background knowledge of gadgets and you just want to start with the step-by-step practical approach to gadget development, you can directly start with the second section, "Developing a Gadget." The third section, "Advanced Samples," is for people who have developed a gadget and want to go beyond the basics of gadget development. Each chapter in the third section is actually an advanced sample dealing with a particular type of gadget in a scenario of its own.

Special Features and Notations

This book is meant to be a definite, precise, and concrete guide for gadget development. By pruning redundant information and filtering and highlighting the information that is more crucial, we have tried to make it as comprehensive as possible. This book includes various features and conventions that help you get the most out of the book.

HTML, CSS, and JavaScript code blocks will be shown as follows:

```
<HTML>
Code in HTML, CSS, and JavaScript
</HTML>
```

Sample single code lines will look like this:

```
Statement one;
```

```
Statement two;
```

Other comments will also show up in the code with two backslashes

```
// Comment one
// Comment two
```

The book also uses the following boxes for important information:

NOTE

A Note includes extra information to broaden your understanding of a topic.

TIP

A Tip provides alternative, shortcuts, or insider information of the topic being discussed.

CAUTION

A Caution warns you of potential traps and pitfalls.

Supporting Website

The book has a supporting website where you can download all the codes and gadgets. The website also has blogs I have written on Sidebar gadgets and some of my personal views on gadget development. You are invited to check that site and contact me personally. You will also find errata and most updated information there.

Visit www.innovatewithgadgets.com

PART

I

The Foundation

IN THIS PART

Innovate with Windows Vista Sidebar Gadgets

"…the only reason to invest in companies in the future is their ability to innovate…"

—Jeffrey Immelt, CEO, GE

Introducing Gadgets and the Vista Sidebar

For many people, Sidebar gadgets are the coolest new feature in the Windows Vista operating system. Gadgets are small, lightweight applications that reside on the Windows Vista Sidebar or Windows Vista desktop. They provide ready-to-use information and easy access to frequently used features and tools.

Gadgets offer a diverse range of functionality, from giving you an at-a-glance view of your upcoming appointments, to listing online contacts, to displaying a picture slideshow of your Flickr account, to offering an easy way to control your media player. Gadgets can have any number of dedicated purposes. As shown in Figure 1.1, they can be clocks, calculators, games, sticky notes, and more.

FIGURE 1.1   Gadgets can be placed anywhere on the Vista desktop, but most are organized on the Windows Sidebar.

Windows Sidebar

The Windows Sidebar is a pane on the side of the Microsoft Windows Vista desktop and is used to place and organize the gadgets. You can easily customize the Windows Sidebar to suit your preference: always on top or resting below maximized windows. If you don't want to keep your gadgets on the Windows Sidebar, you can drag them to your desktop and hide the Sidebar. The Windows Sidebar can also be activated from the icon in the system tray.

Gadgets can have multiple instances, both in the Sidebar as well as on the Windows desktop, and these can be configured with different settings. For example, you can have two instances of a Clock Gadget, one showing the current time for San Diego, California and the other one for Paris, France.

A Vista Sidebar gadget consists of HTML, CSS, JavaScript, and image files, all coordinated to accomplish a variety of tasks. You can host a mini web page, call a web service, integrate with a business application, or even call operating system APIs to create a custom application.

Technology Behind Gadgets

Gadgets are developed using standard web technologies, namely HTML, CSS, and JavaScript, but they can also use technologies such as DHTML, Ajax, and ActiveX COM for advanced functionalities. A gadget can be thought of as an HTML Application (HTA) with advanced features and properties. All the interfaces used in the gadget, the gadget main window, the settings page, as well as the flyout window, all are HTML pages.

A gadget can also use advanced plug-ins such as Adobe Flash, Windows Media Player, and Microsoft Silverlight. Anything that can be hosted in a web page can be used in gadget development.

Figure 1.2 gives an overview of the technology and related platforms used for gadget development. Most of the technologies overlap in a number of applications.

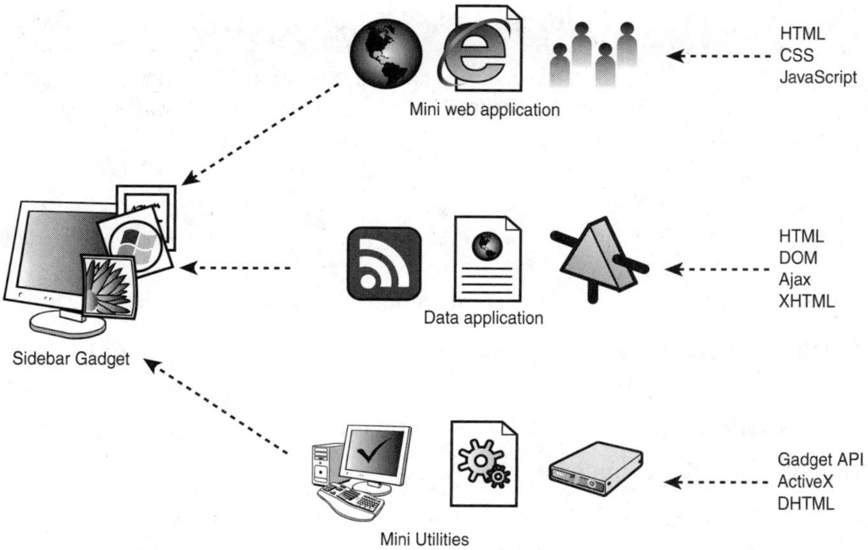

FIGURE 1.2   Different types of applications require different technologies in gadget development.

In the next section we discuss these technologies in more detail.

Different types of applications can be created using Sidebar gadgets:

- **A mini web application**—Mini web applications use HTML, CSS, and JavaScript and can display a small web page from a website or part of the functionality of an existing web application. Or they can just show an existing website on the flyout window.

- **A data application**—Data applications that collect and aggregate data are quite popular nowadays because of the interoperability advantage an XML file provides. XML data is available all over the Internet in the form of RSS/atom feeds, plain XML files, XHTML pages, and web services providing XML data.

  DHTML, XML, XHTML, and Ajax are the tools for development of data applications.

- **A lightweight application that uses the Gadget Object Model and Windows APIs to give shortcuts to frquently accessed tools and features**—Quick information and shortcuts to frequently used features, tools, and applications are also among the attractive options for developing gadgets. You can use gadget APIs to develop utilities, which exposes system functionalities such as hardware information, files and folders, network, memory, CPU, and so on.

Brief History of Gadgets

Windows XP includes a feature called *Active Desktop*, which provides the functionality of hosting web pages and channels built with Microsoft's Channel Definition Format (CDF) on the desktop. This is significant because it provides some of the features now found in desktop gadgets. Vista Sidebar gadgets are the logical evolution from Active Desktop.

NOTE

Channel Definition Format (CDF) is a standard XML file that helps web masters organize their websites. It is used to store website information and image file locations related to a website in a hierarchical format.

More information can be found at http://msdn2.microsoft.com/en-us/library/aa768024.aspx (keyword "Create Channel Definition Format").

Gadgets have evolved as a result of different trends in computing:

- Efficient use of desktop space with respect to the current trend for widescreen monitors/dual monitors

- Better personalization of the desktop experience

- Need for lightweight applications

- New dashboard-style presentation of data, which permits access to a variety of different data sources and formats

Sidebar gadget technology is much more structured than Active Desktop and follows an extensible model. It comes with a full set of APIs to support rich and powerful applications.

Innovate with Gadgets

A Sidebar gadget provides information and interacts with the user in a unique way. It extracts useful information from a variety of sources, an application running in the background, RSS feeds, an enterprise solution, or a web application (see Figure 1.3). There are endless possibilities for what you can do with a gadget.

The gadget platform gives you quick access to both desktop and web applications, which make it a platform on which you can innovate and implement ideas in unique ways. It reduces the gap between useful information and the user by providing information in a ready-to-use format in the Windows Sidebar.

For example, you no longer have to open a website to read news. Instead, a news gadget displays the latest news in your Sidebar; the RSS Reader Gadget makes your favorite blog available at your fingertips.

Some of the things a Sidebar gadget can do include the following:

- Host a web page, read an RSS feed

- Connect to a web service

- Use an online streaming server to play audios/videos

- Provide system information

- Host calculators, games, calendars, and so on
- Connect to an enterprisewide application such as Microsoft SharePoint

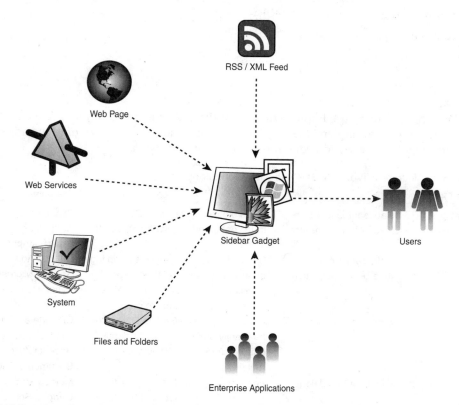

FIGURE 1.3   Gadgets extract information from multiple sources and present it to the user.

Consider an example of a utility gadget. Many users like to know what their CPU utilization is, which up to this point required you to start the Windows Task Manager. With the availability of gadgets in Vista, you need only hold down the Windows key and press the spacebar (the shortcut for showing the Sidebar on the desktop) and then look at the CPU Meter Gadget. If you have a widescreen monitor or dual monitor it's even simpler to just keep the Sidebar and the gadgets you need on display full time.

Imagine an application that can use a native Windows application along with real-time online data, providing you information you want in the way you want it. For example, you might make a Radio Gadget for your favorite radio channel from your hometown, or a media player combined with a real-time streaming audio server, or a section of a web page hosted in a gadget, for which you needed to go to the website. These are some of the time-saving capabilities and fingertip information that make a gadget very useful.

Types of Gadgets

Gadgets can be broadly classified into four major types:

- Information gadgets

- Application gadgets

- Utility gadgets

- Fun gadgets

This classification affects the implementation of the gadget and determines the technology to be used for that implementation. Table 1.1 offers a brief rundown of each gadget type, and the following sections dig into each type in more detail.

TABLE 1.1   Different Types of Gadgets with Technology and Usage

Type of Gadget	Type	Usage	Technologies	Examples
Information	Data source is online feed/XML web service	News/blogs/ traffic data, and so on	HTML, CSS, JavaScript, DOM	RSS Feed Gadget, Live Search Maps
Application	Data from other enterprise applications	Subset features of an enterprise application	Windows Scripting, .VBS, enterprise application APIs, and so on	Outlook Add-on Gadget, Microsoft Dynamics Gadget
Utility	Standalone application	Quick access to frequently used features and tools	Gadget Object Model, Dynamic Link libraries	CPU Meter, Drive Info Gadget, Recent Office Documents Gadget
Fun	Can be a standalone application or get data from an RSS feed	For fun	DHTML, Gadget Object Model, Ajax, and so on	Minesweeper Gadget, Soapbox Video Gadget

Information Gadgets

Information gadgets provide easy access to relevant content from a web page, RSS feed, or web service. Some examples of this class of gadgets are a stock ticker, RSS feed reader, currency converter, or a gadget showing real-time traffic data. Figure 1.4 shows an example of a gadget that tells you the local weather.

The gadget acquires its data from an online web service. You can see the similarities in the data related to the weather of San Diego, in the gadget, and in the website in Figure 1.5.

The Weather Gadget queries the web service located at the URL http://weather.msn.com for data related to the climatic condition of a particular city. The web service returns the current weather information to the gadget in text format. The data is then rendered in the gadget, along with other user-friendly images that are available with the gadget. In the example of Figure 1.4 and Figure 1.5, the city queried to the web service is San Diego, California. And based on the data returned (72 degree Fahrenheit) the image of a bright sun is shown.

FIGURE 1.4   The Weather Gadget is an example of the Information gadget type.

FIGURE 1.5   The Weather web service at http://weather.msn.com provides the data for the current conditions based on location.

Application Gadgets

Application gadgets are those that rely on other applications to get the information required. Examples include an Outlook Gadget that shows upcoming appointments from Microsoft Outlook and a Messenger Gadget that displays online contacts from an instant messenger application (see Figure 1.6). Obviously, these gadgets are not of much use without the main application, but they do serve as valuable tools for quickly accessing baseline information.

The application gadgets shown in Figure 1.6 use Windows APIs and Registry information to get access to frequently used data related to the corresponding application. Most Recent Used (MRU) lists are maintained by the Windows operating system in the Registry.

The Recent Documents Gadget lists the most recently used Microsoft Office documents and the Outlook Appointment Gadget shows the upcoming appointments from Microsoft Outlook.

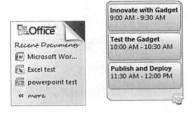

FIGURE 1.6   The Recent Documents Gadget and Microsoft Outlook Gadget provide quick access to current data.

You can access these application-related information sources by using either Gadget Object or ActiveX technology.

Utility Gadgets

Utility gadgets are standalone mini-applications designed to enable fast access to frequently used features such as the CPU Meter, Calendar control, and so forth (see Figure 1.7).

FIGURE 1.7   The Clock Gadget for Time and CPU Meter Gadget showing real-time CPU usage are examples of Utility gadgets.

A utility gadget normally uses the local computer's resources to provide quick access to useful information. These gadgets use Windows APIs to get access to advanced features of the operating system.

Fun Gadgets

Fun gadgets are the most popular kinds of gadgets. Unlike other gadget types, they don't have a specific implementation. They can use an online feed to display interesting information like an information gadget, and even be a standalone game with properties similar to those of a utility gadget. A fun gadget can use images stored in the local computer to display a slideshow and also act as an application gadget. The purpose of these gadgets is to provide fun and entertainment.

They normally take the shape of Utility gadgets and are standalone lightweight applications for fun and games, such as the Minesweeper Gadget. But developers are also creating them as information gadgets and even application gadgets. Developers all over the world are coming up with ideas that combine online feeds, Windows applications, and more for the purposes of making a gadget platform for fun.

Figure 1.8 shows a Video Gadget, which takes an RSS feed from soapbox.msn.com and shows video in a Flash player embedded in the flyout window.

FIGURE 1.8   The Video Gadget gets the data from the RSS feed provided by http://videos.msn.com and plays the media in a Flash Player plug-in.

Ultimately, gadgets are all about enhancing productivity and personalizing the user's experience for visualizing information. They open a world of new and innovative ideas that hasn't been widely exploited on the Windows platform up to this point.

Gadgets in Depth

To understand gadgets in further detail you need to know what the limitations of the gadget are, what gadgets are meant for, and what gadgets are not. You need to know the different views of the gadget and how to customize the gadget.

Some of the topics worth discussion are

- What gadgets are not
- Different views of the gadget
- Opacity level and Always on Top property
- Using flyout for more information
- Other customization options

What Gadgets Are Not

Gadgets are task-specific applications. They aren't designed to replace a fully functional application, but are instead designed to either live on their own with a small set of functionality or complement an application.

As a gadget developer, remember that gadgets are lightweight. There is no need to try and squeeze too much information into a gadget. Just provide the most interesting information to users and then let them go and navigate to a website or an application to examine that information in more depth.

Gadgets are not fully fledged applications, so there are number of things to consider when creating a gadget:

- Gadgets are not executable files.

- Gadgets do not run as individual processes but on the Sidebar pane and can be dragged onto the Windows desktop.

- Gadgets are not available in the Start menu or Task Manager, and cannot be accessed using Alt +Tab keys.

- Gadgets don't have window dialogs with menus, toolbars, or Maximize and Minimize buttons.

- Gadgets are not complete web pages: You cannot navigate links inside a gadget.

Different Views—The Three Hats of the Gadget

Based on the user's choice, the gadget can provide information in three different views:

- **Docked view**—The gadget is placed on the Windows Vista Sidebar (see Figure 1.9). It provides the basic information of the gadget and there is an optional flyout window for more information. This is also the default view of all gadgets.

FIGURE 1.9   Gadgets, when added, are docked in the Vista Sidebar. This is the default state of the gadget.

- **Floating view**—A floating gadget can be dragged from the Sidebar pane to the desktop, which gives a bigger and better view of the information (see Figure 1.10).

- **Multiple view**—You can also have multiple instances of the gadget, both in the Sidebar pane as well as on the desktop. Multiple views are useful when you want information filtered by different criteria displayed in individual instances of the gadget. For example, to compare weather for two different locations, all you need to do is add two instances of the gadget, each customized for an individual location.

FIGURE 1.10   Gadgets can be dragged from the Sidebar and can be placed anywhere in the user's desktop.

Opacity Level and Always on Top Property

Gadgets provide a unique level of customization. When the gadget is in a floating view, you can right-click a gadget and check the Always on Top property (see Figure 1.11). This enables a gadget to remain above all the running windows and makes it more efficient and useful. For example, while running a CPU-intensive application you can see the CPU meter on top of it and monitor the usage in real time.

FIGURE 1.11   The Always on Top property ensures the visibility of the gadget even above maximized windows of other applications.

Gadgets also have an Opacity property, which enables users to customize their opacity levels. The opacity level is defined in terms of percentage. For example an opacity level of 50%, used along with the Always on Top property, gives a translucent effect to a gadget when it is above other applications.

Using Flyout for More Information

Gadgets also have an optional flyout window that can be used for providing further interactive information based on user choice (see Figure 1.12).

A flyout is an excellent tool for displaying additional information related to the limited amount available within the gadget. It also enables the user to interact with the gadget and to navigate to another resource from the gadget. If you click on the desktop or any other window on the desktop, the flyout window automatically hides.

FIGURE 1.12   A flyout window in a Feed Headlines Gadget is used to display details on the feed selected by the user.

Customization

All gadgets have a settings and configuration page that you can access by clicking on Options in the context menu (which is displayed by right-clicking on the gadget) or clicking on the Settings icon as shown in Figure 1.13. The Settings page enables users to customize the gadget the way they want, providing a much more personalized experience. It is particularly helpful when you want multiple views of the gadget with different data.

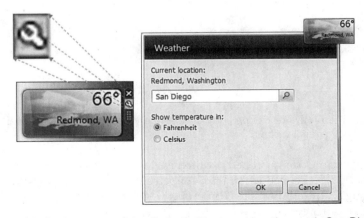

FIGURE 1.13   The Settings page of the Gadget with current location set to San Diego in a Weather Gadget. Note the option for changing the temperature in Celsius or Fahrenheit.

Multiple Platforms for Gadgets

This is fast becoming an era of gadgets. Microsoft gadget platforms have three different kinds of gadgets:

- Sidebar gadget (Windows Vista Desktop)
- Web gadget (Live.com or Live Spaces)
- SideShow gadget (auxiliary hardware devices)

Sidebar gadgets are aimed at the desktop; web gadgets run in a web browser either on the Live.com page or Live Spaces, whereas SideShow gadgets are aimed at auxiliary hardware devices.

Sidebar gadgets use DHTML as a development platform and are meant for the desktop. The gadgets that you write for Windows Sidebar are developed with the Gadget Object Model, which lets you interact with your desktop as well as with web services. They do not run on a web browser, but rather on a Sidebar or desktop as small mini-applications.

The web gadgets are usually understood to reside on Live.com (see Figure 1.14). They are written in DHTML with Ajax libraries. They run with in any web browser and are hosted in either live.com or Live Spaces.

FIGURE 1.14   An example of a web gadget, the Weather Gadget is hosted by the Live.com web page.

NOTE

A web gadget for Live.com and Live Spaces is hosted on a web server rather than a Sidebar and runs inside a browser. Developers develop these gadgets using JavaScript libraries provided by Microsoft, along with the platform to host them. More information on development of Live Gadgets can be found at http://microsoftgadgets.com/livesdk/index.

SideShows are hardware devices that can be found, for example, on the side of a laptop PC (see Figure 1.15), on smart portable devices, or even on mobile phones.

FIGURE 1.15   A Windows SideShow device can be a part of laptop, a smart portable object device, or a cell phone with SideShow capabilities.

SideShow gadgets are written with applications developed with C++ and are more device oriented. A gadget for Windows SideShow is a mini-application running on the PC that sends data to devices with the Windows SideShow platform. The gadget retrieves data from a data source such as an application or web service, and sends this data to the Windows SideShow platform, which sends it to the appropriate devices. A gadget can communicate with the Windows SideShow platform, using one of the following options:

- C++ with SideShow COM APIs
- SideShow-managed APIs with C# or Visual Basic .NET
- Microsoft Sidebar gadget, using the SideShow object model

The SideShow devices are especially interesting because they still function when the laptop is turned off, closed, or in sleep. You therefore have access to information that the Sidebar gadget has sent to the device.

Meeting Points for Different Gadgets

The different platforms on which you can develop different gadgets are also similar in many ways. Their unified goal is to provide quick information from different applications, web services, and XML feeds.

Most of the web gadgets can be tweaked to run as Sidebar gadgets. A widget box is a Sidebar gadget that can include any number of web gadgets in the Sidebar. Check Appendix B for more details on Widgetbox Gadgets.

A Sidebar gadget also can create data on SideShow devices, such that a Sidebar Weather Gadget can send the information to the device on the side of the laptop, as illustrated in Figure 1.16.

FIGURE 1.16   A web gadget can be converted to a Sidebar gadget and a Sidebar can send data to SideShow devices.

The Development Platform

Different gadget platforms use different development platforms:

- Sidebar gadget uses Gadget Object Model, HTML, CSS, and JavaScript.

- Web gadget primarily uses DHTML with the Ajax library.

- SideShow gadget uses C++, SideShow COM APIs, and SideShow-managed APIs with managed code.

Table 1.2 shows a comprehensive chart of the differences between the different gadget platforms.

TABLE 1.2   Gadget Platforms Differ in Use, Technology, and the Target Host

Gadget platform	Target	Use	Technology	Example
Sidebar gadget	Windows Vista desktop	Information at your fingertips	Gadget Object Model, HTML, CSS, JavaScript	RSS Feed Gadget, Live Search Maps
Web gadget	Live.com, Live Spaces	Sharing information between websites	DHTML with Ajax library	HTML Sandbox
SideShow gadget	Laptops, smart devices, auxiliary hardware devices	Accessing information from hardware devices	C++, SideShow COM APIs, SideShow-managed APIs, C#.NET	PowerPoint SideShow gadget

Gadget Ecosystem

Microsoft Gadgets have an online community at http://gallery.live.com, which enables users to browse through the huge number of existing ready-to-use gadgets. The Gallery at Live.com not only hosts all kinds of gadget but also provides dedicated forums for each kind of gadgets, with thousands of users from all over the world. These forums prove to be very useful for interacting with other gadget developers and sharing ideas, problems, and solutions.

Gallery.Live.com also hosts a Developer Center, which provides a Software Development Kit for almost all kinds of gadgets.

Other Desktop Gadget/Widget Platforms

Apart from Microsoft, all the popular internet vendors have their own versions of desktop gadgets. Although the terms *gadgets* and *widgets* are interchangeable and in a broad sense both are used for a small, lightweight applications for accessing remote data, there is a classification based on the environment where they are hosted.

- Desktop gadgets reside on a computer desktop.

- Web gadgets are hosted on a web page.

All major software vendors have their own versions of gadgets. Some of them are called gadgets, some widgets. A number of gadgets work on different versions of Windows.

Figure 1.17 shows the gadgets that work on Windows XP and Windows Vista. Note that AveDesk and DesktopX gadgets work only in Windows XP. On the other hand, Adobe AIR, Yahoo! Widgets, Google desktop, KlipFolio, Opera, and Samurize gadgets work on both Windows XP and Windows Vista. Sidebar Gadget, the topic for this book, works only on Windows Vista.

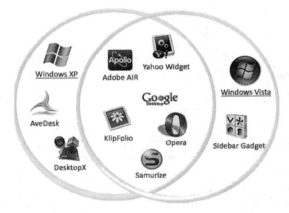

FIGURE 1.17   There are many competing technologies for desktop gadgets.

All desktop gadgets have a common goal: information at the fingertips. The following sections detail a wide range of desktop gadgets/widgets.

Yahoo! Widgets—Konfabulator

Konfabulator is a popular desktop gadget platform from Yahoo!, Inc. Like the Windows Vista Sidebar, Yahoo! widgets also use a pane that can be moved in the desktop and can be used to host number of widgets. More information can be found at http://widgets.yahoo.com/.

Pros:

- Among the first widget platforms, which makes it very popular
- More than 4,000 widgets and a big online community and user base
- Supports both Windows and Mac OS X

Cons:

- Uses a proprietary XML format for development
- Steep learning curve is required to design and develop a widget
- Requires run-times installed in the computer

Apple Dashboard Widgets

Apple's Dashboard is an application that runs on the Mac OS operating system. It hosts a number of widgets that use standard web technologies such as HTML, CSS, XML, and JavaScript for development. As a platform, it is quite popular. More information can be found at http://www.apple.com/downloads/dashboard/.

Pros:

- Based on standard web technologies, JavaScript, HTML, and CSS for development
- Uses existing Ajax libraries and DashCode IDE for writing Dashboard widgets
- Big user base and online community and support

Cons:

- Each widget is a web page, and can take a significant amount of system resources
- Apple's widgets run only on the Mac OS operating system

Google Desktop

Google Desktop started with a desktop search and extended its feature for a Sidebar pane and hosting gadgets. More information can be found at http://desktop.google.com/.

Pros:

- Easy to understand if you know HTML and JavaScript.
- Better platform ties, drag/drop support, and so on.
- Google Gadget Designer, a development tool to write your gadget.
- Not very resource intensive.

Cons:

- Uses its own proprietary XML file, not based on W3C standards.
- Requires download of Google Desktop package.
- Not a great platform for developers.
- No Mac OS X support.

DesktopX Widgets

DesktopX is a widget engine for Windows that was created by Stardock in 2000. It is a desktop enhancement application that helps users add small applications. More information can be found at http://www.stardock.com/products/desktopx/.

Pros:

- Oldest of the group (around 7 years), which makes it a stable, mature platform.
- Integrated COM/ActiveX support.
- Unique animation engine.
- It can export its content as executables.

Cons:

- DesktopX has a run-time version for $14.95.
- You need to download and install the run-time.
- Steep learning curve to create widgets.
- Not a vast developer community.

Samurize Widgets

Samurize is a desktop enhancement engine for Microsoft Windows and is primarily used for tools for system monitoring. More information can be found at http://www.samurize.com.

Pros:

- Easier to create widgets.
- Large library of widgets.
- Lots of easy built in system/network monitoring features.

Cons:

- User interface is more concentrated on features.
- VBScript run-time engine.

KlipFolio Widgets

KlipFolio is a small, personal Dashboard and Sidebar available for Windows XP as well as Windows Vista. More information can be found at http://www.klipfolio.com/.

Pros:

- KlipFolio makes use of files called *Klips* to deliver rich functionality.
- Easily read or parse any XML on the Internet.
- Works on both XP and Windows Vista.
- Great community support, forums, and cookbooks available.

Cons:

- Windows operating system–specific.
- Uses proprietary KlipScript and built-in data structures.
- Steep learning curve for development.
- Need to download and install the engine.

Adobe AIR/Apollo Widgets

Adobe AIR, formerly Apollo, is a cross-platform engine for creating widgets. With AIR, developers can use HTML, Ajax, Flash, and Flex to build and deploy rich Internet applications to the desktop. More information can be found at http://labs.adobe.com/technologies/air/.

Pros:

- Cross platform
- Tight integration with Adobe products Flash and Flex
- Simple development with HTML, JavaScript, and related technologies

Cons:

- Steep learning curve for Flex and Flash
- Primarily meant for creating web applications in the desktop
- Packages whole applications instead of just the widget

AveDesk Widgets

AveDesk is a free widget engine for Windows XP. It's a desktop enhancement application that runs widgets that are called *desklets*. More information can be found at http://www.avedesk.org/.

Pros:

- Community driven.

- AveDesk desklets are powerful plug-ins developed in Visual C++ rather than script.

Cons:

- Users cannot easily create custom-made desklets for AveDesk.

- Supports only Windows XP.

Opera Widgets

Opera is a cross-platform widget technology that works on all popular operating systems and devices. It is developed by Opera Software, based in Oslo, Norway. More information can be found at http://widgets.opera.com/.

Pros:

- Supports many versions of Microsoft Windows, Mac OS X, Linux, FreeBSD, and Solaris.

- Used in mobile devices, game consoles, and interactive televisions.

- Technology from Opera is also licensed by other big software and service vendors.

Cons:

- Opera is proprietary software.

- Development is complex.

Gadget Comparison Chart

With so many different technologies for gadgets and widgets, users have multiple options, without respect to the operating system used. Figure 1.18 shows a world of popular gadgets for different operating systems.

The most important factor that separates Vista gadgets from the herd is that they are based on standard web technologies (that is, HTML, CSS and JavaScript) and do not require a run-time application to be installed. Table 1.3 compares the various gadget/widget platforms (sorted alphabetically).

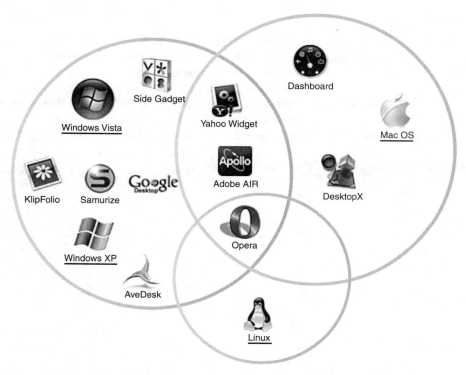

FIGURE 1.18   A lot of different gadget technologies are available for Windows, Mac OS, and Linux.

TABLE 1.3   Comparing the Various Gadget/Widget Platforms

Gadget/Widget	Vendor	Operating System	Technology	License
Apollo	Adobe Inc.	Windows OS, Mac OS	HTML JavaScript, Flash, Flex	Freeware
AveDesk	Andreas Verhoeven	Windows XP	Standard web technologies*, C++	Donation ware
Dashboard	Apple Computer	Mac OS X	Standard web technologies*, C++	Part of Mac OS
DesktopX	Stardock	Windows XP	Standard web technologies*, C++	Shareware
Google Desktop gadget	Google	Windows XP, Windows Vista	Standard web technologies*	Freeware
KlipFolio	Serence	Windows XP, Windows Vista	XML , JavaScript	Freeware
Microsoft Sidebar gadget	Microsoft	Windows Vista	Standard web technologies*, Gadget Object Model, ActiveX	Part of Vista OS

TABLE 1.3   Continued

Gadget/Widget	Vendor	Operating System	Technology	License
Opera	Opera Software	Windows XP, Windows Vista, Mac OS X, Linux	Standard web technologies*	Freeware
Samurize	Gustaf & Oscar Lundh	Windows XP, Windows Vista	JavaScript, C++	Semi-free software
Yahoo Widget	Yahoo Inc.	Windows OS Mac OS	XML, JavaScript	Freeware

Standard web technologies: HTML, CSS, XML, and JavaScript

The Architecture

"The noblest pleasure is the joy of understanding."

—Leonardo da Vinci

Gadgets Overview

A gadget is a set of HTML, XML, JavaScript, CSS, and image files packed into one file. A gadget package with an extension `.gadget` is actually a Zip file that contains these files to run the gadget. Figure 2.1 shows a common layout for a simple gadget.

Normally a gadget contains these folders and files:

- en-US folder
    - `main.html`
    - `Settings.html`
    - `Flyout.html`
    - `Main.js`
    - `Gadget.xml` (with proper mapping)
- Images folder
    - `Dragicon.png`
    - `Logo.png`
    - `Icon.png`

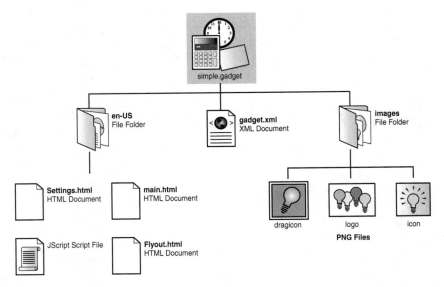

FIGURE 2.1   A gadget contains a few HTML, JavaScript, CSS, and image files.

Table 2.1 explains all the files that come with a gadget. Note that the filenames are not fixed but mapped. Gadget.xml contains the reference to Main.html and other image files and Main.html contains further reference to Settings, Main.Js, and flyout file information.

TABLE 2.1   Different Files in a Typical Gadget

File	Description
Main.html	The main HTML page, which makes the background of the gadget.
Settings.html	Exposes gadget settings for the user to change.
Flyout.html	The HTML file, which will be used for the flyout window.
Main.Js	The core code/script for the gadget.
Gadget.xml	An XML file defining the gadget properties, including name, icon, and description.
Icon.png	For use in the Gadget Picker window.
Logo.png	For display on the lower-right corner of the Gadget Picker window when description is displayed.
Dragicon.png	For display when the gadget is dragged inside the Gadget Picker window.

Figure 2.2 shows Simple Gadget inside Vista's Gadget Picker. Note that the Gadget Picker offers a brief description of the gadget at the bottom of the window.

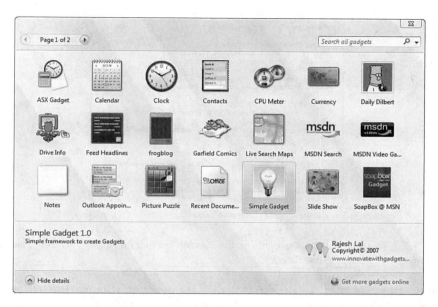

FIGURE 2.2   A Gadget Picker window displays all the gadgets available in the computer in alphabetical order.

The Manifest File `gadget.xml`

The gadget package contains the file `gadget.xml`, which contains all the information needed by the Sidebar to identify and display the gadget, what this gadget is, and how to run this gadget. This is the gadget manifest file. It contains the metadata about the gadget, such as the name, author, information URL, copyright, and so on. The `gadget.xml` file also contains information such as the gadget's icon, the name to display, and any website associated with the gadget. It also contains the reference to an `.html` file that is used to run the gadget.

Figure 2.3 offers a look at the gadget's manifest file. Note the `src`, which is assigned the value `main.html`, decides the gadget's main window.

Most of the parameters in the manifest file are self explanatory; however, Table 2.2 provides further details about some of the parameters of the manifest file `gadget.xml`.

TABLE 2.2   Different Parameters Used in a Gadget's Manifest File

Tag	Description
`<name>`	Name of the gadget as it appears in the gadget selection box.
`<author>`	Name of the person or company that wrote the gadget.
`<copyright>`	Copyright information.
`<description>`	Description of the gadget and what it does.
`<icon>`	Name of the icon file used as the graphic displayed in the gadget selection box.
`<code>`	Name of the HTML file that makes up the gadget.
`<website>`	Website associated with the gadget.

```
<?xml version="1.0" encoding="utf-8" ?>
- <gadget>
    <name>Simple Gadget</name>
    <namespace>Innovate.Gadgets</namespace>
    <version>1.0</version>
  - <author name="Rajesh Lal">
      <logo src="images/logo.png" />
      <info url="http://www.innovatewithGadgets.com" />
    </author>
    <copyright>Copyright© 2007</copyright>
    <description>Simple framework to create Gadgets</description>
  - <icons>
      <icon width="70" height="80" src="images/icon.png" />
    </icons>
  - <hosts>
    - <host name="sidebar">
        <base type="HTML" apiVersion="1.0.0" src="main.html" />
        <permissions>Full</permissions>
        <platform minPlatformVersion="1.0" />
        <defaultImage src="images/dragIcon.png" />
      </host>
    </hosts>
  </gadget>
```

FIGURE 2.3   The Gadget.XML file contains the information that describes and distinguishes the gadget from other gadgets in the Sidebar.

Most of the time, a gadget has three HTML files, for the main window, the settings page, and a flyout window. A gadget can have different style sheet information as well as different JavaScript code files associated with each of these files. Different functionalities can also be encapsulated in different code files. This adds to the complexity of the gadget layout, but helps in the maintenance process. Figure 2.4 shows a layout for such a gadget.

User Interface and Presentation

The structure of the gadget comes from the three HTML pages that make up the user interface:

- Main.html—The gadget's small "home page." You see this page when the gadget is docked in the Sidebar as well as when undocked (displayed on the desktop).

- Settings.html—The page that enables user customization of the gadget. For example, this page would be the one that manages changing the city setting for a weather-based gadget.

- Flyout.html—The HTML page that typically shows information related to the user selection in the main.html page. This is an optional page.

Cascading Style Sheets

Style sheets are normally used to separate presentation of a web page from the structure, that is, the HTML of the page. Cascading Style Sheets (CSS) is used for a similar purpose in a gadget. A CSS file helps in the presentation of the gadget's HTML files. One can encapsulate all the presentation portion of the gadget's HTML pages in a CSS file. An excellent tutorial on CSS and HTML can be found at the following link: http://www.w3.org/Style/Examples/011/firstcss.

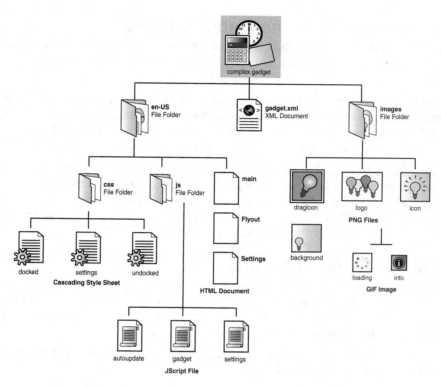

FIGURE 2.4   A complex gadget can have multiple JavaScript and Stylesheet files.

In a typical scenario, a single CSS file helps in the presentation of the main HTML page in the gadget. If the gadget's size changes when the gadget is undocked, having two CSS files, gadget.css and gadgetundocked.css, enables you to change the presentation accordingly.

Different style sheets can be used for the settings page as well as a flyout page. Settings.css is a style sheet for the settings.html page. A flyout can also use a separate CSS file if the flyout presentation is different than the main gadget window.

Style sheet information can also be included in the HTML page itself with a <STYLE> tag, but having a separate CSS file helps in modularity and maintenance in the long run.

The following is a list of different CSS files that can be used in gadget development:

- gadget.css, meant for the main window of the gadget
- undocked.css, used by the gadget when in floating (undocked) mode
- Settings.css, meant for presentation of the settings page
- Flyout.css, for the flyout window

Core Functionality of the Gadget: JavaScript

JavaScript provides the core functionality of the gadget. Structure (HTML) and presentation (CSS) make the bones and the body of the gadget, but it's the JavaScript that adds life to it.

The gadget's core, which makes a gadget dynamic, is one or more snippets of JavaScript code. Normally all these JavaScript files are put together in the js folder. These JavaScript files handle the gadget's functionality and are referenced in the corresponding HTML files (main, settings, or flyout), where the functionality is required.

Other JavaScript files are added for additional functionality, such as updating the gadget through the Internet (autoupdate.js) or adding menus and so on in the Settings.html (settings.js) page. All the CSS as well as JS files are optional; even the names are not hard-wired. Both scripts as well as style sheet information can be included in the HTML page itself, but for modularity are kept in separate files.

Resources, PNG, and Other Files

Images are a very important part of gadget development. They add professionalism to the gadget's look and feel. If you want your gadget to acquire space in the millions of users' desktops, it needs to look good. Images of the gadget are like wallpapers and icons in the computer. Everyone prefers a nice one.

Figure 2.5 shows the images required by a gadget. icon.png, Logo.png, and dragicon.png are found in the Gadget Picker gallery.

The background image is used as the gadget's "wallpaper." It is a semitransparent image that appears in the gadget's background. The loading and info images are typically used for presenting the status to the user. Table 2.3 shows the list of images along with their specific purposes.

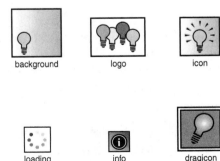

FIGURE 2.5   A typical gadget will contain an icon, a logo, a dragicon, and a background image.

loading.gif and info.gif have very important purposes. The loading.gif file visually informs the user that the gadget is trying to load the data from the Internet, which can be time consuming. Similarly, the info.gif file is used when the data has not loaded or the service is not responding. You'll learn more about using PNG and GIF files in Chapter 3, "An Approach to Design."

TABLE 2.3   Common Set of Images for a Gadget

Title	Purpose
logo.png	Shows up in right corner of the Gadget Picker window, along with description of the gadget.
icon.png	Shows up in the Gadget Picker with the title.
background.png	This is the "wallpaper" for the gadget.
dragicon.png	Dragicon appears in the Gadget Picker window when you drag the gadget.
loading.gif	Meant for displaying the status for some long-running task.
info.gif	Meant to display errors, information, or warnings to the user in the gadget window.

Technology Behind Gadget Development

Gadget development starts with HTML and JavaScript. A basic knowledge of standard web technologies such as CSS, XML, and Document Object Model (DOM Level 1) helps expedite the development process.

DOM Level 1 is a set of specification to access the elements of an HTML page. More information can be found at http://www.w3.org/TR/REC-DOM-Level-1/.

Windows Vista Sidebar exposes a rich Gadget Object Model for gadget development, which is a set of methods to access the files and features of the operating system. This can be used to create gadgets that can access operating system resources. The Gadget Object Model also supports ActiveX technology (COM), which can be further used to extend the gadget's functionality.

Gadget technology can be divided into the following parts (see Figure 2.6):

- The gadget runs as an MSHTML component.

- It uses standard web technologies, HTML, CSS, XML, DOM Level 1, and JavaScript.

- Vista Sidebar exposes a Gadget Object Model for functionality related to the local computer.

- Gadgets also support ActiveX technology (COM) for advanced features.

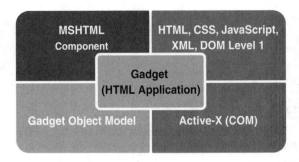

FIGURE 2.6   A gadget is much more than a web page. It can access resources from the local computer, play a media file, or even run an Excel sheet.

MSHTML Component, the Core of the Gadget

The core of the gadget is an inherent object of the Windows Vista operating system called the Microsoft HTML (MSHTML) component. This component provides the hosting capabilities of an HTML page as a miniature web browser page, without any of the associated features such as the address bar, the navigation bar, menus, and so on.

A nice article on MSHTML component can be found at the website for the Microsoft Developer Network (MSDN) at http://msdn2.microsoft.com/en-us/library/bb508516.aspx (or search for it using the keyword "reusing MSHTML").

Gadget developers can use the images, CSS, and JavaScript in a similar way as they do to create web pages. The rich HTML rendering allows for the advanced graphics, user interactions, and cascading style sheets.

Standard Web Technologies

Standard web technologies such as HTML, CSS, and JavaScript make the most of the gadget's structure, presentation, and the behavior. Here is a comprehensive list of the technologies that come together for gadget development:

- HTML
- CSS
- JavaScript/VBScript
- XML/XHTML
- Document Object Model (DOM Level 1)

Document Object Model is the object model of the HTML page that is accessible from the gadget through JavaScript and is used to create dynamic and rich presentations. There is a slight difference between an HTML DOM and the DOM that comes with a gadget. Neither JavaScript alerts nor any kind of modal dialog is allowed in a gadget.

Sidebar Gadget as an HTML Application

A Sidebar gadget is more like an HTML application (HTA) than an HTML web page. A web page cannot access local resources, but HTML applications have access to all the local computer's resources.

The configuration of the core MSHTML component is similar to the set of permissions given to an HTML application or the Local Machine Zone security configuration. This model separates the Sidebar gadget in functionality from a simple web page.

Compared to web pages, gadgets are configured differently in several ways. Gadgets are treated as executable code and they can utilize any installed ActiveX objects. A Sidebar gadget has the Initialized and Script ActiveX Controls option, which, in Internet Explorer, is marked as not safe. Therefore, when programming gadgets, it is important to know the difference between various IE security permissions and any restrictions that apply.

Gadgets can also access data sources across domains: They can aggregate and collect data from multiple websites and web services. Conversely, a local web page trying to access cross-domain data, or another web page, initiates a security warning. Sidebar gadgets can also be made to download and install new ActiveX controls. This feature is disabled in Internet Explorer by default. A gadget can be made to act as spyware or malware, which can compromise the security of the user's computer. See Appendix A for more information on Security.

In contrast to the behavior of web pages, gadgets always

- Run on a secure zone, which means a gadget has permission to access all the system resources.
- Are enabled to initialize and script ActiveX controls without asking the user for permission, as is the case with a web page.
- Can access data sources across domains.
- Are enabled to download and install new ActiveX controls.
- Run with standard privileges and operations.
- Internet Explorer's Protected Mode does not apply.

These configurations in the MSHTML component make gadgets rich in capability, more like typical desktop applications, and for the same reason vulnerable to security issues. A cool-looking gadget can also be a Trojan, which appears to be legitimate, but is designed to have destructive effects. Table 2.3 compares a web page with an HTML application. More information about the HTML application can be found at http://msdn2.microsoft.com/en-us/library/ms536496.aspx.

TABLE 2.3   An HTML Application Is More Powerful Than an HTML Web Page

An HTML Web Page	Gadget as an HTML Application
Cannot access local computer's resources without warning	Can access local computer resources
Cannot access data from different domains	Can access data from different domains, using Ajax methodology
ActiveX controls need to be allowed by the user	No permission required for running ActiveX controls inside HTA
Safe for the user	An HTML application can compromise the security of the user

A gadget coming from an unverified developer can harm your computer. Normally the gadgets that appear on http://gallery.live.com are checked for security-related issues, before they are accepted for public distribution. But gadgets spread all over the Web may not be secure.

CAUTION

As a rule of thumb, if you don't know where the gadget is coming from, don't install it.

Another method is to sign a gadget with certificates to verify its authenticity.

Gadget Object Model

Windows Vista comes with a Gadget Object Model, which is a set of APIs that are exposed to JavaScript, enabling the gadget to interact with the operating system.

The gadget uses these APIs to interact with the operating system within the gadget's pages, to maintain session state, to manage input-output operations, and to access local files and folders in the system. Numerous methods, properties, and functions are available through the Gadget Object Model. The next section discusses the Gadget Object Model and discusses these APIs in detail.

More information on the Gadget Object Model can be found at MSDN keyword "Windows Sidebar Object Reference," http://msdn2.microsoft.com/en-us/library/aa965853(VS.85).aspx.

In later sections we discuss the Gadget Object Model in more detail.

ActiveX Technology

One of the important aspects of gadget development is its support for ActiveX components. ActiveX (COM) technology is used when you need a custom feature available in an already created ActiveX control, or to integrate a custom ActiveX component, such Windows Media Player, inside the gadget. For example, you may want to implement a gadget that displays a part of a Microsoft Excel worksheet in the gadget's flyout window.

An ActiveX component can be integrated in any of the HTML pages inside the gadget, the main window's HTML, the flyout page, or the settings page. Any of the ActiveX controls that are installed in the operating system, or any ActiveX control that you write yourself to interact with your own gadgets, can be used to extend a gadget's functionality.

An ActiveX object can be accessed from a gadget and provides considerable flexibility and power to the gadget:

- ActiveX can be directly embedded in the HTML page.

- Media Player, Microsoft Office, and other Windows applications can be accessed directly from the gadget.

- You can use existing ActiveX COM component by using the method `CreateObject` inside the script.

- You can also create custom ActiveX controls using any technology for use inside a gadget.

Gadget Object Model

The Gadget Object Model exposes a set of APIs available on the Vista operating system (see Figure 2.7). The System Object is the root of all the objects supported in the Sidebar. The available objects and APIs can be divided into four categories:

- APIs for user interaction with the gadget object and Sidebar events

- File system APIs that use the machine and network objects

- APIs for using advanced features with shell and environment objects

- Communication-related APIs for contact and messaging

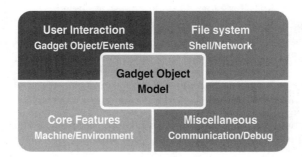

FIGURE 2.7   The Gadget Object Model gives a complete set of APIs to access system resources.

These classes of API are discussed in more detail in the following sections.

User Interaction and Sidebar Events

The Gadget Object Model provides a rich set of methods, properties, and events for user interaction. All these APIs and events can be used inside a script file. User interaction can be divided into the following three sections, which themselves encompass two APIs, and several methods for Sidebar events:

- The core `System.Gadget`

- Sidebar Events

- T Gadget Settings `System.Gadget.Settings`

`System.Gadget` is a namespace that groups all the related APIs for user interaction. It helps the gadget interact with the user by allowing it to respond to user events such as moving the gadget on or off the Sidebar.

Sidebar Events are methods that are called when a particular event occurs in a gadget. These are normally used to set specific properties or user interface changes. For example, if you want to change the size of the gadget when the gadget is undocked (floating on the desktop), you have to use the `OnUndock()` method provided by the gadget.

Events such as `OnDock`, `OnSettingsClosed`, `OnUnDock`, and so on are available through `System.Gadget`. You can see the list of events later in this chapter, in the "Sidebar Events" section.

`System.Gadget.Settings` is used to maintain the session state or information pertaining to the current user. It enables the gadget to interact with various settings. The settings object is particularly important and is most frequently used in gadget development. This is useful to read, write, and update values of local variables and settings.

System.Gadget Objects

Apart from the interaction of a gadget and Sidebar, the Gadget Object Model is also responsible for handling the Sidebar events, settings page, and flyout window, as well as interacting with the SideShow Gadget.

The `System.Gadget` object is further divided into the following subobjects for these operations:

- `System.Gadget`—Used for interaction between the gadget and the Sidebar.

- `System.Gadget.Sidebar`—Used for handling the events and properties specific to the Sidebar, such as the `onDockSideChanged` event.

- `System.Gadget.Flyout`—Used to set the properties of the flyout window.

- `System.Gadget.Settings`—Used to read and write settings.

- `System.Gadget.Sideshow`—Helps to set Sidebar gadget properties and features when the gadget is interacting with SideShow devices.

Sidebar Events

A thorough understanding of the following common gadget events comes in handy in understanding the interaction between the Sidebar and the gadget:

- onDock—When the gadget is docked to the Sidebar, this event is called. It's used to resize the gadget, change images, or even refresh the data.

- onSettingsClosed—This event is useful if the gadget has custom settings and you need to update the gadget with changes to settings.

- onSettingsClosing—This event is triggered when the settings page is being closed. It is useful to save settings and so on.

- onShowSettings—This event fires when the settings page is opened. It's used to initialize defaults or get the current settings from local files or folders.

- onUndock—This event occurs when the gadget is dragged from the Sidebar to the Windows desktop. It's normally used to change the size of the gadget, its image, and so on.

- visibilityChanged—This event fires when the gadget's visibility changes from visible to invisible and vice versa.

Gadget Settings

System.Gadget.Settings is the object responsible for automatically distinguishing between gadgets. A Weather Gadget, for instance, can show weather for San Diego while another instance of the gadget can show the weather for Redmond, WA. This enables the user to create multiple gadgets and the Sidebar remembers which settings are associated with which gadget, automatically.

This object is dependent on the current user's choice and is on a per-user basis. Two important methods are

- System.Gadget.Settings.write("user-variable","value")—This method is used to set a user's reference as a value in a variable.

- System.Gadget.Settings.read ("user-variable")—This method is used to retrieve the same value from the user variable.

These methods are the basis of all the session state management in the gadget development. Please note that there is no setting stored in the local computer; the code in the settings file stores the user's preferences in a session that is managed by the Vista Sidebar.

In the Weather Gadget's settings page, when a city is selected and the user presses OK to close the settings window, the following occurs:

1. The OnSettingsClosing event fires.

2. A variable (for example, WeatherCity) is updated.

3. The variable is set. In this case, it's `System.Gadget.Settings.write`
   (`"WeatherCity"`,`"San Diego"`).

4. When the `OnSettingsClosed` event fires, the gadget's main windows are refreshed
   and updated with the weather related to the selected city—in this case, San Diego. A
   background image is also updated to reflect the current value (see Figure 2.8).

FIGURE 2.8   Two instances of the gadget with different values of the variable `WeatherCity`.

The Vista Sidebar manages the session for the user, even if you close the sidebar or restart
the computer.

APIs to Access the File System

The Sidebar provides the APIs that enable developers to communicate with the file system
and acquire information about the hardware, network, and machine. For example, the
CPU Meter Gadget and slideshow gadgets that come with the Vista operating system are
both great examples of how a gadget uses those APIs rather than ActiveX controls.

The File System API are

- `System.Shell`
- `System.Network`

System.Shell to Access Files and Folders

`System.Shell` provides access to the Windows Vista shell for advanced access to folders,
files, disk drives, and so on. For example, to open a web page, you can call
`System.Shell.execute` with the URL in a couple of different ways.

For example, the following code opens a web browser pointing to the website
www.innovatewithgadgets.com:

```
System.Shell.execute("http://www.innovatewithgadgets.com ");
```

Another example could be to get the path of the Pictures folder (a built-in folder) from
the `System.Shell` object, using the following:

```
var myPicturePath = System.Shell.knownFolder ("Pictures");
```

The `System.Shell.knownFolder` method accepts the following strings and returns the respective folder paths:

- Desktop
- Startup
- StartMenu
- Documents
- Programs
- CommonStartup
- CommonPrograms
- PublicDesktop
- PublicFavorites
- PublicDocuments
- System
- SystemX86
- Profile
- Windows
- Pictures
- Music
- Videos
- ProgramFiles
- ProgramFilesCommon
- ProgramFilesX86
- ProgramFilesCommonX86
- AdminTools
- CommonAdminTools
- PublicMusic
- PublicPictures
- PublicVideos
- UserProfiles
- Downloads
- PublicDownloads
- GadgetsUser
- RecycleBinFolder

The earlier method with the list of strings provides a shortcut to all the frequently used folders in the local computer. This becomes very useful when creating a utility gadget that uses files from different folders.

The `System.Environment` object can also be used to read the path, as in `System.Environment.getEnvironmentVariable ("Folder name")`.

`System.Shell` is further divided into the following objects used to access individual items, folders, the recycle bin, and disk drives respectively:

- System.Shell.Folder
- System.Shell.Item
- System.Shell.Recyclebin
- System.Shelldrive

System.Network

The `System.Network` object is used to determine network connectivity. For example, to access information on a wireless connection, use the following API: `System.Network.Wireless`.

Core Features to Interact with the System

Among other things, operating system functionality, hardware information, and ActiveX controls are handled by these objects:

- `System.Machine`

- `System.Environment`

`System.Machine` is used to determine the machine processor and memory characteristics. For example, if you want to find out the available memory of the computer you can try the `availableMemory` property in the following way inside JavaScript code:

```
VariableforMemory = System.Machine.availableMemory;
```

`System.Environment` is used to determine the information about the system and the logged-in user information. This information is accessed using the `getEnvironmentVariable` method. For example,

```
var tempValue =   System.Environment.getEnvironmentVariable("Temp");
```

gives the path of the temporary folder location of the user Rajesh, which will be `C:\Users\Rajesh\AppData\Local\Temp folder`, if the logged-in user is Rajesh.

The following two APIs are used to access information about the machine hardware and different CPUs on the computer.

- `System.Machine`

- `System.Machine.CPU`

To detect information about the power supply (specifically useful if the machine is operating from battery power), the `PowerStatus` method of the `System.Machine` API is used.

- `System.Machine.PowerStatus`

To access the system's sound and time information the following APIs are available:

- `System.Sound`

- `System.Time`

- `System.Time.TimeZone`

Communication and Other APIs

The Gadget Object Model also supports a set of communication APIs, starting with

- `System.Contact`

- `System.MessageStore`

`System.Contact` and related objects give access to the address book stored in the Contacts database of the local computer. It returns a collection object with all the contacts information.

The following set of APIs allows a gadget to access the information from the Windows Contact data store:

- `System.Contact`
- `System.ContactManager`

`System.MessageStore` gives access to folders collections, which store the emails in the local computer.

The following are useful APIs to access mail and other messages in Windows Mail:

- `System.MessageStore`
- `System.MessageStoreFolder`
- `System.MessageStoreMessage`

Other Miscellaneous Objects

The following two objects are related to debugging and tracing information for a gadget. This object can provide diagnostic capability to a gadget:

- `System.debug`
- `System.Diagnostic.EventLog`

These objects also help to diagnose any error during development of the gadget.

Sidebar Graphic Protocol

The Sidebar gadget also supports a set of objects for presentation in the gadget. They are also called *graphic protocols* and they enable easy access to graphics inside a gadget's HTML pages.

Sidebar has three specific protocols for image manipulations:

- `gBackground`—Background element/object
- `gImage`—Image object
- `gText`—Text object

These methods give you direct access to a lot of image manipulation features.

These gadget-specific protocols are great tools, and give better flexibility in designing gadgets with features such as

- Dynamic generation of thumbnails
- Alpha transparency
- Manipulating images
- Placing text and images over transparent regions
- Background image

For example, an `addShadow` method can be used to add a shadow to an image that is used with the `gBackground` protocol.

```
<g:background id="imageBG" src="images\background.png" />
imageBG.addShadow("black", 40, 40, 0, 0);
```

This adds a shadow with a radius of 40 and an alpha transparency value of 40.

More information on `addshadow` and other methods can be found at MSDN at http://msdn2.microsoft.com/en-us/library/aa359356(VS.85).aspx.

These protocols easily apply special filters on the images used in the gadget, such as shadow, glow, brightness, and so on, without any actual graphic manipulation. Appendix A further details these gadget protocols with a sample gadget GraphicDemo.gadget.

Sidebar Gadgets: The Road Ahead

Are gadgets here to stay, or are they just a phase? Should I be interested in gadget development? What is the future of Sidebar gadgets? With so many different gadget and widget engines available, which one should I use? Should I learn all of them? What is in store for gadget development in the future, if there is one? They're the kinds of questions that always come to mind whenever a new technology or platform shows up on the scene.

The truth is, Sidebar gadgets are here to stay. Microsoft has projected around 200 million sales of Vista operating system in the next two years. Although adoption has been slower than Microsoft would've liked, and although there are always problems successfully launching a new operating system, people have largely started embracing Windows Vista.

Gadgets are already the coolest new tool. Users are finding gadgets to be productive and time-saving applications. Thousands of useful Sidebar gadgets are already available in the Live Gallery (http://gallery.live.com) and the number is growing every day. It can only get better from here.

Fun gadgets and utility gadgets are currently very popular, but users are realizing the potential of gadgets in a business environment. In the future it's easy to imagine gadgets talking to Microsoft SharePoint, giving you updates on regular sales from an inventory management system. You will see gadgets operating on the same data as Microsoft BizTalk and Microsoft Dynamics. You can see gadgets interacting with task-tracking systems, pulling data from databases to give you network information at your fingertips.

The gadget platform is ripe with potential for innovations and products for the future.

W3C Widgets 1.0

Even as I type this, the World Wide Web Consortium (W3C) is working on standardizing widgets, defined as

"…small client-side applications for displaying and updating remote data, packaged in a way to allow a single download and installation on a client machine. The widget may execute outside of the typical web browser interface. Examples include clocks, stock tickers, news casters, games and weather forecasters. Some existing industry solutions go by the names 'widgets,' 'gadgets' or 'modules.'"

Although Microsoft is not directly working with W3C, most of the Microsoft Sidebar gadget design conforms to the standards defined in the Widgets 1.0 standard.

A working draft can be found at http://www.w3.org/TR/widgets/.

The W3C published a working draft in October 2007 based on standard specifications, including the following standards:

- Atom Auto discovery
- CSS 2.1 Specification
- Dashboard Reference, Apple Computer, Inc.
- HTML 4.01 Specifications
- Internationalized Resource Identifiers (IRIs)
- XHTML 1.0
- ZIP File Format Specification

The draft describes possible standardization on widget packaging, the widget configuration file, widget scripting interfaces, widget auto discovery, and the security model.

Most of the Windows Vista Sidebar gadget specifications are along the same lines, so eventually we may see more standardized Sidebar gadgets.

An Approach to Design

"You know you've achieved perfection in design, not when you have nothing more to add, but when you have nothing more to take away."

—Antoine de Saint-Exupery

Design Considerations

This chapter is about gadget design and user interface. Design starts with the factors that determine the type of gadget you want to develop, the information it will display, the user interface, the usage pattern, and the behavior of a gadget.

Design includes the dimensions, the images, the text, and the "look and feel." You also decide how the gadget interacts with the user and how it interacts with the system. This chapter discusses the visual theme, how the gadget can look like a part of Windows Vista, and the overall user experience.

Before you start, keep these two things in mind:

- **Justify the space**—The Windows Vista Sidebar is neither very tall nor wide. It can have—at the most— five or six gadgets at any particular time. Thousands of other gadgets, freely available online, will compete for the same screen space. So, offering the set of features a user critically needs is an important factor. Be prepared to convince users that your gadget justifies the space.

- **Ensure overall quality**—If your users don't experience quality throughout your gadget, they may conclude there is a lack of quality everywhere. This means you need to pay attention to the quality of icons, images, text, background, and interaction. Each of these elements is equally important. A good idea and a great implementation with an average user interface cannot stand up to the competition (see Figure 3.1).

FIGURE 3.1   Two gadgets that perform the same function, one with a nice interface and the other plain and simple. Which one would you prefer?

Consider the following four factors before designing a gadget (see Figure 3.2):

- Information first
- The right user interface
- The gadget's usage pattern
- The gadget's behavior

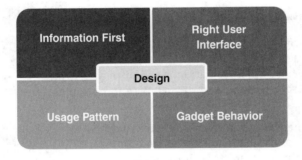

FIGURE 3.2   A gadget's design is an important aspect of development.

Putting Information First

Gadgets are meant for a single task. When designing a gadget, keep in mind that a gadget should have a small set of goals relevant to the specific task. A gadget should show only data suitable for that task and that task only. Information in the gadget window should satisfy the following rules:

- Live data
- Information for quick access
- User's choice
- Brief information for further action

Let's take a closer look at what each of these really means.

Live Data

Gadgets should display only information that changes regularly, such as live feeds, news updates, daily weather, battery status, and so on. Information that is static for more than a day makes a gadget dull.

A user looks to a gadget to see interesting things that are active. Fun gadgets are an exception but can be made more interesting if live data is also added. For example, a subset of a popular game is nice to have in a Sidebar, but it's better if there is live information, like a regularly updated scoreboard, or live updates about the game. If that is not possible, adding a capability to change the gadget's wallpaper (background image) is a good option.

Easy Access to Information

Gadgets are particularly useful at showing information for which users don't have to start an application or open a web page. A good example might be stock values, an event calendar, traffic maps, local fuel cost, and so forth. Any information that saves a user's time makes a gadget worth the space it takes.

Information Relevant to Individual Users

Gadgets are all about user choice and preference. If there are a lot of users for a particular newspaper's crossword puzzle, a gadget that taps into that theme can be an instant hit with them. User-tailored gadgets are very popular, such as a gadget for a Flickr website showing the user's own shared pictures or the user's favorite blog feed.

Information for Further Action

The gadget should show enough information for the user to decide on further action. For example, a website statistics gadget should not show each and every detail corresponding to website usage. It should show statistics for a week or a day and let users decide what further action they want to take.

Case Study: The Soapbox Video Gadget

Imagine you wanted to create a video gadget (see Figure 3.3). The task is to create a gadget for a video feed from http://soapbox.msn.com with the goal of accomplishing the following:

- Listing frequently updated videos from soapbox.msn.com in a simple and aesthetically pleasing way

- Playing a video in the flyout

A video feed normally contains thumbnails of the video, reviews, and ratings from users. A gadget with these goals gives you the following options for design decision:

- Making available the thumbnails and ratings for each video

- Adding capability to browse video by categories

- Functionality to search for videos by keyword

- Video resize option with support for Windows Media Player and Flash Player

- Easy page-wise access to list of videos

Figure 3.3 shows a preview of the Soapbox Video Gadget with all these options. More information about the gadget can be found at http://www.codeproject.com/KB/gadgets/ SoapBoxGadget.aspx.

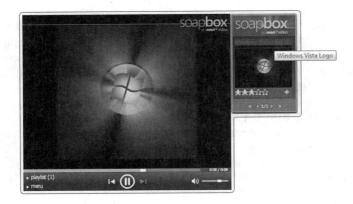

FIGURE 3.3   This fully developed gadget gives quick access to Soapbox video.

Try to make your gadget feature-rich by providing a complete set of functionality related to a specific task (see Figure 3.4). Think like a user. If the gadget shows a list of videos, the gadget should also categorize them and give easy access to all the items in the video feed.

Providing the complete set of functionality does not mean that the gadget should do everything the Soapbox video website is doing. Video sharing and review capabilities in the website may not be a part of the gadget. Complete functionality here means the gadget should give access to all the information from the video feed, which is the gadget's input. The users should be able to filter videos, sort them, search by keyword, and play videos in the way they want. In Chapter 11 we will see how to create a video gadget using YouTube Video feedback.

FIGURE 3.4   This gadget is able to categorize MSN Soapbox videos, giving users easy access to the one they want to see.

Refer to the checklist of guidelines for gadget development and compare that to this gadget. What live information does the gadget display?

- Frequently updated soapbox feed.
- Currently featured videos.
- Recent videos.

Does the gadget offer quick access to the information it provides?

- Ability to click on the thumbnail to play the video in the flyout.
- Ability to browse through the video list.

Does the gadget give the user a choice?

- Settings page gives an option to customize the list of videos.
- Users can select the media player and video size.

Does the gadget provide information that lets the user decide on further action?

- Gadget gives information about the video's ratings, a thumbnail image, and the title in the main window for users to decide to watch the video.
- Gadget gives Previous and Next options for browsing the videos in the feed.

Constructing the Right User Interface

Gadgets are a visual experience and the right user interface makes all the difference. Here are four pointers for creating one:

- Keep the gadget simple and aesthetically pleasing.
- Show only relevant information.
- Make use of visuals such as icons and images, rather than text.
- Be sure that the gadget is not too obtrusive.

Simplicity and Aesthetics

A gadget should look simple and aesthetically pleasing. Take a look at the gadget samples provided in Figure 3.5.

Clearly the objects in the first pair are both simpler and more aesthetically pleasing than the obnoxious clock and difficult-to-read note. If a gadget is going to be part of the desktop, it is something the user will look at every day; make sure it is as clear and aesthetic. The choice of color and fonts can also make a difference.

FIGURE 3.5   Choice of clear image and aesthetically pleasing fonts can make a lot of difference in gadget design.

Show Only Relevant Information

The maximum width of a gadget is 130 pixels. That's not a lot of room to work with, especially if there's a lot of information you want to convey. It can be done, however. Just look at the RSS feed and Calendar Gadgets shown in Figure 3.6.

FIGURE 3.6   The RSS feed Gadget shows the title partially in the gadget window, and the complete title is shown as the tooltip.

So, what is it exactly that makes these well-designed gadgets? For one, titles should generally be only as long as the space allows. With some gadgets, like this RSS news feeder, that isn't possible. But in this case, tooltips are applied to good effect. And, although you can't see this clearly from the black-and-white photos in this book, the fonts have different colors to highlight the title.

The RSS Reader Gadget doesn't try to do too much. It displays only four records at a time, and the Calendar Gadget displays just the current month or the current day, based on the user's choice.

Figure 3.7 shows two more gadgets that are designed to accomplish the same goals, but suffer from an extremely poor design.

FIGURE 3.7   The gadget with scrollbars and the overfilled calendar both try to squeeze too much information into the small space.

The presence of a scrollbar in a gadget is unacceptable. It's far better to use paging because a scrollbar can further reduce the already small space a gadget provides. Providing paging functionality to browse multiple items with previous and next options and page numbers can remove the clutter from the gadget screen. Both the Blog and the Calendar Gadgets have far too much information cramped into a small space. That's the kind of design mistakes you should strive to avoid when designing your own gadgets.

Make Use of Visuals

Make use of icons, images, and signs as much as possible; they give visual clues of the functionality (see Figure 3.8). For example, a Weather Gadget can use pictures of clouds, the sun, and rain instead of corresponding text to depict different weather condition. The proper use of images makes the gadget more user friendly.

Two gadgets are compared in Figure 3.8. Both gadgets show the same information, using different designs. However, the designs in the top row have visuals that give a rich experience to the user. When designing a gadget, check for the following:

- Can any information displayed in the gadget can be replaced by visuals?

- Is the gadget too plain or does it lack design?

Visual themes are covered in more detail in later section.

Good design

Bad design

FIGURE 3.8   Pictures of clouds and sun in the Weather Gadget depict the weather. Computer usage in the form of a CPU meter is more intuitive than plain text.

Not Too Obtrusive

The design of the gadget should not be too obtrusive. The use of buttons and user controls should be avoided at all costs. For example, using a Previous and Next button can make the gadget look ugly. Instead, use proper images and show them when the mouse is moved over the gadget.

Figure 3.9 compares a Picture Slideshow Gadget with two different designs. The lower gadget shows buttons to browse either the previous image or the next one. The buttons are too obtrusive for a good design. The upper images are examples of a good design. The gadget's default view (upper left) is without any Previous or Next buttons. When the mouse is moved over the gadget, previous and next images are shown.

The Picture Slideshow Gadget shows the action buttons (images) on mouse hover. A good mouseover effect (refer to the upper-right image of Figure 3.9) with proper visuals makes a good design. Note that these are not buttons but images that are aligned with the gadget theme.

FIGURE 3.9   The always visible Previous and Next buttons are used to browse images in the Picture Slideshow Gadget (lower image), but they are too obtrusive for the small space.

Usage Patterns

The type of gadget you want to create also has an impact on its design. As discussed previously, there are four broad classifications:

- Information gadget
- Application gadget
- Utility gadget
- Fun gadget

These classifications all have common user interface guidelines, but each has its own specific design pattern that needs to be considered during development.

Information Gadget

Information gadgets collect data from multiple sources and are time sensitive. An information gadget normally uses RSS feeds that contain 10 or more items. To display them all in the gadget proper, page number and previous/next options should be available. The use of such options is also referred to as *paging*. These gadgets refresh their data regularly, so they should not be visually distracting or obtrusive (see Figure 3.10). As stated previously, there should be no scrollbars.

FIGURE 3.10   This example of an RSS Reader Gadget has paging options 1–4 and no distracting images. It reflects good gadget design.

Application Gadget

These gadgets depend on other applications or products for their data and act as a side product or a quick tool for data visualization. These gadgets should be designed with the main product or application in mind. The visual theme should go along with the original application (see Figure 3.11).

FIGURE 3.11   An application gadget mimics the user interface of the original application.

This is an example of a Microsoft Office Recent Documents gadget. The gadget shows the recently used Microsoft Office documents. The corresponding logo of Microsoft Office and icons for Microsoft Word, Excel, and PowerPoint make the gadget look rich and pleasing.

> **CAUTION**
>
> Please note that the gadget shown in Figure 3.11 is developed at Microsoft and it uses icons and images that are copyrighted by Microsoft and should not be used in publicly distributed gadgets without permission. Please check the "Use of Microsoft Copyright content" at https://www.microsoft.com/about/legal/permissions/default.mspx.

Utility Gadget

Utility gadgets provide quick information or shortcuts to frequently accessed tools and features. There should be no gimmicks in a utility gadget. The size should be appropriate: It should be the smallest of all other types of gadgets and should correspond to the feature it provides (see Figure 3.12).

98%
3:51 remaining

FIGURE 3.12   A Battery Monitor Gadget displays percentage and time remaining in appropriate size.

This example shows a utility gadget that indicates the amount of battery life remaining in a mobile PC. The information it provides is the percentage of battery remaining and the time left. The background is an image of a battery with a percentage filled with color. This is a good design. There are no bells and whistles, but the size is appropriate and the design is intuitive.

Fun Gadgets

Fun gadgets are more distracting than other types of gadgets. As a result, users are likely to change them more frequently. Their purpose is to entertain or provide some fun activity to the user. If you are making a fun gadget, you must have a strong understanding of your target users and the gadget should have some dynamic features to keep the user interested for a longer period of time. It should also look visually pleasing (see Figure 3.13).

A visually pleasing experience comes with proper use of colors along with neat and clean images. Keep these quick tips in mind:

- Do not use too many colors; try to stick with two or three colors.
- Do not use more than one bright color in your gadget window.
- Check for good contrast colors or shades of the same color.

TIP

To get a better idea on different colors and contrast effects check http://www.colorsontheweb.com/.

FIGURE 3.13   This Minesweeper Gadget has a visually pleasing interface.

The example shown here is of a Minesweeper Gadget. It uses only a few colors: gray, black and red. It makes good use of contrast between red and black and the color also reflects the personality of the game.

What Gadgets Are Not Meant For

So far we have discussed what the different usage patterns are and what a gadget is meant for. This section gives you an idea what a gadget is not meant for. Keep this set of rules in mind while designing a gadget:

- Gadgets are not meant as a substitute for full applications such as email or instant messaging.

- Gadgets should not be designed as time-sensitive applications.

- Gadgets should contain no direct advertisements.

A gadget is not meant for notification purposes. Notice of new emails or instant messages should not be a gadget's purpose. Applications such as instant messaging and email notification require more robust applications such as MSN Messenger and Microsoft Outlook. A gadget is lightweight and is designed to supplement these applications rather than compete with them.

A gadget is also not meant for notification applications that need immediate attention because gadgets are not executables running in the user's desktop. They reside in the Sidebar and the user might have closed or hidden the Sidebar to avoid distraction. A gadget should not be a crucial application.

Gadgets can be used for advertisement purposes but are not meant to include banner advertisements or text ads. The small size of gadgets does not allow them. Check the next chapter to get details on the gadget's business model.

Gadget Behavior

The behavior relates to the way the gadget interacts with the user. How a gadget should react in particular circumstances, what a gadget is meant for, and what it is not meant for—all this decides the gadget's behavior.

You need to consider the following to ensure proper gadget behavior:

- Gadget configuration

- Refreshing a gadget

- Errors, information, and warnings

- Service not available information

Gadget Configuration

Most gadgets have an optional settings page that can be used to configure the gadget. You access it by clicking on the Option menu in the right-click context menu or by clicking the settings icon in the top-right corner of the gadget (see Figure 3.14).

Gadget configuration is the only option a user has to customize the gadget. It is a single administration page per instance of the gadget. Any configuration change in the settings page is applied to only that instance of the gadget. Choose wisely what changes a user would like to have in the gadget, based on its functionality. For example, if the gadget allows, give a resize option to a mini version of the gadget with absolute essentials. This gives the user the opportunity to add more gadgets to the Sidebar, which means that your gadget has a better chance of being utilized.

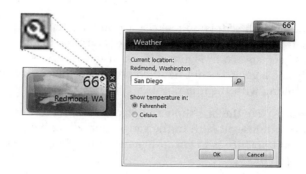

FIGURE 3.14   A settings page of a Weather Gadget enables the user to select a location, as well as choose Fahrenheit or Celsius to display temperature.

A settings page gives the user an option to customize the gadget according to choice. A configuration page gives more flexibility and freedom to the user and so increases a gadget's usability.

Refreshing a Gadget

If your gadget displays live data, you might need to refresh it regularly or on user demand. Keep in mind that if a user has a slow Internet connection, it can take some time for a gadget to reload. Using a loading image in the waiting screen with the message Getting data... or loading... is recommended (see Figures 3.15).

FIGURE 3.15   A Weather Gadget displays a Getting Data screen, along with a Vista busy cursor (image on the left) to display the status.

Errors, Information, and Warnings

The gadget sometimes needs to display status to the user. For example, an RSS Feed Gadget needs to tell the user when the feed is not available, or if there is no Internet connection available to fetch data from the remote server. These messages can also be custom error messages, warnings, or other information. All these status messages should be shown as inline text with standard 16×16 icons, like the ones shown in Figure 3.16, for the type of message. Pop-up dialog boxes are not allowed in a gadget.

FIGURE 3.16   Standard icons for errors, information, and warnings need to be used for the corresponding status.

A gadget is an HTML file with scripts, so make sure you have handled all the possible errors in the gadget. If there is an unexpected error or warning, display it in the same way as the Getting Data screen shown in Figure 3.15, or display the Service Not Available screen. If the error inside a gadget is not handled properly, a default runtime error message is displayed along with the line number.

JavaScript error messages, like the one shown in Figure 3.17, are annoying. One of these messages and the user will lose all faith in the gadget and won't hesitate to remove or even uninstall it. A good practice is to encapsulate each JavaScript function inside an error handler, a try-catch block.

FIGURE 3.17   Typical JavaScript error messages, like this one, are too vague to be useful to the end user.

A try-catch block is a piece of code that ensures the execution of the catch block if any error occurs inside the try block. Here is the example in JavaScript. The code ensures that the user doesn't get a default JavaScript error dialog:

```
try
 {
  // your script code here
 }
 catch (e)
 {
   //set and display your inline error message and icon here
 }
```

Service Not Available Information

Service Not Available is a default screen that is used in most of the common scenarios. Use the Service Not Available screen where appropriate. For example, if the gadget is in a mobile laptop and the laptop disconnects from the Internet, show a screen with the information icon like the one shown in Figure 3.18.

FIGURE 3.18   A Weather Gadget shows a Service Not Available screen when there is no Internet connection, along with the information icon.

Sample code would look like this:

```
If (CheckInternetConnection)
 {
 // your functionality code here
 }
 else
 {
   //set and display your inline "Service not available" message and icon here
 }
```

Challenges for the User Interface

A gadget looks quite simple, but developing a rich and effective gadget takes much more than HTML and JavaScript code. The design of the gadget almost always decides the fate of the gadget. Therefore, while developing gadgets an important factor to keep in mind is size limitations.

So far, we have approached gadget design in a methodical way. If you take care of information first and consider the usage pattern, you can develop a good user interface and ensure the behavior of the gadget. It's time to give boundaries to the gadget. Note that by *boundaries*, I mean the actual dimensions of all the interfaces of the gadget.

A gadget should not be treated as a web page. For example, the Zodiac Sign Gadget in Figure 3.19 outgrows the width of the Sidebar and has scrollbars. This is not a good design. The size of the gadget window should not be larger than the Sidebar when docked. A larger size is desirable only in the undocked mode.

FIGURE 3.19   A Zodiac Sign Gadget with width greater than that of the Sidebar looks cumbersome in the desktop.

Knowing the standard dimensions to use when designing specific gadget types is essential for you to have success in gadget development.

Standard Dimensions

All the interfaces in a gadget are HTML pages, each with recommended and allowed dimensions. These dimensions are set in the corresponding CSS files. There are different recommended dimensions for the different types of pages you might use. These page types include

- Gadget page when docked

- Undocked gadget

- Settings page

- Flyout page

Each of these types is documented in more detail in the following sections. Table 3.1 summarizes the recommended and maximum dimensions for each page type. These dimensions are recommended by Microsoft. More information on guidelines can be found at http://msdn2.microsoft.com/en-us/library/aa511443.aspx.

TABLE 3.1   The Maximum Dimensions for Each Page Type

Type of Page	Recommended Width×Height	Maximum Width×Height	Minimum Width×Height
Gadget main page when docked	130 pixels×150 pixels 5 pixels transparent border (2 left/3 right)	130×200	130 pixels×57 pixels
Gadget page when undocked (floating)	250 pixels×180 pixels	400 pixels×400 pixels	130 pixels×57 pixels
Settings page	280 pixels×180 pixels	300 pixels×400 pixels	Variable
Flyout page	320 pixels×240 pixels	400 pixels×400 pixels	Variable

Gadget Page When Docked

A gadget width when docked should be not more than 130 pixels. The Sidebar width is 150 pixels. The image used for the gadget's background needs to have two pixels on the left and three pixels on the right side for the gadget's drop-shadow effect. These five pixels are also sometimes kept transparent (see Figure 3.20).

The minimum height for a gadget is 57 pixels, which accommodates the Settings and Drag icons in the upper-right corner. The maximum height for a docked gadget is 200 pixels. Remember that a gadget that utilizes space efficiently is more likely to be used.

The recommended size for a docked gadget is 130×150 pixels.

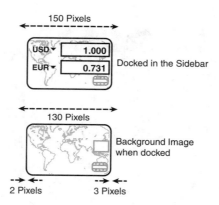

FIGURE 3.20   The Currency Gadget docked size is 130 pixels wide and 83 pixels high.

Undocked Gadget

An undocked gadget size should differ according to the gadget's functionality. If the gadget needs more real estate when undocked to show more information, the size changes accordingly. The maximum size is 400×400 pixels, and the recommended size is 250×180 (see Figure 3.21).

FIGURE 3.21   The undocked size for the Currency Gadget is 254×196 pixels.

Settings Page

The size of the settings page, like the one shown in Figure 3.22, depends on the amount of customization given to the user. For example, a Weather Gadget just needs to have an option for city and for temperature unit. The maximum allowed size for a settings page is 300×400. The recommended size is 278×180.

Flyout Page

The flyout window is meant for extra information and is optional. The maximum size allowed for a flyout page is 400×400 pixels. The recommended size is 320×240.

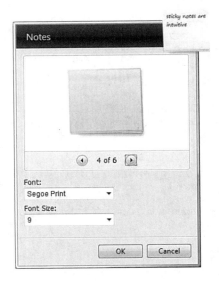

FIGURE 3.22   The settings page for the Notes Gadget is 278×310.

Other Interface Guidelines

The following is a list of other interface guidelines that should be considered:

- Use Windows styles for text, cursors, icons, and so on. Because gadgets reside within the Vista operating system, the images, text, and icons used should go along with the Vista theme.

- Use a similar style for the gadget's docked and undocked states. The style used for fonts, colors, and sizes should not be completely different between docked and undocked state.

- A gadget should be self-explanatory, with no need for help files. A gadget is a lightweight application and should be simple to understand and use.

- After installation, the gadget should start working. Initial gadget configuration makes a gadget look cumbersome. A gadget should come with working default settings. For example, a Weather Gadget shows the weather of a default city as soon as it is installed. The user is able to customize it later. Asking the user for a configuration as soon the gadget is installed is not the norm and should be avoided.

- An option to resize the gadget in its docked state is absolutely essential in a good design. A gadget that comes with an essential mini version in the docked state becomes an instant favorite of users.

- Flyouts should be used for additional information, but keep in mind that they automatically hide when the focus is in any other window. Flyouts cannot be used to display live data updates.

Visual Themes

The visual theme determines the look and feel of the gadget. Visual theme is about images, text, fonts, colors, sizes, and styles—everything together. It is all about what users see and also what they don't see. They all work together to present a unified theme to a user. Here is the list of items to consider when developing a theme for your gadget:

- Title
- Icon
- Drag image
- Background image
- Controls
- Text and style

A gadget's visual theme starts at its icon and title, which appear in the Gadget Picker window after installation.

Title

Keep the gadget's title to two or three meaningful words, 15 letters maximum, so that it displays properly in the Gadget Picker. For example, for a Google Search Gadget, use the title "Google Search" rather than "Google.com Search bar." Figure 3.23 shows two gadgets in the Gadget Picker window. The first one has the name "Currency" and the second one is called "MyMoneyGadget," which displays as "MyMoneyGad...." You can avoid this undesirable result by keeping the title short.

Icon

A transparent icon gives a rich look. The `icon.png` file is an image file whose dimensions are 64×64. Figure 3.23 shows two versions of a gadget that compares different currencies of the world. The left image uses a meaningful title and an attractive icon. The right image, MyMoneyGadget, is not a meaningful title and the icon is very crude. This is not a good design.

FIGURE 3.23   To avoid turning off potential users from the start, gadgets should have an attractive icon and short title.

Drag Image

The drag image appears when you try to drag an image from the Gadget Picker window to the Vista Sidebar. The source of the drag image is drag.png. It's meant to show the screenshot of the actual working gadget in its docked size (see Figure 3.24).

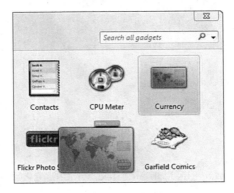

FIGURE 3.24   When a clock gadget is dragged in the Gadget Picker window, it shows the drag.png image.

Background Image

The gadget's background image is the wallpaper for the gadget. It is normally a plain image with rounded curves. The image is selected based on the gadget's functionality. An image of a world map for a Currency Gadget, for example, is appropriate (see Figure 3.25). Multiple images are used for the gadget for different modes, like docked and undocked. The images used can also be different for different sizes of the gadget.

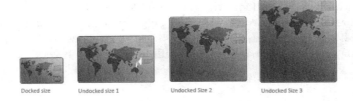

FIGURE 3.25   A Currency Gadget uses different images to display the gadget's background in different sizes.

When the gadget is docked, the image should have a shadow of 2 pixels on the left and 3 pixels on the right. When the image is undocked, the shadow should be more prominent—10 pixels to the left and 18 pixels to the right.

You can add the shadow to an image by using photo-editing software or the graphics protocol provided by the Vista Gadget Model. A black shadow with an opacity level 25%

can be used for the docked image for a two-three-pixel shadow, and an opacity value of 75% can be used for a 10-pixel shadow in images for undocked gadgets.

Controls

For any controls or action buttons that need to appear on the gadget, only the glyph images consistent with Windows should be used. Figure 3.26 shows a number of these glyphs with possible actions they can each represent. If the action buttons need to be shown in the gadget's main window, always try to keep them hidden by default and have them activate only on mouse hover or when the gadget is active. All these glyph images can be found in the Extras section in the book download.

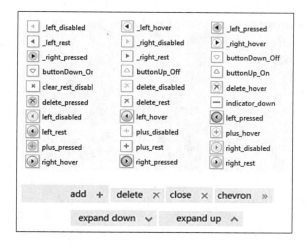

FIGURE 3.26   The glyph images that are consistent with the Windows Vista user interface should be used in the gadget.

Figure 3.27 shows an example of a gadget with controls that are hidden until the user hovers the mouse over the gadget.

FIGURE 3.27   The Notes Gadget by default (left image) does not show the action buttons. When the mouse is moved on the Notes Gadget (image on the right), the action buttons are visible.

Text and Style

The fonts and the styles used to format text in the gadget are also very important while designing a gadget. The style sheet is a language used to describe the presentation of an HTML page. A gadget can use multiple sStyle sheets for different pages of the gadget window, such as the settings page and the flyout page. The style sheet and font you should use depend on the gadget's functionality and theme, and can vary with different gadgets. Here is a link that can further help you understand HTML and CSS: http://www.w3.org/Style/Examples/011/firstcss.

Here is some of the standard style information as applied to the different pages. These styles help the gadget to display a consistent look with Windows Vista.

For the gadget window:

```
Font: Calibri or Segoe UI
Style:
body
{
    margin: 0px;
    padding: 0px;
    color: #000;
    font-family: Calibri, Tahoma, sans-serif;
}
```

For the settings window:

```
Font: Segoe UI
Style:
body
{
    padding: 0;
    margin: 0px;
    font-family: Segoe UI, Tahoma, sans-serif;
    font-size:12px;
}
```

For the flyout:

```
Font: Calibri
Style:
body
{
    margin: 0px;
    padding: 0px;
    color: #ffffff;
    font-size: 10px;
    font-family: Calibri, Tahoma, sans-serif;
}
```

> **NOTE**
>
> These are merely recommendations for suitable style sheet information. Users should change it according to the feature set that the gadget provides. For example, the Notes Gadget shown in Figure 3.27 uses italic fonts.

Transparent Images in the Gadget

The images used in a gadget window have a shadow effect and sometimes semitransparent oval shapes. These images use either a PNG or a GIF image format. The recommended images used for the gadget are in a PNG format. The next few sections describes these formats in more detail.

Alpha Transparency

Microsoft started supporting PNG icons with alpha transparency in Windows Vista. Creating an alpha transparent image is a process of combining two images: a central image laid on top of a background image to create an appearance of partial transparency. It is used to display an image that has transparent or semitransparent pixels.

Alpha transparency is used extensively in the images used for gadgets to create the shadow or oval shape effect.

Portable Network Graphics File

PNG is an abbreviation for Portable Network Graphics. It's an advanced graphics format with 48-bit color. It's one of the standard formats that is beginning to replace the use of GIF images, which are limited to 8-bit colors (256 colors). It also includes an alpha channel for showing transparency.

This is the standard format used in all the images for a gadget. A PNG file allows every pixel (dot) to have any level of transparency, from completely opaque to completely transparent and anything in between.

The PNG image format combines the best features of GIF and JPG/JPEG. It supports binary transparency along with alpha transparency, meaning that each pixel of the image can also have one of 256 different levels of transparency. PNG format produces a file with approximately the same file size as that of an equivalent GIF image, assuming that they have the same number of colors. Appendix A shows how to create a PNG image in Adobe Photoshop.

GIF File Limitations

Graphics Interchange Format is a popular bitmapped graphics file format developed by CompuServe. To date, it is the most widely used graphics format on the Web. Given that GIF files can also be transparent, you might wonder why you would not want to use them in favor of PNG. There are three reasons for not using a GIF format:

- GIF files support only 100% transparency; you cannot create a translucent shadow effect.

- GIF images are limited to 8-bit colors, so they're not very rich.

- PNG format is endorsed by the World Wide Web Consortium (W3C), an organization responsible for managing standards for the World Wide Web.

About Accessibility

Accessibility is a way of producing applications accessible to the broadest range of people. This includes people with disabilities such as poor eyesight, motor impairments, and so on, and also to people who prefer to use keyboards for fast access, people with limited bandwidth, with older computers, people using applications such as text-only browsers, screen readers, and other devices to access applications. To learn more about adding accessibility to an application, visit the Microsoft Accessibility Developer Center at http://msdn2.microsoft.com/en-us/accessibility/default.aspx.

For a Sidebar gadget, accessibility relates to theme colors, high color contrast, and HTML accessibility in general. Adding accessibility to a gadget means taking care of gadget design in terms of the following:

- Keyboard access

- HTML accessibility

- Theme colors and contrast

Keyboard Access

One of the fundamental accessibility scenarios is that some users use only their keyboards. This is also a requirement from power-users who love the speed of using the keyboard rather than a point-and-click device such as a mouse. So, specifically, the Sidebar and the gadgets themselves should be accessible from the keyboard.

The keyboard support listed in Table 3.2 is provided by the Sidebar

TABLE 3.2   Shortcut Keys to Access Sidebar Gadget

Keyboard Access	Action
Windows logo key + Spacebar	Brings all gadgets to the front and puts focus on the Windows Sidebar
Windows logo key + G	Cycles through the gadgets

After your gadget is in focus, you have to make sure all its features are accessible through the keyboard. The following lists important points to keep in mind when adding accessibility:

- Focus should be put on the gadget when it is loaded.

- Users should be able to tab through the controls and links in the gadget.

- The Enter key should act like a mouse click to push a button or follow a link and should call the `onclick` event of the control or link.

- The `onfocus` and `onfocusout` functions should be called to simulate the mouse hover effect.

- Apart from the gadget main page, a gadget's Flyout and Settings page should also be accessible from the keyboard.

The, "About Accessibility," section in Chapter 6, "Design Patterns and Standard Practices," shows you how to implement these in a gadget.

General HTML accessibility

Because all the pages used in a gadget (the main gadget window, Flyout, and Settings pages) are HTML pages, accessibility rules apply to them as well. To adhere to these rules you should attend to the following:

- Provide text alternatives for images and links. Set the `ALT` tag in the image and `Title` tag in the `Anchor` element. The alt text as well as the title act as a short description of the image that serves the same purpose as the image or the link itself. If the image is purely a decoration, then set alt="". For example, if the gadget has a weather image, then set alt="Cloudy" or alt ="Partly sunny". Reflecting what the image conveys fulfills this requirement.

- Create content in a modular way so that the structure of the page (HTML), presentation (CSS), and behavior (JavaScript functionality) are in separate pages and the HTML page is accessible without the CSS file.

These guidelines are from the W3C Initiative Web Content Accessibility Guidelines 2.0, which can be found at http://www.w3c.org/TR/WCAG20/.

Theme Colors and Contrast

When adding accessibility to a gadget, you next need to consider the colors used in the background, images, HTML page elements, and so forth.

- Pick contrasting foreground and background colors to make your gadget information more visible. This is especially important for the color of the text against the background color. Contrast is a function of lightness, hue, and saturation. Here's a resource from the Lighthouse for the Blind, an expert in vision disabilities: http://www.lighthouse.org/accessibility/effective-color-contrast/.

- Avoid using red and green combinations because people with red-green colorblindness cannot distinguish between red and green. There are other types of colorblindness, but red-green is the most common.

- Do not use color alone to convey information.

Selling Your Gadget

"Make service your first priority, not success, and success will follow."

—Anonymous

Gadget Revenue Model

The Sidebar gadget development platform is new, but it uses standard web technologies such as HTML, CSS, and JavaScript. These technologies have matured in the last few years and have a large community of developers. Sidebar gadgets have a much shorter development life cycle than regular software: quick development, easy deployment, and almost no maintenance. This makes the Sidebar gadget development platform very attractive for developers. It's a platform rife with the opportunity to innovate. It's a new approach for providing quick information and tools.

The revenue model of an Internet-based service company depends on one thing: traffic. And Sidebar gadgets have the potential to drive traffic. There will be more than 100 million Windows Vista users in next few years. If your gadget is popular among 1% of them, just imagine your gadget on 1 million users' desktops. A reference to your website will also drive them directly to your online business portal. How you use this new way of interaction and this new set of customers coming to your website depends on you and your own individual service.

A Sidebar gadget is a mini application with the simplicity of a web application and the power of a Windows application. It is a small and lightweight tool. A Sidebar gadget is not meant to be created as a complete software application, whether sold as a download-able product or a "try before buy" tool. The revenue model of a Sidebar gadget works best as a free service to drive traffic to your website or as a side product of a bigger application.

It is debatable right now whether you can make millions from a Sidebar gadget, but the potential is there and the possibilities are endless. Do the math yourself; assuming that your gadget is popular:

- There will be 100 million Windows Vista users in the next year (predicted by Microsoft).

- A popular gadget used by 1% of those users means 1 million users.

- If 5% of those 1 million users to become customers, you have 20,000 potential customers.

- Potential revenue equals 20,000 multiplied by $ x (sales per user).

Users will be using the gadget for free; *customers* are those 5% among the gadget users who go ahead and buy a service from the gadget provider's website. We discuss this in detail in the later sections.

The type of gadget you build depends on which revenue model you want to use to attract potential buyers:

- **Pull model**—A free utility that pulls customers to the website

- **Push model**—A tool that enhances an existing application or service

We discuss both these models in the following sections.

Pull Model

In the pull model, you create new ways to market your online business by distributing a useful Sidebar gadget freely on the Web. The gadget should have a subset of features you want to sell to buyers and it needs to have enough information to keep users interested and eventually convert at least some of them to buyers.

Gadgets utilizing the pull model should have a link to the website providing the product or service.

> **TIP**
>
> There are two keys to creating a successful gadget with the pull model:
> - Using the gadget platform to create a free innovative service to pull the customers to your website.
> - Creating a website that sells online service(s) and uses gadgets as a marketing tool by providing free basic services in the form of Sidebar gadgets.

Steps and Different Roles in the Model

A pull model needs a series of steps along with the development of sidebar gadgets. Companies that already have an online service or product to sell can also utilize this model. In action, the model follows these general steps, which are also illustrated in Figure 4.1:

- You have a website that provides the service(s) and/or product(s) you want to sell.

- Choose a subset of the service that you can provide as a basic free service.

- Create a Sidebar gadget that delivers this free service to users.

- Build a user base.

- Drive interested users (potential customers) to the website where more complete services are offered (for a price).

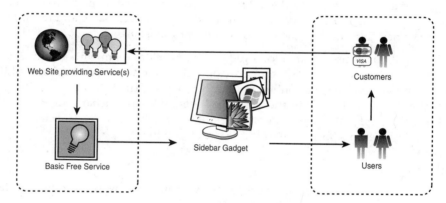

FIGURE 4.1   A pull model uses a gadget to drive traffic to the website.

The gadget provides a basic service that is available for free to all in a public server. The basic service should be sufficient enough to create user interest in related products and services.

Case Study: Rare Book Seller Website

TrickofMind, a Fictitious dot-com company with few developers and resources, wants to sell rare puzzle books on the Internet. It has a catalog of books and a payment gateway set up, but what it lacks is users that may become customers.

You, as an analyst, have come up with a plan to leverage the Sidebar gadget platform by following these steps:

1. Create a Trick of the Day Sidebar Gadget. This has a puzzle trick every day in the form of an RSS feed.

2. Track your RSS feeds with online tracking tools such as feedburner.com. Appendix A contains a section about tracking RSS feeds.

3. Deploy your Sidebar gadget on a publicly available server, such as
    http://gallery.live.com, for users to find and download. Don't forget to add
    keywords and tags to make it easily searchable.

4. Provide a consistent service to users, such as the trick question every day and also
    some kind of interaction through the Sidebar gadgets, such as a reply link or a link
    to the website.

5. Provide a link to the website for users interested in puzzle books. Make your website
    dynamic, informative, and interesting enough for users to return to on a regular basis.

Websites that provide tricks, puzzles, or questions every day already exist, but a Sidebar
gadget providing puzzles at your desktop would make yours more usable. A daily trick
delivered to your desktop is a very attractive service for puzzle lovers.

Gadgets offer a new approach to the old model, "basic free service, paid pro service."
Almost all Internet companies try to use this model to generate traffic and revenue. The
model is not new, but the approach utilizing sidebar gadgets is.

Every day, millions of users search for a gadget that provides them with a daily dose of
their favorite hobby. There are websites providing these daily services, but most of them
deliver them by mass emails or online forums. Nobody—at the time of this writing—
delivers them to your desktop in the form of a state-of-the-art Sidebar gadget. Use the
gadget platform and grab those customers before somebody else does. Check the
TrickofMind gadget in Appendix B in the "Extras" section.

Push Model

The push model relies on enhancing existing service and increasing customer satisfaction.

This model works where you already have an online business with a customer base. Use a
Sidebar gadget to enhance your customer experience and provide that "extra" service
exclusively to your customers. This will not only boost the satisfaction of the existing
customers but also act as a great marketing tool for new customers. Use the Sidebar platform to create an add-on service that provides users with quick and ready-to-use information that benefits them. Any information that changes daily and is needed by your
customer can be provided as an information gadget.

> **TIP**
>
> Consider an appropriate authentication method to ensure that only your paying users have
> access to the gadget's features.

Steps and Different Roles in the Model

A push model starts with an existing web service, but an existing customer base is what
distinguishes the push model from the pull model. There is lot more potential for marketing in a push model where you already have a customer. Your users are already coming to

your website for frequently updated data or information. The following list, which is illustrated in Figure 4.2, describes the components of a push model:

- Existing web application or service

- Existing customer base

- Ready-to-use information gadget based on an existing service

- Gadget deployment in the web portal

- Increased satisfaction for the existing customers, relative to the pull model

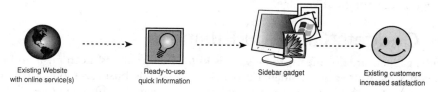

FIGURE 4.2   A push model uses the existing customer base.

Case Study: Real Estate Web Service

Imagine you have a website that displays home rental listings for property managers. Your website receives updates from multiple agents and private sources. Currently, property managers go to the website and filter the results based on their preferences, such as area, price range, and date. The information is dynamic in nature and changes every day. The property managers are always searching for new rental listings, but it's easy for them to miss some of the listings.

As an analyst, you come up with a plan to leverage the push model for Sidebar gadgets.

1. Make global listings available in XML format as RSS feeds, with date and region as parameters.

2. Create a Recent Listing Sidebar gadget that uses settings specific to the rental listing to filter the feed data into a set of top 20 listings. Let the gadget update the feed every hour.

3. Deploy your Sidebar gadget in your web application exclusively for property managers.

Here is the list of benefits:

- Use of the gadget ensures proper flow of important information.

- The gadget makes listings available to property managers without requiring them to go to the website. With multiple instances of the gadget, the property manager can set up different search criteria.

- This results in better flow of information, reducing search costs and potential missed listings.
- Use of gadgets results in increased satisfaction among property managers.

The push model facilitates the property manager in viewing useful information quickly and efficiently. With the power of the Sidebar gadget, the property managers can manage more properties in less time, which increases both their revenue and customer satisfaction.

The push model can be used with many online businesses with an existing customer base. Think of this new way of providing features to your customers as something that offers you a significant competitive edge.

How Gadgets Give You Business

Typically, gadgets are not meant to be sold as individual products. Both push and pull revenue models utilize a Vista Sidebar gadget as a tool to do business more efficiently. The platform provides a unique way to interact with customers. The business model of a gadget is not to sell and make profit out of the gadget itself but rather out of the information, service, or product that the gadget supports.

The reason is simple. Sidebar gadgets are based on HTML, CSS, and JavaScript, so the gadget's source code actually goes with the gadget when you deploy it. The .gadget extension is nothing but a .zip extension in disguise. Anybody with this information can open the source of the HTML file and make changes to it. In addition, thousands of gadgets are freely available online, delivering all kinds of services, which makes it difficult—if not impossible—to sell a gadget.

Four kinds of gadgets can generate revenue (see Figure 4.3):

- Ad Gadgets, which are gadgets used as advertising tools
- Gadgets that are side products for enterprise-level applications
- Utility Gadgets, which provide a watered-down version of a utility
- Free Information Gadgets, which collect trends and usage statistics

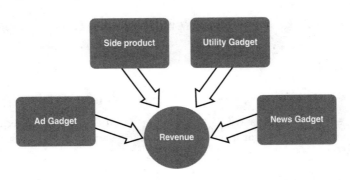

FIGURE 4.3   These four types of gadgets are all capable of generating revenue.

The Ad Gadget

The Ad Gadget is meant for advertisement of a service. It is based on the pull business model in which you create a free subset of a service, but compel the user to subscribe for an advanced set of features. An Ad Gadget becomes the starting point of an already existing service on the web and helps business in the following ways:

- Free basic service in the Sidebar gadget acts as an advertisement for the actual service on the website.

- The service on the website can be free, with a revenue model derived from advertisement banners on the website.

- The service on the website can be a paid subscription for a Pro Account. Revenue here comes from subscribers.

> **TIP**
>
> The Ad Gadget is not meant for displaying advertisements but to be used as an advertisement tool for a particular service.

Case Study: Site Statistics, Ad Gadget with Pull Model

A website statistics provider company such as sitemeter.com shows statistical information about visitors for a particular customer's website. It gives free information for the last single month. The statistics provider company's revenue model is based on advertisement banners on the website and paid professional accounts.

In addition to offering a free basic service (statistics for last month), what if the organization created a Sidebar gadget for advertising its free service? The information in the gadget would whet users' appetites, and compel them to visit the website for more detailed statistics.

Here is how the pull model works for the Site Statistics Gadget (also see Figure 4.4):

- Free basic statistics in the Sidebar gadget pull users to the website. The gadget has a link to the website, which provides detail statistics. Users visit more often through the gadget than they do by actually navigating to the website.

- The gadget provides a subset of the free basic service and still pushes users to go to the website for detail statistics. This helps drive in the revenue from banner advertisements on the website.

- The gadget helps in driving traffic to the website. It also acts as a tool for marketing the paid subscription for the Pro Account. The revenue model of a paid subscription is strengthened by the presence of the gadget.

FIGURE 4.4   Ad Gadget for Site Statistics provides a subset of free basic service on the Vista Sidebar.

The pull model here has two modes of revenue: revenue from advertisements on the website and revenue from the users who come from the link in the Sidebar gadget. Eventually there will also be revenue from users who become subscribers to the Pro Account, an account that provides the detailed annual statistics and other advanced services and that comes with a paid subscription.

Benefits of Using an Ad Gadget

An Ad Gadget not only provides an advertisement of the web service but also acts as a marketing tool that is freely available in online communities. Following lists the benefits of an Ad Gadget:

- Free advertisement of the service through the gadget.
- Wide availability (The gadget can be made available in free online communities such as http://gallery.live.com, which gives the service exposure to millions of users.)
- Increase in number of users for your service.
- More satisfaction among existing paid account holders.

Gadget as a Side Product

A gadget as an add-on to an enterprise-level application is also a great selling tool. This kind of gadget follows the push model and is targeted toward existing users.

Any enterprise-level application, such as a Customer Relationship Management (CRM) or Enterprise Resource Planning (ERP) application, deals with a lot of frequently updated data. Users sometimes find it difficult to filter down data relevant to them for a particular scenario. A sidebar gadget providing the ready-to-use data can be very useful in this kind of scenario (see Figure 4.5).

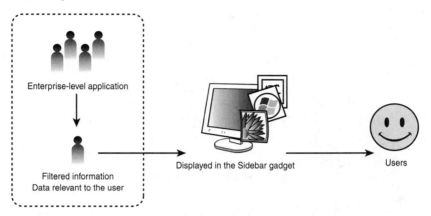

FIGURE 4.5   A Sidebar gadget used as a side product increases both the usability of the main application as well as customer satisfaction.

A gadget as a side product becomes a useful tool for existing customers. To enable a gadget for an enterprise-level application, you have to make sure of the following:

- First of all, expose required data to be displayed in the gadget in an open XML format (recommended RSS feed format).

- Enable a way to authenticate users to display data filtered by the individual user.

- Use existing web technologies such as Ajax and SOAP to access secure data from an XML web service.

This kind of gadget works as a complementary product to the actual application and is primarily used for displaying user-relevant information, as well as frequently updated data.

Case Study: Microsoft CRM Gadget, Gadget as a Side Product

Microsoft Dynamics Customer Relationship Management is a powerful enterprise-level application. Its capability to integrate with Microsoft Office applications, Microsoft Outlook, and Blackberry mobile devices makes it a state-of-the-art application.

One important feature of the CRM is that it acts as a central repository for all customer-related data and accounts related to a particular member. Normally a member has to log in to Microsoft Dynamics and access information filtered by different criteria, using a user interface provided by the application, an intranet application, or a website. Creating a gadget that displays the list of accounts and contacts associated with a current member is of immense help. The user no longer has to start Microsoft Dynamics and go to the accounts page to get this information. This is possible because the enterprise application enables gadget development by supporting the following (as illustrated in Figure 4.6):

- Microsoft CRM is exposes data through web APIs.

- Authentication for the member is possible from the gadget.

- The enterprise application provides a web service for accessing data.

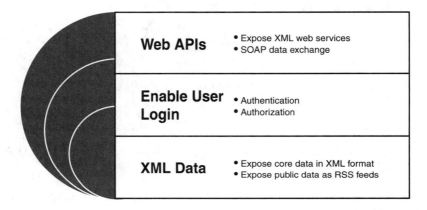

FIGURE 4.6   An enterprise-level application needs to expose data through web APIs and should support the technologies for gadget development.

Benefits of Using Gadgets as Side Products

A gadget used as a side product compliments the main application. The case study showed how a member of an enterprise-level application can benefit from the use of the gadget. A gadget as a side product increases the usability of the main product by doing the following:

- Providing ready-to-use information.

- Providing filtered and relevant data.

- Displaying data related to the logged-in member.

- If you use multiple instance of the gadget, enabling the member to search information with different filters.

Utility Gadget

A utility gadget normally is a watered-down version of a Windows application, giving access to quick tools and features provided by the operating system. Some utility gadgets provide information on CPU usage or available drive space. This kind of gadget can be used to create revenue within the pull model.

A utility gadget can be both a basic version of the main application or a side product complementing the application. For example, a basic utility in the form of a gadget can be distributed freely over the Internet, and a more feature-rich application with advanced features can be purchased from your website. If the gadget is popular, it will drive traffic to your website and eventually help sell the application.

In the actual implementation, a utility gadget typically is a watered-down version of the full application. This functionality can be exposed as an active component to be called and used by the gadget. In this scenario, the full-featured application exists on the provider's website and the Sidebar gadget platform is used in the following ways:

- A Sidebar gadget with a basic or watered-down version of the application

- A gadget that acts as a side product to the application

Trial software is quite standard for companies selling products and doing business online. The addition of the sidebar gadget can be a major advertisement for the utility and can be leveraged as a trial version of the software.

Case Study: Backup Software Utility Gadget

DBKP, a fictitious backup software company, provides robust, reliable, and complete backup software. The company provides a "trial version" of the software implemented as a gadget, providing some basic free services.

The company creates a gadget that provides quick access to the application's popular features, using APIs exposed in a dynamic link library that the application also uses.

Benefits of the Utility Gadget

The utility gadget can be both a free service for advertisement of the company as well as a side product for the actual application. It provides the following benefits to the company:

- The right set of features in a Sidebar gadget can make it instantly popular, resulting in lot of traffic to the website.

- The gadget provides quick access to the features of the backup application and makes the application more useful.

A utility gadget's feature set, which is meant for driving users to buy the actual product, has to be carefully chosen so that it drives potential users to purchase the product and become customers.

Free Information Gadget

A free information gadget, as the name suggests, provides regularly updated information as a free service. In turn it collects usage statistics from the gadget users. This can be thought of as similar to the process of mining web logs, where web logs are analyzed for page usage statistics. Information such as page views, durations on a page, and number of visits are used to make decisions. The only difference is now you are making the data available through the gadget and tracking the RSS feed instead of web pages.

The free information gadget's revenue model is based on the current trend in advertising, which values user choice. That is to say, this revenue model depends greatly on the statistics related to the number of users who views a particular piece of information. Data related to information that was shared a greater number of times or commented or viewed are used for advertisement purposes.

For example, a gadget providing video feed can use the statistical information on which video was shared or played the most. The demand for this kind of information becomes the basis of the free information gadget. These gadgets also promote a parent website and help generate revenue from banner advertisements.

You'll find more information on collecting usage statistics from the gadget in Appendix A.

A free information gadget can even use live data streaming for things such as broadcasting or podcasting. It can also have built-in advertisements, just like a real radio or video channel.

These gadgets take data in the form of an RSS feed from the provider website and display the data, formatted, to the user. The data in the information feed can contain links to pictures, audio, video, or just plain text or HTML. The gadget provides the title and a short description of the information. The user can click on either one to read the information or play the audio or video related to it.

This revenue model is based on the usage statistics of the information and also the ad banners in the website. The whole advertisement network is switching toward this trend, which is based on this kind of usage information.

To create a free information gadget, follow these steps:

1. Make your data available in the form of an RSS feed.

2. Track the usage of individual items in the feed.

3. Provide a link from the gadget to the actual website.

Case Study: NYBC News Gadget, a Free Information Gadget
NYBC, a New York broadcast company, provides access to the news from its website but consumers don't seem to be using the service. It provides a lot of options for users to add their opinions, ask questions, interact with the reporters, and rate and share news with others.

The company provides top local news in the form of an RSS feed that is freely available in the website. The data available is in a variety of formats: audio, video, and HTML with pictures. NYBC also provides streaming servers for live commentaries. The customers are local to New York and it has a lot of presence in the newspaper market. What it's aiming for is an online presence.

The company leverages a Sidebar gadget platform to solve this problem. As an analyst in the company you come up with a News Gadget for New Yorkers. The gadget provides the following:

- Frequently updated news in the form of an RSS feed

- A radio feature built into the gadget for live streaming

- Links to the news website

Benefits of the Gadget

Having a gadget on your desktop, which gives you regularly updated news in the form of text, audio, and video, is far more attractive than visiting a website to access information. The gadget platform can provide the following benefits in the current scenario:

- Subscribers love the easy-to-use gadget for their favorite newspaper.

- Online activities will increase because each news item will have a corresponding link to the website.

- The RSS feed can be tracked easily for usage information.

- The streaming server can also include audio and video advertisements.

Supporting Your Gadget

Supporting a gadget is similar to supporting any product, but in many ways it is relatively easier. Gadget support is crucial because if you are developing a gadget for revenue, you have to make sure that it works properly.

Because no help file comes with the gadget, if you want to include some kind of tutorial, it has to be done in the support page. Remember that gadgets are all about interactivity. A forum dedicated to the gadget is very helpful in acquiring feedback from users in the form of suggestions and new feature requests. As with any software product, you need to provide an upgrade path for new features and services.

Support features that can help maintain a gadget include the following:

- A link to the support page, which describes the features.

- An email link to contact the developer or the company that provides the gadget.

- An online forum that provides a mechanism for users to communicate with each other and the developer/company for issues. A link to a forum in the gadget is helpful.

- A page dedicated for suggestions, new features, and so on.

- Auto-update functionality. Detailed further in Appendix A.

Links should be provided in the Settings page to enable the user to visit the corresponding web page.

TABLE 4.1   Differences Between an Application and a Sidebar Gadget

Application	A Sidebar Gadget
Normally has a help file associated with it.	No help file.
Has about a page that contains company or developer information for contact.	A gadget's settings page can be used to add an email address or website information.
Products normally have dedicated forums for support and a huge user community.	Contact information in the form of email address. A support/suggestions page is desirable. A lightweight forum for a discussion board is also helpful.
Comes with auto-update functionality.	Needs to be upgradeable and needs user's interaction for upgrade.
Products normally have dedicated forums for support.	Contact information in the form of email address. A support/suggestions page is desirable. A lightweight forum or discussion board is also helpful.
Flyout page.	320 pixels×240 pixels.

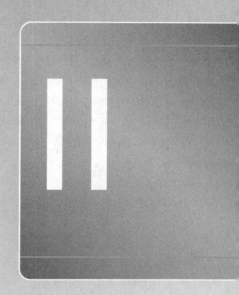

PART

II

Developing a Gadget

IN THIS PART

Creating a Simple Gadget with RSS/Atom Feed

"The ability to simplify means to eliminate the unnecessary so that the necessary may speak"

-Hans Hoffman

Feed Gadgets

One type of information gadget is the feed gadget, a gadget that uses an online feed to display data. A feed typically uses an XML data format, which contains all the data along with the information about the data—the metadata. A typical feed icon is shown in Figure 5.1.

A feed can be in the form of RSS 2.0 or Atom 1.0. Both these formats store metadata in the form of an XML file.

Brief Background on Feeds

Really Simple Syndication (RSS) and Atom are the syndication formats used for blog feeds. RSS was developed by Harvard University. It is a closed standard and cannot be extended, whereas Atom, which is based on RSS, is the newer, open, and extensible format. It supports all kinds of payloads, such as XML, XHTML, base64-encoded binary, and so on, along with text and HTML, as originally supported by RSS. More information on RSS can be found at the Harvard website, http://cyber.law.harvard.edu/rss/rss.html, and about the Atom syndication format at http://tools.ietf.org/html/rfc4287.

FIGURE 5.1   A standard feed icon. A website with this icon indicates that the contents are available in the form of RSS syndication.

Another difference also comes in the way the formats store data. Here is a simple example of a node in an Atom and an RSS format. Note the difference in the metadata fields and content type.

ATOM 1.0 node:

```
<entry>
  <title>WidgetBox: A Windows Vista Sidebar Gadget</title>
  <link href="http://www.innovatewithgadgets.com/2007/07 "/>
  <id>2786381406870346951</id>
  <published>2007-07-25T17:39:00.000-07:00</published>
  <updated>2007-07-26T11:35:05.078-07:00</updated>
  <content type='html'>  ...Actual content of  of the blog...    </content >
</entry>
```

RSS 2.0 node:

```
<item>
  <title>WidgetBox: A Windows Vista Sidebar Gadget</title>
  <link>http://www.innovatewithgadgets.com/2007/07</link>
  <description>       ...Actual content of  of the blog...       </description>
  <pubDate>Tue, 04 September 2007 04:00:00 GMT</pubDate>
  <guid> 2786381406870346951</guid>
</item>
```

As you can see from these samples, an individual entry in an Atom node starts with the field tag `<entry>`, whereas an RSS node starts and ends with `<item>`. The other noticeable difference is the content, which in RSS is stored inside a `<description>` tag, whereas in Atom it's inside a `<content>` tag. RSS allows text and HTML in the description section, whereas content in Atom can be of type XML, XHTML, image (in the form of base64-encoded data), and is specified in the attribute `type` as in this example, which is `<content type='html'>`.

In development, during the parsing of an XML file, you just have to switch the tags for each type of the syndication format. If you are reading a date, you have to look for `<pubDate>` in RSS format and `<published>` in Atom format.

About the MyBlog Gadget

The MyBlog Gadget is an information gadget that displays data from an online blog feed. It supports both RSS 2.0 and Atom 1.0 feeds. This example needs the title of the blog, which is to be displayed on the Sidebar. The gadget also fetches the blog entry, the actual content of each blog, and the date published from the web feed.

The MyBlog Gadget is designed to display the last five blog titles in the Gadget window, and when the user clicks on the title, the description of the blog is shown in the flyout window (see Figure 5.2). For this example, when the gadget is loaded for the first time, it reads the blog available at www.innovatewithgadgets.com/atom.xml.

The user has the option to change the feed URL from the Settings page.

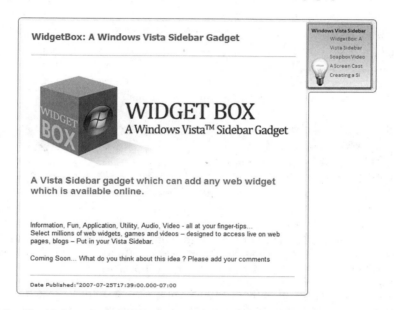

FIGURE 5.2   The MyBlog Gadget displays the last five titles from my blog from an online feed. It also displays full blog entries in the flyout window.

The goal of the first version of the MyBlog Gadget is to create a simple gadget with the following:

- The gadget displays the last five titles of the blog.

- It displays the contents of the blog, with dates, in the flyout window.

- The gadget supports both RSS 2.0 and Atom 1.0 formats.

- It enables the user to change the feed.

Basic Framework of the MyBlog Gadget

To create a Sidebar gadget you need an HTML editor and a way to group related files. Dreamweaver, Visual Studio, Visual Studio Express Edition (free download), and Microsoft Expression Studio are some of the HTML editors you can use for this purpose. Visual Studio Express editions can be downloaded at http://www.microsoft.com/express/download/.

All the examples in the book are created using Visual Studio 2005. To create a gadget, follow these steps:

1. Create a new website in Visual Studio (Shift+Alt+N), choose the location as file system and Empty Web Site among the Visual Studio Installed templates, and enter the path as %userprofile%\AppData\Local\Microsoft\Windows Sidebar\Gadgets\MyBlog.Gadget. This creates a folder for it, called MyBlog.Gadget, in %userprofile%\AppData\Local\Microsoft\Windows Sidebar\Gadgets\.

> **NOTE**
>
> %userprofile% is equivalent to the user's profile folder. For example, if your username to log in to Vista is John, the %userprofile% translates to C:\Users\John. Try typing `%userprofile%` in Windows Explorer.

2. Create a new folder inside the project and name it Images to store the images related to the gadget. Creating a gadget directly in the standard gadget folder makes it available for side-by-side testing while in development.

3. After you have the required files in the MyBlog.Gadget folder, the gadget can be added in the Sidebar through the Gadget Picker window.

4. To directly view the gadget files and structure of the gadget that comes along with the book, install the gadget MyBlog.Gadget and then open a web project inside Visual Studio 2005.

5. Choose the location type as file system, browse, and give the path as %userprofile%\AppData\Local\Microsoft\Windows Sidebar\Gadgets\MyBlog.Gadget.

Required Files

To create a Sidebar gadget you need at least two files: an HTML file that becomes the main window of the gadget, and an XML manifest file with the name Gadget.xml, which is the gadget configuration file. All other files are optional.

Two other HTML files are needed if we want functionality: one for the Flyout window and one for the gadget's Settings panel. You also need a script file for the core features and a stylesheet file for the gadget presentation. Granted, a script and stylesheet can also be included in the Gadget.html file, but it is normally a good practice to have them as separate files.

The list of files required for the MyBlog Gadget includes:

- `Gadget.html` for the gadget's main window

- `Gadget.css` for the gadget stylesheet

- `Gadget.js`, the gadget script file that provides the core functionality

- `Flyout.html` for the flyout window that displays the blog entry

- `Settings.html` for the Settings dialog page

- `Gadget.xml` to maintain the gadget configuration

In all, the MyBlog Gadget requires six files to be placed in the MyBlog.Gadget folder and a few images for the icon, background, and logo inside the Images folder.

Directory Structure

The directory structure of a gadget consists of a folder named MyBlog.Gadget, which contains three HTML files: `Gadget.HTML`, `Flyout.HTML`, and `Settings.HTML`. There is also one stylesheet file, `Gadget.css`, one JavaScript file, `Gadget.js`, and a manifest file, `Gadget.xml`, with a subfolder, Images (see Figure 5.3).

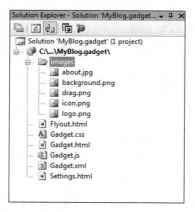

FIGURE 5.3   The directory and file structure of a simple gadget contain some HTML files, a JavaScript file, a stylesheet file, and an XML file.

Adding a folder inside MyBlog.Gadget with the name of the locale—for example, en-US for English, fr-FR for French (France), and so on—and adding the entire file list inside the folder makes the gadget available for that locale (see Figure 5.4).

Having a locale-specific folder helps when you need to create multiple versions of the gadget for multiple locales. For example, consider a gadget that displays text in French in France but in English in the United States. The gadget can have two folders, for example: one en-US, that contains English versions of the files, and the other fr-FR with French versions of the same folders inside. The Vista Sidebar automatically checks for the locale folder and displays the appropriate language accordingly. More details can be found in Chapter 7, "The MyBlog Gadget Revisited."

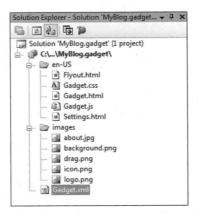

FIGURE 5.4   The directory and file structure of a simple gadget with locale information.

CAUTION

The gadget shown in Figure 5.4 works only in the English-locale computers, but the gadget with structure as shown in Figure 5.3 works in all locales.

The Images folder contains image files related to the gadget. The paths for these files need to be referenced in the gadget manifest file as well as in the gadget's main window's HTML file.

Here is the list of image files used in the MyBlog Gadget:

- `about.png` is used on the settings page to display the About This Gadget image.

- `background.png` is the gadget's wallpaper.

- `drag.png` is displayed when the gadget is dragged in the Gadget Picker.

- `icon.png` is used to distinguish different gadgets in the Gadget Picker.

- `logo.png` is used for branding and is displayed when the user clicks on more details in the Gadget Picker window.

You can see what each of these files looks like in Figure 5.5.

In Table 5.1 you can see a summary of each file necessary to create the MyBlog gadget.

FIGURE 5.5   A set of images is used for a sidebar gadget.

TABLE 5.1   A Gadget Uses at Least the Following Set of Files

File Type	Filename	Description
Manifest	Gadget.xml	An XML file defining the gadget properties, including name, icon, and description
Main window	Gadget.html	Defines the main window of the gadget
Flyout	Flyout.html	The flyout window
Settings file	Settings.html	Exposes a UI for user settings
Script	Gadget.js	Gadget core functionality
Stylesheets	Gadget.css	Stylesheet to be used for main window
Background	Background.png	The gadget background
Other Images	about.png, icon.png, drag.png, logo.png	Used in the Gadget Picker window

How the MyBlog Gadget Works

So far we discussed the files needed to make a gadget and the gadget's directory structure. This section goes deeper into the gadget's workings and tries to lay out the steps involved, from the first time the gadget is loaded to the point when it displays the data and what happens when user changes the settings.

Figure 5.6 shows a detail layout of an information gadget. The figure shows a gadget inside a Vista Sidebar, which reads a feed from an online blog website. In this case, the blog is http://innovatewithgadgets.com/atom.xml. All the different files are also shown to give you an idea of their role in the Vista Sidebar. As you can see, Gadget.html becomes the gadget's main window of the gadget and Gadget.xml is used to configure the gadget and is explicitly used by the Vista Sidebar to distinguish between different gadgets.

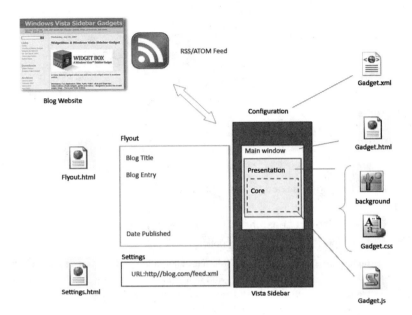

FIGURE 5.6 The figure shows a complete layout and the architecture of the MyBlog Gadget.

The following list describes the steps taken by Windows Vista Sidebar when the gadget is loaded:

1. Windows Vista Sidebar reads the `Gadget.xml` manifest file to find the HTML file used for the main window (`Gadget.html` in this example).

2. `Gadget.html` is loaded inside the gadget window; it has the reference to the `Gadget.css` stylesheet as well as the `Gadget.js` script file.

3. The gadget's main window retrieves and displays style information from `Gadget.css`.

4. The core gadget code is defined inside the `Gadget.js` JavaScript file, which has code to fetch the online feed, using the default feed.

5. The Settings page (`Settings.html`) is used to change the default feed.

6. After the data is fetched, the feed's title is written in the gadget's main window and other required information, such as details, date published, and so on, is stored in memory to be displayed in the Flyout window.

The Manifest File

The gadget's root file is the `Gadget.xml` manifest file. It contains gadget-level configuration information that the Windows Vista Sidebar requires to identify each gadget, including its name, author, and so on. It also contains the name of the HTML file that defines the gadget's layout. Here is the content of the manifest file for the MyBlog Gadget:

```xml
<?xml version="1.0" encoding="utf-8" ?>
<gadget>
  <name>Blog Gadget</name>
  <namespace>Innovate.Gadgets</namespace>
  <version>1.0</version>
  <author name="Rajesh Lal">
    <logo src="images/logo.png" />
    <info url="www.innovatewithgadgets.com" />
  </author>
  <copyright>Copyright&#169; 2008</copyright>
  <description>Display XML Feeds from blogs</description>
  <icons>
    <icon width="70" height="80" src="images/icon.png" />
  </icons>
  <hosts>
    <host name="sidebar">
      <base type="HTML" apiVersion="1.0.0" src="gadget.html" />
      <permissions>Full</permissions>
      <platform minPlatformVersion="1.0" />
      <defaultImage src="images/drag.png"/>
    </host>
  </hosts>
</gadget>
```

Figure 5.7 shows the gadget in the Gadget Picker window. Gadget.xml directly translates to the values displayed in the Gadget Picker. The name of the gadget and the icon are shown among other gadgets. The logo, description, author, copyright, and info URL are shown in the detail section when the user clicks on the gadget and selects View Details in the bottom left corner.

Table 5.2 lists the keywords found in the gadget.xml file, along with their value and description.

TABLE 5.2   A List of the Most Commonly Used Fields and Their Values

Keyword	Value	Description
<name>	Blog Gadget	Name of the gadget as it appears in the gadget selection box
<author>	Rajesh Lal	Name of the person who wrote the gadget
<logo>	Images/logo.png	Will be used in the Show Details portion of the Gadget Picker
<copyright>	Copyright 2008	Copyright information, including name and copyright date
<description>	Display XML Feeds from blogs	Description of the gadget and what it does
<icon>	Images/Icon.png	Name of the icon file with relative path, the graphic displayed in the gadget selection box
<src>	Gadget.html	Name of the HTML file that makes up your gadget
<info url>	www.innovatewithgadgets.com	Website associated with the gadget

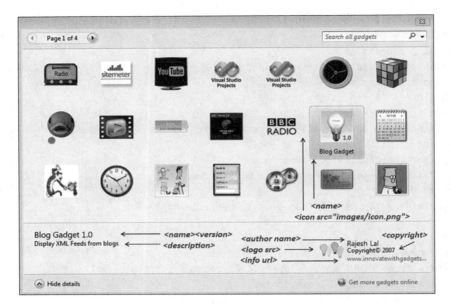

FIGURE 5.7   The Gadget Picker window, showing the MyBlog Gadget. Notice how the corresponding values of `gadget.xml` display in the Gadget Picker window.

These values are used in the Gadget Picker window.

> **NOTE**
>
> The Gadget Picker is the window used to install and uninstall a gadget. It's the window that appears when you click Add Gadgets in the Vista Sidebar.

Apart from the configuration, the user also needs to know where the Settings page is and how to customize the gadget's values; in this case, the feed the gadget is intended to track. This topic is covered in the next section.

Gadget Settings

The Settings page is an HTML file which can be used to change the values for the current session. The MyBlog Gadget uses the Settings page to enable the user to change the feed URL, as shown in Figure 5.8. All changes made by the user are stored in memory and are managed by the Vista Sidebar.

The default feed URL, until changed by the user, is an Atom format feed with the URL www.innovatewithgadgets.com/atom.xml. This default feed is set in the gadget `load` function in the `Gadget.js` file. This can also be thought of as initialization with a default value, which occurs when the gadget is loaded for the first time. The Settings page enables the user to change the default value for the feed URL. This change is effective when the Settings page is closed, with the gadget taking the new value from memory.

FIGURE 5.8   The Settings page is an HTML file that enables the user to change the default feed.

The following JavaScript code initializes the value of the feed URL in the gadget's main window. It checks whether the user has set the feed URL and, if not, sets the URL to the default value. After the user sets the feed URL, the gadget fetches the data from the new URL.

```
if (System.Gadget.Settings.read("FeedURL")=="")
    {
       DefaultFeed = "http://innovatewithgadgets.com/atom.xml";
       System.Gadget.Settings.write ("FeedURL", DefaultFeed);
    }
```

FeedURL is the variable that stores the URL of the feed in the memory and fetches the data based on the source specified in the value.

The Settings page uses two JavaScript functions to load and save the URL feed information. LoadSettings, as shown here, loads the initial value of the feed URL:

```
function loadSettings()
{
if  (System.Gadget.Settings.read("FeedURL") == "")
  {
  document.getElementById('TextBoxFeedURL').value =
  "http://innovatewithgadgets.com/atom.xml";
  }
  else
  {
```

```
document.getElementById('TextBoxFeedURL').value =
System.Gadget.Settings.read("FeedURL");
  }
}
```

Next, the function SaveSettings saves the value that the user enters:

```
function saveSettings()
{
System.Gadget.Settings.write("feedChanged",true);
System.Gadget.Settings.write("FeedURL", document.getElementById➥
('TextBoxFeedURL').value );
}
```

TextBoxFeedURL is the text box that takes the feed's value in the settings page as shown previously, in Figure 5.8.

The variable feedchanged is also set along with the FeedURL to let the gadget know that the feed has been changed and the data needs to be refreshed from the new online source. document.getElementById is the method used to get the value of the text box.

Both of these functions need to reside in the Settings page as JavaScript code. If you open the Settings.html file in Visual Studio designer, you can see both these functions.

Parts of the MyBlog Gadget

The gadget can be further divided into three parts: the data that is fetched from the online feed in the form of an XML file in RSS/Atom format, the core function(s) that fetches the data, and finally the presentation of the data (see Figure 5.9).

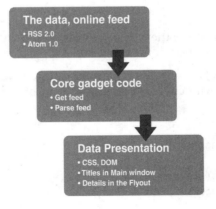

FIGURE 5.9   The gadget comprises data, core functionality, and the presentation.

The following sections address these three parts in more detail.

The Data

- The title of the online feed, such as "Blog on Windows Vista Sidebar" or "XYZ's Blog"

- The author of the blog

- The titles of last five blog entries posted

- The description of the last five blog entries (to be displayed in the flyout window)

- The date published for each of the blog entries (to be displayed in the flyout window)

The first thing required is to find out whether the online feed is in RSS or Atom format.

Here's a typical Atom feed:

```
<? xml version="1.0" encoding="UTF-8" ?>
<feed xmlns="http://www.w3.org/2005/Atom" xml:lang="en">
   <entry>
      <title></title>
      <content></content>
      <published></published>
   </entry>
         <entry>... </entry>
</feed>
```

This is what a typical RSS feed looks like:

```
<? xml version="1.0" encoding="UTF-8" ?>
<rss version="2.0">
   <channel>
     <item>
         <title></title>
         <description></description>
         <pubDate></pubDate>
     </item>
     <item>...</item>
 ...
   </channel>
</rss>
```

The root node of an Atom feed is identified by the `<feed>` tag and each item in the feed is a child node of the `<entry>` tag, whereas the root tag in RSS is `<rss>` and each child node is inside a `<channel>` tag and identified by the `<item>` tag.

The data needed for this gadget are in the `<title>`, `<content>`, and `<published>` tags in an Atom file. In the case of an RSS feed, this same data is inside the `<title>`, `<description>`, and `<pubDate>` tags.

Core Functionality of the Gadget

The core code of the MyBlog Gadget is actually a set of JavaScript functions inside the Gadget.js file. This includes functions that set up the gadget for the first time, communicate with the online feed, and download and parse the data. This file also includes code for storing the downloaded data in memory and displaying it in the main window and the flyout window. Finally, the code for managing the user settings and displaying the flyout windows is also found in the Gadget.js file.

The core JavaScript file Gadget.js is included in three files: the main gadget file Gadget.html, the settings file Settings.html, as well as the flyout window Flyout.html with the help of the <script> tag as shown in the following line. The functionality of the Settings page was already discussed in the last section. This section deals with the core functionality surrounding the main window Gadget.html and the data displayed in the flyout window.

```
<script src="Gadget.js" type="text/javascript"></script>
```

Gadget.html uses the core functions for the following:

- Set up the gadget for the first time
- Set up the path of the flyout and settings HTML
- Set the default feed URL
- Get the feed using Ajax
- Parse the feed
- Save the data in memory to display in the flyout window

The Settings.html file embeds JavaScript to load settings and save settings. And finally, the Flyout.html file embeds JavaScript to create the content dynamically based on the title, which is clicked and the data corresponding to the title is stored in the memory.

Main Gadget Window

The first step is to set up the gadget for the first time. Gadget.html calls a *body on load* function Setup(), which is defined inside the Gadget.js.

The Setup function takes care of

- The sizing and position of elements of the main gadget
- Setting the flyout windows and the Settings window
- Calling the getFeed function with the default settings

When this is done, it's time, with the help of the Gadget API, to set up the path of the Settings window and the flyout:

```
System.Gadget.Flyout.file = "Flyout.html";
System.Gadget.settingsUI = "Settings.html";
```

Now you need to get the feed using Ajax. The GetFeed() function makes the remote call and downloads the online feed. This process uses an XMLHTTPRequest object to make an asynchronous call to open the feed URL and call a function when done. The callback function, parseFeed(), is responsible for parsing the XML file received.

> **NOTE**
>
> JavaScript Object Notation (JSON) is a lightweight data-interchange format and is comparable to XML. More information on JSON can be found at http://www.json.org.

XMLHTTPRequest is an object JavaScript uses to fetch data through the Internet. The data can be in the form XML, HTML, Text, or JSON. This is the core component of AJAX (Asynchronous JavaScript and XML), which is what makes an information gadget work. For any gadget that needs to fetch data from the Web, you need to use the XMLHTTPRequest object.

To create an XMLHTTPRequest object, enter the following:

```
var req = new ActiveXObject("Microsoft.XMLHTTP");
```

The common methods and properties of the object are listed in Table 5.3.

TABLE 5.3   Common Methods and Properties of the XMLHTTPRequest Object

Method	Description
abort()	Stops the current request
getAllResponseHeaders()	Returns complete set of headers (labels and values) as a string
getResponseHeader("*headerLabel*")	Returns the string value of a single header label
open("*method*", "*URL*"[, *asyncFlag*[, "*userName*"[, "*password*"]]])	Assigns the destination URL, method, and other optional attributes of a pending request
send(*content*)	Transmits the request, optionally with postable string or DOM object data
setRequestHeader("*label*", "*value*")	Assigns a label/value pair to the header to be sent with a request

Property	Description
Onreadystatechange	Event handler for an event that fires at every state change
readyState	Object status integer: 0 = uninitialized 1 = loading 2 = loaded 3 = interactive 4 = complete
responseText	String version of data returned from server process
responseXML	DOM-compatible document object of data returned from server process

TABLE 5.3   Continued

Property	Description
Status	Numeric code returned by server, such as 404 for "Not Found" or 200 for "OK"
statusText	String message accompanying the status code

The GetFeed function uses the XMLHTTPRequest object to get the data from the URL:

```
rssObj = new ActiveXObject("Microsoft.XMLHTTP");
rssObj.open("GET", System.Gadget.Settings.read("FeedURL"),true);
rssObj.onreadystatechange = function()
 {
    if (rssObj.readyState === 4)
 {
        if (rssObj.status === 200)
 {
        rssXML = rssObj.responseXML;
        parseRSS();
        }
        else
 {
        error.innerText = " Service not available";
        chkConn = setInterval(getFeed, 30 * 60000);
        }
        }
    else
        {
    loading.title = "Connecting...";
        }
 }

rssObj.send(null);
```

NOTE

readyState = 4 denotes that the XMLHttpRequest object has completed the data-fetching process and 200 is the numeric code returned by the server. A status of 200 means the data has been successfully received.

In this code we try to load the feed URL and, on state change, call the function, which checks for the current state and either calls parseRSS(), if the status returned is 200, or sets the Service Not Available screen.

The act of parsing the XML actually scans the data received and filters the information the application requires. After the XML feed is loaded in the rssXML object, check whether the feedType is Atom or RSS, and based on the feedType, store the values in an array. The code checks the XML data, rssXML, for the tag name entry and based on that decides whether the feed type is RSS or Atom.

```
if ( rssXML.getElementsByTagName("entry").length > 0 )
    {
    feedType = "Atom";
    }
    else
    {
    feedType = "RSS";
    }
if ( feedType == "Atom" )
    {
    rssItems = rssXML.getElementsByTagName("entry");
    blogTitles = rssXML.getElementsByTagName("title");
    blogAuthor = rssXML.getElementsByTagName("author")[0].firstChild.text;
    myblogTitle = blogTitles[0].text + " - " + blogAuthor ;
    }
else
    {
    rssItems = rssXML.getElementsByTagName("item");
    blogTitleChannel = rssXML.getElementsByTagName("channel");
    myblogTitle = blogTitleChannel[0].firstChild.text;
    }
```

Because the data also needs to appear in the flyout window, the next step is to create arrays and store the values in those arrays, as in the following code:

```
var Descriptions = new Array();
var Titles = new Array();
var PublishedList = new Array();
var Authors = new Array();
```

As you have seen, the gadget's core functionality comes from the code in the script file. The gadget first sets up the gadget's flyout window and Settings page, initializes the feed URL, and then fetches the data using Ajax technology. After the data is received, the parseFeed function parses the data and stores the value in the arrays in the memory.

Presenting with CSS and DOM

The final part of the gadget deals with the presentation of the data in the gadget window, the flyout, and the Settings page. The presentation uses the fetched data to make the structure of the gadget display; that is, the HTML portion of the gadget. The CSS file associated with the gadget is used for the gadget's presentation. The raw data is styled with standard font face and size as defined in the CSS file. The CSS file also determines the gadget's dimension and the location of the HTML elements in the gadget. Finally, the

Document Object Model (DOM) is used to dynamically set the value. You have already seen the use of the functions `GetElementById` and `GetElementByTagNames`. These are the standard functions used to access the elements of the document.

CSS

A cascading stylesheet is used for the presentation of the data. It helps to separate the data's structure from the window style.

You can use a single CSS file for all the HTML files (`Gadget.html`, `Settings.html`, and `Flyout.html`). All you need to do is link the CSS file in the corresponding HTML file.

In the MyBlog Gadget, `Gadget.html` is linked to the CSS file with this statement:

```
<link rel="stylesheet" type="text/css" href="gadget.css" />
```

CSS information can also be put directly in the HTML file, as is done in the `Flyout.html` file. The stylesheet is defined inside the <head> tag of the HTML file as follows:

```
<style>
body
  {
    font-family: Calibri;
    font-size: 2px ;
    width:500px;
    height:620px;
    margin:0px;
    padding:0px;
    overflow: auto;
  }
</style>
```

Notice how the `overflow` property of the body ensures that a scrollbar appears in the flyout window if the HTML page content is longer than the specified height.

The content in the main window HTML files is wrapped in DIV blocks, which are used in the CSS file for applying the appropriate style. DIV blocks also allow the JavaScript to access the elements inside the DOM.

```
<div id="blogtitle">Windows Vista Sidebar </div>
<div id="content">
<div id="loading" title ="Connecting...wait"></div>
<div id="error"></div>
<a href="http://www.innovatewithgadgets.com" title ="blog website" >
<div id="mylogo" title ="Go to Gadgets Blog Website">
```

The `blogtitle` block has the following entry in the CSS file; this ensures that the blog title appears at the upper-left corner (10px, 10px) and is displayed in the color navy:

```
#blogtitle
{
    position:absolute;
    left:10px;
    top: 10px;
    color: Navy;
    font-weight:bold ;
}
```

DOM

Document Object Model is a standard representation of an HTML file. It enables scripts to dynamically access and update the content, structure, and style of documents.

For example, to set the text inside the `blogtitle` block, you need to call

```
document.getElementById("blogtitle").title ="Vista Gadget";
```

The `getElementById` function is a standard function in DOM to access the elements the HTML document.

Here are some more examples of DOM accessing the DIV blocks mentioned earlier. The following DOM methods are called inside the gadget's `resize` function:

```
document.getElementById("contenttable").height = "90%";
document.getElementById("content").style.top ="24px";
document.getElementById("content").style.width = "80px";
document.getElementById("content").style.left = "38px";
document.getElementById("content").style.fontsize ="11px";
document.getElementById("mylogo").style.left ="2px";
document.getElementById("mylogo").style.top ="70px";
document.getElementById("mylogo").style.height="70px";
```

Titles in Main Window   When the data is fetched, the `parseRSS` function first updates the title in the gadget's main window. The DIV blocks in the `Gadget.html` page need to be updated with the last five titles in the blog. The following code shows the first DIV element that will be updated with the blog title. The `id` is `cell0`. The five elements are `cell0`, `cell1`, `cell2`, `cell3`, and `cell4`, which are updated with the blog entry titles.

```
<table id="contenttable" width="100%" height="100%"  border="0"
➥cellpadding="0" cellspacing="0">
<tr>
 <td class="title" valign="middle"
 onmouseover="this.style.background='url(images/shadow.png)';"
 onmouseout="this.style.background='none';">
 <div title="Hello" id="cell0"></div>
 </td>
</tr>
</table>
```

The following code adds the title of the blog entry to each of the five DIV elements, using a loop:

```
for (i=0; i<5; i++) {
if (feedType == "Atom" )
{
if (rssItems[i].getElementsByTagName("title")) { rssTitle =
➥ rssItems[i].getElementsByTagName("title")[0].text; }
if (rssItems[i].getElementsByTagName("content")) { rssSummary =
➥ rssItems[i].getElementsByTagName("content")[0].text;  }
if (rssItems[i].getElementsByTagName("published")) {rssPubDate =
➥ rssItems[i].getElementsByTagName("published")[0].text; }
}

else
{
if (rssItems[i].getElementsByTagName("title")) {rssTitle =
➥ rssItems[i].getElementsByTagName("title")[0].text;}
if (rssItems[i].getElementsByTagName("description")) {rssSummary =
➥ rssItems[i].getElementsByTagName("description")[0].text; }
if (rssItems[i].getElementsByTagName("pubDate")[0]) {rssPubDate =
➥ rssItems[i].getElementsByTagName("pubDate")[0].text; }
}
Titles[i] = rssTitle
Descriptions[i] = rssSummary;
PublishedList[i] = rssPubDate;

document.getElementById("cell" + (cell)).innerHTML =
'<div align="left" onclick="showFlyout(\'' + i + '\');">'
+ Mid(rssTitle,0,12) + '</div>';

document.getElementById("cell" + (cell)).title = rssTitle;
}
```

This code shows how the DIV elements are set for the blog entry titles. Notice the showFlyout function, which is also added in the cell's innerHTML. The showFlyout(i) function is called when the title is clicked on in the gadget window. Both the ShowFlyout and HideFlyout functions use the Gadget Object Model's built-in namespace System.Gadget.Flyout to show or hide the flyout window.

```
function showFlyout(i)
{

    if (System.Gadget.Flyout.show == false)
    {
```

```
            myWidthVariable =System.Gadget.Settings.read("FlyoutWidth");
            myHeightVariable =System.Gadget.Settings.read("FlyoutHeight");
            System.Gadget.Settings.write("currentClickedCell", i);
            System.Gadget.Flyout.file = "Flyout.html";
            System.Gadget.Flyout.show = true;
    }
    else
    {
            hideFlyout();
    }
}
function hideFlyout()
{
   System.Gadget.Flyout.show = false;
}
```

When the flyout window is loaded, the startUpPage function is called, which sets the width and height of the flyout window. The following code is the HTML for the flyout window:

```
<body  onload="startUpPage()">
<table cellpadding = 10 cellspacing = 10 width=100% height = 100%><tr>
➥<td valign=top>
<script  type="text/javascript">BuildMyBlog();</script>
</td></tr>
</table>
</body>
```

Here is the startupPage function in the Gadget.js file:

```
function startUpPage()
 {
document.body.style.width = System.Gadget.document.parentWindow.
➥myWidthVariable;

document.body.style.height = System.Gadget.document.parentWindow.
➥myHeightVariable;
 }
```

The main function, which creates the content of the blog, is the BuildMyBlog function. This function takes the values from the parent window Gadget.html arrays:

```
function BuildMyBlog()
{
    var BlogTitle= System.Gadget.document.parentWindow.Titles;
    var BlogDescription = System.Gadget.document.parentWindow.Descriptions;
```

```
    var BlogPublished = System.Gadget.document.parentWindow.PublishedList;
    var i = System.Gadget.Settings.read("currentClickedCell");

try
    {
    document.write('<h3><font face ="Calibiri" color="#006699">' +
     BlogTitle[i] + '</font></h3><hr noshade="true" size="1"><font face
    ="Calibiri" size = "2">' + BlogDescription[i] + '</font><hr
    noshade="true" size="1"> <font face ="verdana" size = 1>Date
    Published:"' + BlogPublished[i] + '</font>');
    }
catch(e)
    {
    document.write('Error occured !')
    }
}
```

The `BuildMyBlog` function uses JavaScript's `Document.Write` to create the content dynamically, based on the value of I and the corresponding value stored in the array `BlogTitle`, `BlogDescription`, and `BlogPublished`.

Putting It All Together

It's time to look at the complete picture. So far there are three HTML pages, all of which are linked with `Gadget.js` files. The main window is responsible for initialization of the gadget, fetching the data, and parsing and storing the data in the list. The Settings page loads the settings from memory as well as enables the user to change the settings, which are, again, stored in memory. And last of all, the flyout window, based on the parsed data stored in the parent gadget window array, displays the blog entries and the date published. The flyout window also sets its own dimension on startup.

Here is a list of JavaScript functions used for the MyBlog Gadget. You can get a visual sense of how each of these functions is used from Figure 5.10.

Main window:

- Setup

- Settings

- Resize

- Get feed—parse feed

- Save in memory

- Settings closed

Settings page:

- `LoadSettings`
- `SaveSettings`

Flyout page:

- Startup page
- Build blog

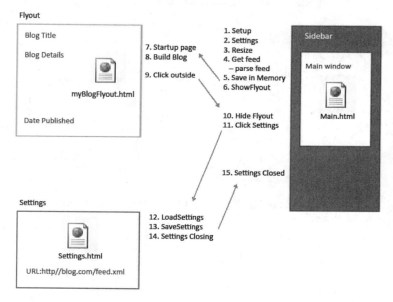

FIGURE 5.10   The figure shows the sequence of functions called in the gadget.

After all the files have been created and the gadget tested in the local machine, you need to zip the complete folder as `MyBlog.zip` and change the extension from `MyBlog.zip` to `MyBlog.Gadget`.

CAUTION

Sometimes a zip folder also includes the folder structure. This is not a valid package for the gadget. To do this correctly, open the MyBlog.Gadget folder, select all the files *inside* the folder, choose Send To in the context menu, and select Compressed (Zipped) Folder from the submenu. The zip file will be named after one of the files in the folder. When you are finished, rename the zip file to the name you want for the gadget and then change the extension of the zip file to `.gadget`.

You are ready to deploy and share the gadget. You can distribute your gadget as a single file with the extension .gadget. To install the gadget the end user needs to double-click the gadget file, which automatically installs the gadget.

In Figure 5.11, you can see how the Windows compression tool is used to create the zip file.

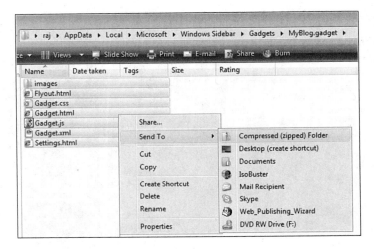

FIGURE 5.11   Rather than choose MyBlog.Gadget to zip, select the files inside the MyBlog.Gadget folder to zip.

Design Patterns and Standard Practices

"Design is the conscious effort to impose a meaningful order."

—Victor Papanek

Design Patterns

Design patterns refer to tried and tested solutions to recurring problems. Standard practice points to the reuse of known methods for developing functionality common to similar applications.

Although gadgets are lightweight applications and don't follow a complete software development life cycle (SDLC), developing a gadget is similar to developing software. Knowledge of existing patterns and practices and taking a standardized approach helps a lot in gadget development and ensures a smooth development process.

What is the common functionality of a particular type of gadget? What factors in gadget development enable you to extend an existing gadget, to customize a gadget according to new requirements? These are some of the questions you need to answer before developing a gadget. Chapter 5, "Creating a Simple Gadget with RSS/Atom Feed," concentrated on the gadget's basic functionality. This chapter takes a more methodical approach. The basic goal is to create a gadget that can be dynamic and loosely coupled so that it can adapt and extend itself.

This chapter lists a set of design patterns and standard practices to help in gadget development. This provides a consistent and standard framework for development. This list is not intended to be comprehensive but rather one that gets you thinking about design patterns within the context of gadget development.

The following standard patterns and practices, which are illustrated in Figure 6.1, have important benefits with regard to gadget development:

- Maintainable
- Customizable
- Extensible

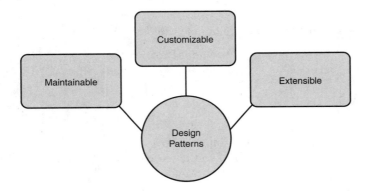

FIGURE 6.1   Following a design pattern benefits the developer in the long run.

The following section discusses each of these aspects in more detail.

Maintainable

Having a standard design pattern helps to maintain the gadget and makes it easier to add new features. After the gadget is uploaded you might receive a number of requests from users all over the world for improvements, enhancement, and new features.

For example, although the MyBlog Gadget covered in Chapter 5 is functional, after you start using it you might want to add new features. It becomes easier to upgrade a gadget if you write the gadget with good development practices.

Customizable

A gadget may need to be customized to meet a specific user need. For example, the MyBlog Gadget can be used for any existing blogs, but if you need to customize it for a specific blog with a unique set of features, it is to your advantage if the gadget is written with the possibility of customization in mind. Imagine a gadget that displays a trick of the day from a blog (www.trickofmind.com, for example). It has a normal question every day but Fridays, however, when it instead has a big puzzle. You can take advantage of this by creating a Trick of the Day Gadget, based on the MyBlog gadget, that has custom actions if the day is Friday or when the question is a long one.

Extensible

One of the desirable traits of a gadget is extensibility. That way a gadget can be used to extend existing functionality. For example, Ticker Counter Gadgets, which count down the number of days to an event are very popular, but if you create one that can extend itself to accommodate events in Microsoft Outlook, it also becomes a useful tool.

A design pattern gives a generic layout and structure to a gadget's development, which helps to solidify the gadget's foundation. It helps you to create the gadget based on the existing template, which has all the common files and functionalities. It also helps you understand each component of the gadget individually.

Elements of Design Patterns

Implementation of a gadget can be divided into three main parts with respect to the design pattern (see Figure 6.2):

- Layout of the physical file structure
- Reusability of the functionality
- Customized display and presentation

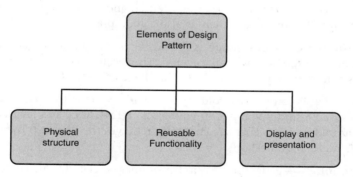

FIGURE 6.2   Design patterns help in reusability of the gadget.

In the preceding chapter you learned how to create a simple gadget. In this chapter we will extend that gadget and make a framework with a standardized version of all three above mentioned patterns. The first is the file and directory structure. Having a modular file structure is very important because this separates each entity into a single file that can be individually modified without affecting the gadget as a whole.

The second important aspect of reusability is the standard functionality common to all the gadgets. The MyBlog Gadget is an information gadget. If you create a core template that has all the common functionality of an information gadget, it can be easily extended to create any kind of information gadget.

And finally it's important to address the issue of a customized display and presentation, one that is specific for the actual gadget being implemented. Although gadgets use requirement-specific images and presentations, the design pattern can start with a default image and presentation. This makes a gadget framework ready to use immediately.

Standard Layout for Files and Folders

A standard gadget contains the following files:

- An XML file
- HTML files
- JavaScript files
- Cascading stylesheet (CSS) files
- Images
    - For configuration in Gadget Picker
    - For use in the gadget

Standard practice for the gadget involves three aspects of the gadget layout:

- **A modular file structure**—A modular practice for a gadget has HTML files with associated stylesheet (CSS) files. These files have JavaScript functionality for interacting with the Gadget Object Model, the Internet, and with each other. Having separate JavaScript files for each of them is also a good practice.

- **Locale information**—Localization is the process of adapting the gadget to the language and culture of a particular region. The localization strategy for Microsoft Sidebar is automatic and directory-based, as are JavaScript files.

    This means that if you create a folder with a name specific to a particular locale, en-MX, for example, and if you put all your XML, HTML, CSS, and JavaScript files inside that folder, the sidebar automatically retrieves the files in those directories when it is under that locale.

- **Image grouping**—A gadget has a number of images related to it. These images can be divided into standard gadget configuration images, as well as images that are displayed in the gadget's HTML files. The standard images are the icon, drag icon, and the logo. These images are used to identify and describe the gadget in the Gadget Picker window. All other images are to be used by the gadget windows.

Gadget Directory and File Structure

Let's go through the gadget's current directory structure. The MyBlog Gadget has a simple directory structure, as shown in Figure 6.3.

FIGURE 6.3   Simplistic layout and file structure of the MyBlog Gadget.

The directory structure shown here is not modular. All JavaScript files are inside a single gadget.js file. The flyout and settings HTML files have style information embedded in them. All the files are grouped together in the root folder and graphics in the images folder. The MyBlog Gadget also does not accommodate localization. So, in this chapter, we'll create a standard MyBlog Gadget and name it MyBlog Standard. The name of the folder inside, which will have all the files, is MyBlogStandard.Gadget.

To follow a standard layout pattern, three things must be done:

- Modularizing the file structure so that each file has its own associated CSS and JavaScript files

- Categorizing images into root-level configuration of images and gadget images

- Accommodating specific locale information for the gadget

The Sidebar looks for files to accommodate localization starting with specific localization folders, and then searches more generally, along this sequence:

1. Language – Country folder (for example: en-US)

2. Language folder (for example: en)

3. The root folder (in this case MyBlogStandard.Gadget).

Standard Layout

If you were to modify the MyBlog Gadget directory structure with the layout of the standard practice, you would have a structure like the one in Figure 6.4.

This is the standard and extensible structure for all kinds of gadgets. Notice how each HTML file has associated CSS and JavaScript files. This separates the HTML structure from its behavior (JavaScript) and its presentation (CSS).

GadgetUndocked.css, as the name suggests, is used to style the gadget window when the gadget is undocked. The number of files has increased after applying the standard design, but the files are now much smaller, more modular, structured, and self-explanatory.

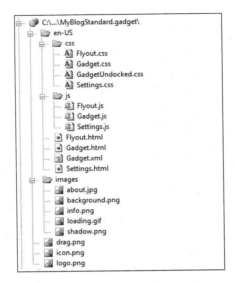

FIGURE 6.4   Standard layout and file structure with locale information.

This structure can also accommodate multiple languages. For each language you want to include, you need to add a folder similar to the en-US folder already shown, like en-MX (Spanish Mexico), and then add the HTML files (gadget, settings, and flyout), as well as the images related to that locale. This added advantage comes with a bit of complexity and is useful only if you want to have your gadget available in multiple locales. For each locale, you need a local-specific folder.

If you just want to support the operating system with the entire available locale without customizing the gadget for a particular locale, all you need is to place the gadget files in the root folder. In this case, a directory structure similar to this is the best option (see Figure 6.5).

This structure is used for the sample framework, going forward.

As you can see, Figure 6.5 shows a detailed hybrid directory structure that falls in between the raw structure of the MyBlog Gadget and a complete structured framework. This is both user friendly as well as maintainable and customizable.

Reusable Functionality

All the functionality of the gadget is wrapped in the JavaScript code associated with each HTML file. After restructuring, there are three different JavaScript files for each of the three HTML files: gadget window, flyout, and settings. Most of the functions in the JavaScript are common to all information gadgets and can be wrapped in the framework for an information gadget (see Figure 6.6).

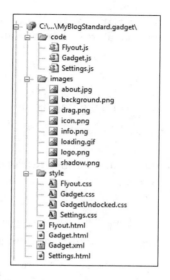

FIGURE 6.5   Standard layout with simplified folder and file structure.

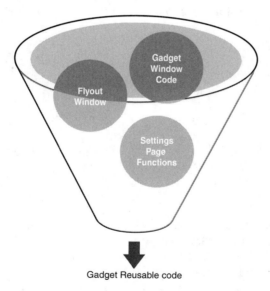

Gadget Reusable code

FIGURE 6.6   Modularity of the code helps in reusability.

Let's see each of the three modules, one-by-one. First, the gadget window.

Gadget Window Code

The gadget window is the main window displayed in the Vista Sidebar when it is docked, and floats on the Windows desktop when undocked. The gadget window code is the core of the gadget functionality and can be further divided into the following list. The list includes standard functions common to all the gadgets related to the gadget window.

- Functions for gadget configuration
- Settings-related functions
- JavaScript code to generate and configure the flyout window
- Functions related to the type of the gadget

Functions for Gadget Configuration   Functions for gadget configuration can be thought of as the JavaScript code related to the gadget initialization. A framework for the function setup() is required, as follows:

- On Load function to set up the gadget for the first time
- Gadget setup to set up all the default values and configuration
- Setup size to configure the size of the gadget's dimensions
- OnDock to reconfigure the gadget when docked
- OnUndock to set dimensions and so on when the gadget is undocked (optional)

Here is the sample code:

```
function setup()
{
    SystemSetup();
      Resize();
    getFeed();
    window.setInterval(getFeed, (30 * 60000));
}

function SystemSetup()
{
  System.Gadget.Flyout.file = "Flyout.html";
  System.Gadget.settingsUI = "Settings.html";

  if (System.Gadget.Settings.read("FeedURL")=="")
    {
     DefaultFeed = "http://innovatewithgadgets.com/atom.xml";
     System.Gadget.Settings.write("FeedURL",DefaultFeed);
    }
  if (System.Gadget.Settings.read("FlyoutWidth")=="")
    {
     System.Gadget.Settings.write("FlyoutWidth",600);
    }
  if (System.Gadget.Settings.read("FlyoutHeight")=="")
    {
```

```
    System.Gadget.Settings.write("FlyoutHeight",600);
  }
}
```

In this code the Setup function is common to all gadgets and is called when the gadget is loaded. The SystemSetup() and Resize() functions are also needed by all gadgets but getFeed and window.setinterval functions are specific to information gadgets. Note that the SystemSetup() function initializes the flyout windows, the Settings page, the default feed URL, and the dimensions of the flyout window. These values can be changed dynamically but need to be initialized before use.

Settings-Related Functions   The settingsClosed function is quite an important function because it decides whether the gadgets need to be refreshed for the data according to the new settings.

You might be wondering why we need a settings-related function in the gadget window code. The answer is because the gadget window needs to be updated when the user closes the Settings page.

Here is the sample code to give you an idea. The first thing is to initialize the property System.Gadget.onSettingsClosed with the name of the settingsClosed function.

```
System.Gadget.onSettingsClosed = settingsClosed;

function settingsClosed(event)
{
    if (event.closeAction == event.Action.commit)
        {
            if (System.Gadget.Settings.read("feedChanged"))
            {
            page=0;
            Refresh ();
            }
        }
}
    function Refresh()
    {
        Resize();
        getFeed();
}
```

The event.closeAction property tells the gadget whether the OK button or the Cancel button was pressed in the Settings page. The event.Action.commit property declares that the user clicked the OK button in the settings. This, along with the value of feedchanged variable for the example, decides whether the contents of the gadget window need to be refreshed. The refresh function is a subset of the Setup function discussed in the previous section.

Flyout-Related Functions   Flyout related functions have two functions:

- ShowFlyout, which displays the flyout when needed

- HideFlyout, which hides the flyout when it isn't needed

Here's some sample code:

```
//Flyout-related funtions
    function showFlyout(i)
    {
        if (System.Gadget.Flyout.show == false)
        {
            myWidthVariable =System.Gadget.Settings.read("FlyoutWidth");
            myHeightVariable =System.Gadget.Settings.read("FlyoutHeight");
            System.Gadget.Settings.write("currentClickedCell", i);
            System.Gadget.Flyout.file = "Flyout.html";
            System.Gadget.Flyout.show = true;
        }
        else
        {
                hideFlyout();
        }
    }
    function hideFlyout()
    {
        System.Gadget.Flyout.show = false;
    }
//End Flyout-related funtions
```

Functions Specific to the Type of the Gadget   Finally, we have two functions that are specific to the type of gadget being developed:

- GetFeed

- ParseFeed

This portion differs for different types of gadget. These functions are related to the Feed Gadget.

Flyout Window

The next part of the gadget reusability code comes under the flyout window. Two functions are can be reused in a flyout window:

- An Initialize function to set up the dimension of the window

- A BuildContent function to render the HTML in the flyout window

The `Flyout.html` page contains references to both these functions. A flyout window can render simple HTML (as in the MyBlog Gadget) or it can be used to render an embedded Flash or Microsoft Silverlight object.

Following is an example of building the HTML content dynamically in a `BuildContent` function of the flyout window:

```
function StartUpPage()
    {
        document.body.style.width =
        ➥System.Gadget.document.parentWindow.myWidthVariable;
        document.body.style.height =
        System.Gadget.document.parentWindow.myHeightVariable;
    }
    function BuildContent ()
    {
    var BlogTitle= System.Gadget.document.parentWindow.Titles;
    var BlogDescription = System.Gadget.document.parentWindow.Descriptions;
    var BlogPublished = System.Gadget.document.parentWindow.PublishedList;
    var i = System.Gadget.Settings.read("currentClickedCell");

    flyoutHtmlString  = "<h3>" + BlogTitle[i] + "</h3>";
     flyoutHtmlString += BlogDescription[i] ;
     flyoutHtmlString += BlogPublished[i] ;
    document.write(flyoutHtmlString);
}
```

The key thing to note here is the way value is passed from the parent gadget window to the flyout window. The value of the current cell is stored in the variable `currentClickedCell`, which is also the selected index for the arrays. It stores the title, description, and dates related to a blog entry.

Settings Page Functions

Last of all is the Settings page. Three standard functions are required for the Settings page; if you know them you know almost everything about customizing the gadget with the Settings page:

- `LoadSettings`
- `SaveSettings`
- `SettingsClosing` (event is passed as parameter)

The `LoadSettings` function sets the default configuration in the Settings page or loads the user's saved settings. Similarly a `SaveSettings` function is required to save the settings if a user changes the gadget's configuration. These settings are normally stored in the JavaScript variables, which remain in memory and are managed by the Sidebar. These settings are not persisted when the computer is shut down or restarted. Settings can also be loaded from and saved to a local text or XML file, which enables the gadget to preserve configuration settings between reboots.

The following is a sample `LoadSettings` and `SaveSettings` function for the MyBlog Standard Gadget. Note that the `FeedURL` variable is loaded for the first time if not already available in the memory.

```
function loadSettings()
{
    if  (System.Gadget.Settings.read("FeedURL") == "")
        {
          document.getElementById('TextBoxFeedURL').value =
           "http://innovatewithgadgets.com/atom.xml";
        }
        else
        {
          document.getElementById('TextBoxFeedURL').value =
          System.Gadget.Settings.read("FeedURL");
        }
          document.getElementById('txtWidth').value =
          System.Gadget.Settings.read("FlyoutWidth");
        document.getElementById('txtHeight').value =
        ➥System.Gadget.Settings.read("FlyoutHeight");
}
function saveSettings()
{
        System.Gadget.Settings.write("feedChanged",true);
        System.Gadget.Settings.write("FeedURL",
        document.getElementById('TextBoxFeedURL').value );
        System.Gadget.Settings.write("FlyoutWidth",
        document.getElementById('txtWidth').value );
        System.Gadget.Settings.write("FlyoutHeight",
        document.getElementById('txtHeight').value );
}
```

The last essential function is fired when the Settings' OK button or Cancel button is clicked. It is the `SettingsClosing` function, which takes the event action as the parameter. The event could be `event.Action.commit` or `event.Action.cancel`.

This function is triggered automatically when the Settings page is closed. If the user clicks the OK button, the `Commit` event becomes the parameter of the `SettingsClosing` event, and if the Cancel button is clicked the `Cancel` event becomes the parameter (see Figure 6.8).

Based on the event, further action is taken. If the event is `commit`, `SaveSettings` is called. If the event is `cancel`, the Settings page is simply closed without saving any settings.

FIGURE 6.7   Settings page with two default buttons: OK and Cancel.

Similar to the SettingsClosed event in the gadget main window, the SettingsClosing event occurs at the Settings page. The name of this event also needs to be initialized in the onSettingsClosing property of the gadget, as shown here:

```
System.Gadget.onSettingsClosing = settingsClosing;
function settingsClosing(event)
{
    if(event.closeAction == event.Action.commit)
    {
        saveSettings();
    }
    else if (event.closeAction == event.Action.cancel)
    {
     //do nothing
    }
}
```

Display and Presentation

So far in the design pattern you've seen the standardized approach to the layout and the file structure. You've also examined all the functions and events that are common to most gadgets. The last part of the design pattern is the visuals of the gadgets; that is, the images and icons used to make the gadget visually attractive. Although most of these images need to be different for different gadgets, a standard naming convention can be reused, which helps in the development process.

The presentation also includes the styles applied to all three windows: the gadget window, the Settings page, and the flyout window.

Display and presentation includes the following:

- Common images
- Standard images and background
- Gadget stylesheet

Common Images

Common images, as the name suggests, can be reused across multiple gadgets. These are standard icons and animated GIF files that can be used in all gadgets. The first example is the standard icons used to convey special messages to the user, such as a warning, error, or other information (see Figure 6.8).

FIGURE 6.8   The red cross is used to convey error status; the blue i image is used for information; and the yellow exclamation point image is used to convey a warning message to the user.

Another example of a common image could be the animated loading image used to display the wait status to the user while data is fetched (see Figure 6.9).

FIGURE 6.9   Animated loading GIFs are used to display the wait status to the user.

Standard Images and Background

Each gadget needs a separate graphical representation for icons, logo, and the drag icon. The logo image is meant to be displayed in the description of the gadget in the picker window.

Some standard images can be used to start with. These include the background image, a rounded square image with alpha transparency, the info.png image for information, and the loading animation that appears when the gadget is loading the feed or is doing any time-intensive operation. The example here uses the standard images shown in Figure 6.10, which were created for the MyBlog gadget in the framework. You can change these images to customize the gadget.

FIGURE 6.10   Standard images for the framework. These may be changed for each gadget.

Gadget Stylesheet

Finally, the stylesheet files determine the presentation of the gadget. In this example, you'll create four different stylesheets for the gadget presentation. A gadget window has two stylesheets: one for the docked state and one for the floating state. The floating state style is optional and is needed only if your gadget requires a different stylesheet when in the floating state. Here are the stylesheet files commonly found in gadgets:

- `Gadget.css` defines the stylesheet when the gadget is docked, and `GadgetUndocked.css` defines the stylesheet when the gadget is floating on the user's desktop

- `Flyout.css` defines the stylesheet for the flyout window

- `Settings.css` defines the stylesheet for the Settings page

The following describes the standard stylesheet information for the respective gadget windows. These fonts and style information are the defaults for the Windows Vista operating system.

For the gadget window

```
Font: Calibri or Segoe UI
Style:
body
{
    margin: 0px;     padding: 0px;
    color: #000;
    font-family: Calibri, Tahoma, sans-serif;
}
```

For the Settings window

```
Font: Segoe UI
Style:
body
{
    padding: 0;     margin: 0px;
    font-family: Segoe UI, Tahoma, sans-serif;
    font-size:12px;
}
```

For the flyout

```
Font: Calibri
Style:
body
{
    margin: 0px;     padding: 0px;
    color: #ffffff;
```

```
    font-size: 10px;
    font-family: Calibri, Tahoma, sans-serif;
}
```

Although the stylesheet information also changes for each gadget, the framework provides a starting point for each of them so that later you can make changes to them individually and test for the best visual effect without affecting other gadgets.

Common Assumptions

To make a gadget robust, you have to do more than just apply a standard design. You also have to tighten up the gadget so that it is protected from common pitfalls and assumptions that can cause a gadget to break. Standard practices can help you avoid the common assumptions. Here is a list to start with:

- The gadget will always work.
- An Internet connection will always be there.
- There will be regular updates.
- Current data will be accessible from the cache.
- It's okay to just store everything in system memory.

The Gadget Will Always Work

The first and foremost assumption is that the gadget will work with all users. This normally is not the case. Because a gadget is not a compiled executable, even the best functional gadget throws a JavaScript error at times (see Figure 6.11).

FIGURE 6.11   A typical JavaScript error dialog showing the line number of the error.

There could be many different reasons for this. A gadget using a media player plug-in or using system folders can work on one Vista machine that has the media plug-in, but can throw an error on another that doesn't.

Here is one of my personal experiences. I downloaded a video gadget from live.gallery.com. When I loaded the gadget I got the error shown in Figure 6.11. I clicked on No and proceeded; the gadget worked in most of the cases, but threw JavaScript errors every now and then. I added a comment in the gadget author's page about the error. The author instantly replied that he is not able to simulate the error in his computer and said maybe the fault was at my side. Well! I could agree that the fault could be at my side, but I was trying to help. I therefore suggested that because the gadget worked fine even with the error message, it might be a good idea to add error handlers to avoid those messages. He never replied back, neither has he added the error handlers I suggested; I still get the same error when I load his gadget. This taught me a very important lesson: Don't assume that your code will always work.

Even if the functionality remains intact, this message can cause the user to lose faith in the gadget.

An important technique in defensive programming is to create error handlers by encapsulating each JavaScript function inside a `try-catch` statement. This prevents the user from seeing a JavaScript error and instead presents a more meaningful message to the user, as the following example illustrates:

```
try
    {
    // do gadget complex function
    // which may cause error
    }
    catch(e)
    {
    document.write('Error occurred in gadget function!');
    }
```

This is a very simplistic example of a `try-catch` statement. In the gadget you might want to display the error icon along with the message as per the design guidelines.

Internet Connection

The second assumption involves the availability of the Internet connection. When creating a gadget that uses the Internet to fetch data, the "no Internet" scenario should be covered. If the Internet connection is not available, the gadget should either load the required data from a local cache or show a message to the user regarding the status of the Internet connection.

The gadget also needs to check the Internet connection at regular intervals to automatically change from a local state that uses cached data state to a connected state that uses live data without requiring the user's intervention.

Here is a sample code for testing for the presence of an Internet connection. This function takes the `URLtoTest` (a website URL) as an input parameter and uses Ajax to determine the Internet connection's current status.

```
var InternetConnected;
Checkinternet(URLtoTest)
    {
        try
        {
        rssObj = new ActiveXObject("Msxml2.XMLHTTP");
        rssObj.open("GET", URLtoTest, false);
        rssObj.onreadystatechange = function() {
            if (rssObj.readyState === 4)
            {
                if (rssObj.status === 200)
               InternetConnected = true;
                    else
               InternetConnected = false;
            }
        }
    catch(e)
        {
        document.write('Error occurred in check internet function!');
        }
    }
```

URLtoTest can be the URL from which you are getting the data or a plain website such as google.com, just to test the Internet connection. InternetConnected is a global variable that can be checked before you call the function to fetch data.

Regular Feed Updates

The other aspect that has to be addressed is automatic updates. A gadget that relies on an online feed needs to keep itself updated with respect to the online feed, which can change any number of times in a day. If your gadget is based on a news feed, you might want to check for updated feeds as often as every five minutes. A blog feed may be set to check every few hours.

JavaScript includes a standard timer function that should be set up the first time the gadget defaults are set:

```
window.setInterval(function, delay in milliseconds);
```

And here is the function with values:

```
window.setInterval(getFeed, (60 * 60 * 1000));
```

This code sets the interval to one hour, which means the function getFeed is automatically called every hour. If you remember the initialize function setup(), the SetInterval function is added to the getFeed function inside that function.

```
// Initialize functions
function setup() {
    SystemSetup();
     Resize();
    getFeed();
    window.setInterval(getFeed, (60 * 60 * 1000));
}
```

This needs to be done just once and every hour the function is called automatically. Isn't that great?

Caching of the Feed Data

The other issue that shows up when creating a gadget that uses an online feed is caching. Because the gadget is based on an MSHTML component, it caches the feed data the first time it fetches from the online source. The cached data is then stored in the computer for faster later access. This feature comes with a drawback: Sometimes the online feed has been updated but the MSHTML component still reads the data available in the cache.

To make sure that you get the latest data from the feed, you need to fool the MSHTML component that you are fetching a new URL every time you fetch the data. Because your feed URL will be fixed, you need to add a parameter to it that includes a random number to make the whole URL unique. This is more of a hack that is applied to fetch the data every time the feed is opened.

This is the default fetch code that gets the cached data:

```
rssObj.open("GET", "http://innovatewithgadgets.com/atom.xml",true);
```

Adding a random number at the end ensures that the gadget fetches the data from an online resource every time rather then taking it from the cache.

```
rssObj.open("GET", "http://innovatewithgadgets.com/atom.xml" + "?randomid=" +
Math.random()*1 ,true);
```

Memory and Session Management

System variables and data stored in the gadget are stored in the computer's local memory and are managed by the Sidebar. If the gadget is storing a lot of information in memory, it can eventually degrade system performance.

Bulk information should be stored in a local text or XML file rather than in memory. A common practice is to use LoadXML and SaveXML functions, which will store bulk data and display it from the local file dynamically rather than from memory.

Here is a partial function to load the XML file. Note that the file needs to be parsed before displaying information.

LoadXML

```
function loadXML(localfilename)
{
var xmlDoc;
xmlDoc=new ActiveXObject("Microsoft.XMLDOM");
xmlDoc.async=false;
xmlDoc.load(localfilename);
return(xmlDoc);
}
```

The LoadXML file uses Microsoft XMLDOM ActiveX to load an existing XML document.

SaveXML

```
function SaveXML(localfilename,  element)
{
xmlDoc = new ActiveXObject("Microsoft.XMLDOM");
xmlDoc.async="false";
xmlDoc.load(localfilename);
xmlObj=xmlDoc.documentElement;
rssAddedItems= xmlObj.getElementsByTagName("item");
rssAddItems[0].appendChild(rssItems[i]);
}
```

The SaveXML function uses the Microsoft XML document to create XML elements and save the data back to the XML file. These two functions are discussed in more detail in Appendix A, "Tools, Tips, and Tricks."

Adding Accessibility

In Chapter 3 we saw an overview of adding accessibility in the Gadget. In this section we go deeper and see how to implement them in the gadget.

One great design principle is to make sure all the features of the gadget are accessible through the keyboard. The following lists important points to keep in mind when adding accessibility.

- Put the focus on the gadget when it is loaded.

- Users should be able to tab through controls/links in a gadget.

- The Enter key should act like a mouse click to push a button or follow a link, and should call the onclick event of the control/link.

- Enable the mouse hover effect by using the `onfocus` and `onfocusout` functions.

- Apart from the gadget main page, the Gadget's Flyout and Settings pages should also be accessible from the keyboard.

Let's go through each of these points and see how full accessibility can be achieved.

Putting the Focus on the Gadget when It Is Loaded

To put the focus on the gadget after it is loaded, add the following `document.body.focus()` on the body of the HTML page in the `onload` event, along.

```
<body onload="setup();document.body.focus();" >
```

This line of code ensures that the gadget is on focus when it is loaded and the user can use the keyboard to navigate through the links or controls in the gadget. Note that if multiple gadgets are loaded at the same time, this event is fired in the sequence for each gadget as it is loaded and the last gadget receives the final focus.

Adding Tab Controls

Users should be able to tab through every control or link in a gadget. To enable this functionality, add `tabindex` in each of the links and controls. This can be done directly in the HTML page, on an element. It can also be set dynamically on an element using the following code:

```
<td class="subtitle"  tabindex="1" id="blogtitle"
➥ondblclick ="Refresh();">Sidebar Gadget</td>
```

Note the `tabindex` is set to 1 for the title in the HTML page in the preceding code and is set to 2 in the following code, which is generated dynamically. The former denotes the first tab stop and the latter second.

```
var akey  = 2; //accesskey for second tab stop
myitem.innerHTML = '<a class="title"  tabindex="'+akey+'"
align="left" href="JavaScript:ShowFlyout(\'' + i + '\');">
<div  class="title" >' + Mid(rssTitle,0,11) + '</div></a>';
```

The Enter Key Acting Like a Mouse Click

This is the most important part of the keyboard accessibility section. You need to simulate the `onclick` event from the keyboard. There are two ways of doing this.

- Change the `onclick` event to an `href`.

- Capture the element's `onkeyup`, `onkeydown`, or `onkeypress` events

The next two sections examine each of these methods.

9

Change the onclick Event to an href

Change the element that has an onclick event to an anchor element (A) and set the href property to the original onclick event. The anchor element is commonly used as an HTML tag for creating a link to another page.

As an example, assume you have this element:

```
<div class="testclass" id='testElement' onclick='doThis();'></div>
```

Change it to this:

```
<a class="testclass" id='testElement' href="JavaScript:doThis();'></a>
```

The anchor element automatically takes care of the Enter keypress event. The href property is automatically called when the focus is on an anchor element and the user presses Enter. There is no need to capture the Enter button keypress event.

Please note that I have used JavaScript before the function call. This ensures the link is meant for a JavaScript function, otherwise the gadget parses all href tags as href links and not as a JavaScript function.

Capture the onkeyup, onkeydown, or onkeypress Events of the Element

If you cannot change the element to use an href, the other option is to capture keypress events such as onkeyup, onkeydown, and onkeypress.

Let's look at the Blog Title code again with the onkeyup event added to it. Note that there is a Refresh() function that is called by the doubleclick event of the Blog Title element:

```
<td class="subtitle"  tabindex="1" id="blogtitle" valign ="middle" onkeyup=
➥"keyboardAccess('refresh','0');" title="Double click to refresh"
➥ondblclick ="Refresh();">Sidebar Gadget</td>
```

Note the addition of the keyboardAccess function, which is called when the onkeyup event is fired.

```
onkeyup="keyboardAccess('refresh','0');"
```

Here is the code for the keyboardAccess function:

```
// for Keyboard Access
function  keyboardAccess(from,id)
{
    switch (window.event.keyCode)
    {
      case 13: // Simulate onclick event on Enter keypress (key code 13)
         {
         if (from==="refresh")
         Refresh();
```

```
      else if (from==="item")
      ShowFlyout(id);
      else if (from==="paging")
      ChangePage(id);
      else if (from==="changefeed")
      ChangeFeed(id);
      break;
      }


   }
}
```

This function calls different methods to simulate the mouse click, depending on where the user pressed the Enter key.

Using the onfocus and onfocusout Events for Mouse Hover Effect

Gadgets often use the mouse hover effect. It is also important to reproduce that behavior when navigating the gadget using the keyboard. As an example:

```
<td width="4"  tabindex="8"  align = right class="arrow"  onfocus=
➥"ShowArrowTitle();" onfocusout="HideArrowTitle();" onkeyup="keyboardAccess
➥ ('changefeed',-1);" onclick="ChangeFeed(-1);" align="right"><div id=
➥"larrowtitle"  onfocus="ShowArrowTitle();" onfocusout="HideArrowTitle();"
➥  style="visibility:hidden;cursor:hand;"  title="previous
blog">&lsaquo;</div></td>
```

This HTML code simulates the mouse hover functionality using the onfocus and onfocusout events. For a list of DHTML events available to elements, visit http://msdn2.microsoft.com/en-us/library/ms533051(VS.85).aspx.

Making the Gadget's Flyout and Settings Page Keyboard Accessible

To make the Flyout and Settings page accessible, first use the tabindex keyword as discussed in the section "Adding Tab Controls".

It is important to be able to close the Flyout using just the keyboard. The simplest approach is to add an anchor element, Close, and add the HideFlyout function in the onclick/href property.

```
<a  tabindex="1" href="JavaScript:hideFlyout();">Close</a>
```

Note that when the Flyout is visible, the keyboard events go to the Flyout rather than to the main gadget window.

You should consider a few other things for additional options:

- If the gadget has HTML controls, use the accesskey attribute for keyboard shortcuts. You can then access the controls by using the Alt key in conjunction with the access key. The accesskey attribute is very helpful if you have HTML controls such as buttons and text boxes on the page. Here is a code example:

```
<button type="button"  name="addText" accesskey="a" id="btnAddText" title=
➥"Add text" tabindex="2" onclick="addText(txtTextInput.value)">Add text</but-
ton>
```

  The access key *a* is used here to access the button, which the user can now do by pressing Alt+a.

- Left/Right Arrow keys can be used for previous/next functionality.

- Top/Down Arrow keys can be used to move through a drop-down list.

- If gadget uses scripts, use device-independent functions so the user can call the scripts with just a mouse or keyboard.

The following URL lists all the codes you need for keyboard access.

http://www.innovatewithgadgets.com/Extra/Key-Codes-for-Keyboard-Access.htm

The MyBlog Gadget Revisited

"Always design a thing by considering it in its next larger context—a chair in a room, a room in a house, a house in an environment, an environment in a city plan."

—Eliel Saarinen, Architect

Recapping the MyBlog Gadget

The MyBlog Gadget gets you started with what can be done with the gadget platform. Most of the information gadgets use an online feed in the form of Atom or RSS syndication. This feed is downloaded using Ajax technology and extracted using JavaScript code. The information is stored in the memory and is displayed on the flyout window.

The MyBlog Gadget in Chapter 5, "Creating a Simple Gadget with RSS/Atom Feed," had a simple objective: display the last five blogs posted from an online feed. It was implemented with the following characteristics:

- Displays the last five titles in the gadget window
- Displays blog entries, with dates, in the flyout window
- Supports both RSS 2.0 and Atom 1.0
- User can change the default feed URL and dimensions of the flyout window

Creating a feature-rich gadget requires more options for the data as well as for user customization than those listed here.

In a real scenario, users should not be limited to just one blog. The user should be able to view and manage multiple blogs in the same gadget. There should be options to add and edit blogs from the gadget with a customizable size for the flyout window. Because the data in the feed may not be completely available in RSS or Atom feeds, the user might have to follow the link in the feed to go to the respective page, which can be coded in HTML or XHTML. There are lots of features that can be added to the gadget if you consider MyBlog Gadget in a larger context.

But just adding features to a gadget doesn't make it more attractive. You have to decide what features are actually required and add real value to the gadget. The right set of features and proper implementation is the key to a successful, popular gadget.

Keep these two questions in mind while adding features to the gadget:

- Is the feature required and does it add value to the gadget?

- How do you implement the feature without adding complexity to the user experience? Simplicity should always be the guiding principal.

The first version of the MyBlog Gadget is a simple implementation of an information gadget and it does exactly what it says (see Figure 7.1). But as this chapter demonstrates, it needs additional features to be a truly usable gadget.

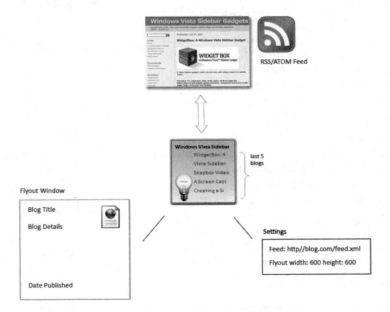

FIGURE 7.1   The simple layout of the first version of the MyBlog Gadget.

Taking the MyBlog Gadget to the Next Level

Although the MyBlog Gadget covers the basic functions and file structures required for the framework, it's not complete. An information gadget needs customizability and more data options. In the MyBlog Gadget, if you have to display another blog you have to create another instance of the gadget (see Figure 7.2).

FIGURE 7.2   The gadget showing feeds from three different blogs.

Instead, the user should be able to add any number of blogs to the gadget and should be able to easily traverse through them. The gadget is also limited to showing only the last five blog entries. There should be a way to include multiple pages (also called *paging*) for the blog entries in the gadget.

Figure 7.2 shows three instances of the gadget, using three different feeds:

- http://widgets-gadgets.com/atom.xml
- http://trickofmind.com/atom.xml
- http://innovatewithgadgets.com/atom.xml

Optimizing the space of the gadget is also desirable. Exercising the option to decrease the size of the gadget can improve its usability.

Finally, it should provide an option to customize the flyout window width and height for each data feed.

The next version of the MyBlog Gadget supports advanced paging so that the user is not limited to the last five blog entries, but can traverse through all the data available in the feed. It will also have a Mini Me version for optimum usage of space. Figure 7.3 illustrates an overview of the gadget you will see built in this chapter. It can take data from any number of online feeds and has advanced paging schemes.

The advanced MyBlog Gadget framework includes the following features:

- Multiple feeds
- Advanced paging
- Docked and Mini Me version
- Unobtrusive traversing

- Advanced display and presentation
- HTML and XHTML data

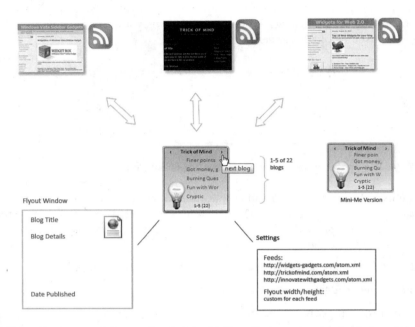

FIGURE 7.3   The layout of the next level of the MyBlog Gadget, showing feeds from three different blogs.

The following sections go through each of them one by one.

Adding Multiple Feeds

To accommodate multiple feeds, options must be added in the gadget window as well as the Settings page. The gadget window needs the following additions:

- In-memory storage for the multiple feed URLs
- Default feeds to display when the gadget runs the first time
- HTML code to display the title of the blog, along with left and right arrows to traverse between the blogs
- changeFeed() function to traverse the feeds

As illustrated in Figure 7.4, the Settings page requires the following additions:

- View feeds
- Add, edit, and delete feeds
- Reset feeds to defaults

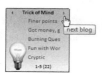
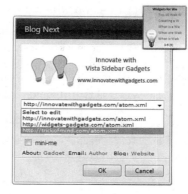

FIGURE 7.4   The Settings page includes the option to include multiple blogs, and the gadget window in the top left enables the user to navigate between blogs by clicking on left and right arrows.

Adding an Option for Multiple Feeds to the Gadget Window

To store multiple feeds in memory, you need three arrays to store the URLs and the corresponding width and height of the flyout for those feeds:

```
var URLFeeds = new Array();
var URLFeedsW = new Array();
var URLFeedsH = new Array();
```

Next, you need to configure the default feeds to display when the gadget runs for the first time. To do this, you must create a function that resets the arrays to their default values.

```
function DefaultFeeds()
{
    URLFeeds[0] = "http://innovatewithgadgets.com/atom.xml";
    URLFeedsW[0] = 600;
    URLFeedsH[0] = 600;

    URLFeeds[1] = "http://widgets-gadgets.com/atom.xml";
    URLFeedsW[1] = 700;
    URLFeedsH[1] = 600;

    URLFeeds[2] = "http://trickofmind.com/atom.xml";
    URLFeedsW[2] = 400;
    URLFeedsH[2] = 300;
}
```

Now you need some HTML code to display the blog's title, along with some navigation arrows. The following table is appended with the left and right navigation arrows and with a call to the `ChangeFeed()` function which is executed when the user clicks on the navigation arrows.

```
<table width="100%" height="20"  border="0" cellpadding="3" cellspacing="2">
    <tr align="center" valign="middle">
    <td class="arrow" onclick="ChangeFeed(-1);" >
    <div id="Div1" style="visibility:hidden;"><b>&lsaquo;</b></div>
    </td>
    <td class="subtitle" id="Td1" valign ="middle" >Vista Gadget</td>
    <td class="arrow" onclick="ChangeFeed(+1);">
    <div id="Div2" style="visibility:hidden;"><b>&rsaquo;</b></div>
    </td>
    </tr>
</table>
```

At this point it's nearly time to code in the `ChangeFeed()` function, which allows the gadget to traverse the various feeds. Before calling the `ChangeFeed` function, however, you first need to use the `Reset()` function to reset the blog titles in the gadget window.

```
function Reset()
{
cell0.innerHTML = '<div title ="Not available">- / -</div>';
cell1.innerHTML = '<div title ="Not available">- / -</div>';
cell2.innerHTML = '<div title ="Not available">- / -</div>';
cell3.innerHTML = '<div title ="Not available">- / -</div>';
cell4.innerHTML = '<div title ="Not available">- / -</div>';
}
```

Why invoke this `Reset()` function? First, assume that the old feed had five blog entries and the new one had only four blog entries. So, if you don't reset the blog titles, the fifth DIV element will still have the old entries. With that done, you can proceed to the `ChangeFeed()` function.

The `ChangeFeed()` function has a parameter indicating the traversing direction as +1 to go forward or –1 to go backward through the feed list. `URLFeedsCurrentId` is a variable to store the index of the currently displayed feed. Note in the following code that the code handles wrap from beginning to end and end to beginning:

```
function ChangeFeed(val)
{
    hideFlyout();
    reset();
try
{
    URLFeedsCurrentID = URLFeedsCurrentID + val;

    if (URLFeedsCurrentID == -1)
    {
```

```
    URLFeedsCurrentID =URLFeeds.length -1;
    }
    if (URLFeedsCurrentID == URLFeeds.length)
  {
  URLFeedsCurrentID =0;
    }

System.Gadget.Settings.write("FeedURL",URLFeeds[URLFeedsCurrentID]);
flyoutWidth= URLFeedsW[URLFeedsCurrentID];
flyoutHeight = URLFeedsH[URLFeedsCurrentID];

System.Gadget.Settings.write("FlyoutWidth",flyoutWidth);
System.Gadget.Settings.write("FlyoutHeight",flyoutHeight);
page=0;
Refresh();
document.getElementById("blogtitle").title ="loading...";
}
catch(exception)
{
   document.write('Error occurred in changeFeed!');
}
}
```

Now let's see what's going on in the code. The ChangeFeed function takes the parameter val, whose value can be a plus one or a minus one. If the user clicks on the forward arrow, ChangeFeed(+1) is called, and for the backward arrow, ChangeFeed(-1) is called.

URLFeedsCurrentID is a global variable that stores the index of the current feed among all the feeds stored in the array. When the gadget is loaded, URLFeedsCurrentID is initialized to the value zero and the first feed from the feed array is taken as the default feed. Based on the current value, the URLFeedsCurrentID is updated first, and then the global variable for FeedURL is updated based on the value of URLFeedsCurrentID.

```
System.Gadget.Settings.write("FeedURL",URLFeeds[URLFeedsCurrentID]);
```

URLFeedsCurrentID also decides the index for arrays, which store width and height for the flyout window corresponding to the feed,

```
flyoutWidth= URLFeedsW[URLFeedsCurrentID];
flyoutHeight = URLFeedsH[URLFeedsCurrentID];
```

and the corresponding global variables for width and height are updated:

```
System.Gadget.Settings.write("FlyoutWidth",flyoutWidth);
System.Gadget.Settings.write("FlyoutHeight",flyoutHeight);
```

So all the `ChangeFeed` function does is change values of the global variables and call the `Refresh` function, which reninitializes the gadget with the current values of those global variables: `FeedURL`, `FlyoutWidth`, and `FlyoutHeight`.

The `Refresh` function calls `getFeed` with the new `FeedURL` and displays it:

```
function Refresh()
  {
    SystemSetup();
    Resize();
    getFeed();
 }
```

Adding Settings Page Code

To make the multiple feeds available in the Settings page, the feeds array from the gadget's window is scanned for all the available items and inserted into the drop-down list in the Settings page. This routine is called in the `LoadFeed` function, which looks like this:

```
function LoadFeeds()
{
        BlogFeeds= System.Gadget.document.parentWindow.URLFeeds;
        BlogFeedsW= System.Gadget.document.parentWindow.URLFeedsW;
        BlogFeedsH= System.Gadget.document.parentWindow.URLFeedsH;
        document.getElementById("rssFeed_SelectId").length = 0;
        AddItem("Select to edit","http://innovatewithgadgets.com/atom.xml");

        for (i=0;  i<BlogFeeds.length ;  i++)
        {
        AddItem(BlogFeeds[i],BlogFeeds[i]);
        }

        document.getElementById("rssFeed_SelectId").selectedIndex = 0;
         document.getElementById("TextBoxFeedURL").innerText =
        ➥document.getElementById("rssFeed_SelectId").value;
}
```

The `LoadFeed` function takes the arrays for `URLFeeds`, `FeedWidth`, and `FeedHeight` from the `parentWindow` and adds the values to the drop-down.

Next, the `AddItem` function is called to insert the item value with the index in the drop-down control `rssFeed_SelectId`.

```
function AddItem(Text,Value)
    {
        // Create an Option object
        var opt = document.createElement("option");
```

```
        // Add an Option object to Drop Down/List Box
        document.getElementById("rssFeed_SelectId").options.add(opt);
        // Assign text and value to Option object
        opt.text = Text;
        opt.value = Value;
    }
```

After all the items are added, the textbox in the Settings page is also updated with the current feed URL text.

Next you need some functionality to add multiple feeds (see Figure 7.5). The AddFeed function takes the values from the input boxes and updates the URLFeeds array. It also checks whether the feed is already available.

FIGURE 7.5   The Settings page enables the user to add more feeds to the MyBlog Gadget.

```
function AddFeed()
{
 var feedrepeat  = false;
 try
 {
    for (i=0;i<System.Gadget.document.parentWindow.URLFeeds.length;i++)
    {
    if (System.Gadget.document.parentWindow.URLFeeds[i] ==
document.getElementById("TextBoxFeedURL").value)
    {
    document.getElementById("statusid").innerText = "Feed already exists!";
    feedrepeat = true;
    break;
    }
    }
```

```
    if (feedrepeat == false)
    {
    System.Gadget.document.parentWindow.URLFeeds.push
    (document.getElementById("TextBoxFeedURL").value);
    System.Gadget.document.parentWindow.URLFeedsW.
    push(document.getElementById("txtWidth").value);
    System.Gadget.document.parentWindow.URLFeedsH.push
(document.getElementById("txtHeight").value);

    document.getElementById("statusid").innerText = "Feed added!";
    LoadFeeds();
    }
}
catch(exception)
{
document.write('Error occurred in AddFeed!');
}
}
```

It's time to go into details of the AddFeed function. There are two parts of the function.
The first one checks whether the feed already exists (this portion can also be encapsulated
as a separate function as CheckFeedExists for modularity) in the array. If it does exist, the
message Feed already exists is added to the label statusid in the Settings page and is
displayed to the user. If the feed does not exist, the value of the feedURL text box,
TextBoxFeedURL, as well as the txtWidth and txtHeight are saved in the array, using the
method push of the array, and the label statusid is updated with the message Feed
added!.

```
System.Gadget.document.parentWindow.URLFeeds.push
(document.getElementById("TextBoxFeedURL").value);
```

Remove and Update Feed

Finally, you need to add the capability to remove and update feeds (see Figure 7.6). For
that you need to use the RemoveFeed and UpdateFeed functions, which respectively
remove a feed from the URLFeeds array and update an entry in the URLFeeds array.

```
function RemoveFeed()
{
    try
    {
            System.Gadget.document.parentWindow.URLFeeds.splice
            (document.getElementById("rssFeed_SelectId").selectedIndex-1,1);
            System.Gadget.document.parentWindow.URLFeedsW.splice
            (document.getElementById("rssFeed_SelectId").selectedIndex-1,1);
```

```
        System.Gadget.document.parentWindow.URLFeedsH.splice
        (document.getElementById("rssFeed_SelectId").selectedIndex-1,1);

        LoadFeeds();
        document.getElementById("statusid").innerText = "Feed removed !";
    }
    catch(exception)
    {
    document.getElementById("statusid").innerText = "Error in RemoveFeed!";
    }
}
```

FIGURE 7.6   The Settings page also enables the user to edit, delete, and reset feeds.

The RemoveFeed function uses the splice method of an array to remove the selected item from the array.

```
function UpdateFeed()
{
  try
    {
    for (i=0;i<System.Gadget.document.parentWindow.URLFeeds.length;i++)
      {
      if (System.Gadget.document.parentWindow.URLFeeds[i] ==
➥document.getElementById("TextBoxFeedURL").value)
        {
        System.Gadget.document.parentWindow.URLFeedsW[i] =
        ➥document.getElementById("txtWidth").value;
        System.Gadget.document.parentWindow.URLFeedsH[i] =
        ➥document.getElementById("txtHeight").value;
```

```
        document.getElementById("statusid").innerText = "Feed updated !";
        }
    }
}
catch(exception)
{
document.getElementById("statusid").innerText = "Error in UpdateFeed!";
}
}
```

Simillarly, the UpdateFeed function is called when the user clicks on the Save icon. It takes the values from the txtWidth and txtHeight and updates the value of the arrays with the currently selected index.

Managing Multiple Pages in the Gadget Window

One of the important features in a feed gadget is the capability to traverse through multiple pages of blog entries. The goal is to let the user easily navigate between all the blog entries. Figure 7.7 shows how page numbers with arrows are implemented and can be used for traversing through all the blog entries of a feed.

FIGURE 7.7   Managing multiple pages in the MyBlog gadget.

Managing multiple pages requires the following changes in the gadget:

- HTML page display changes

- Changes to page function

- Logic integrated into the parseFeed function

In the following HTML I've added markup for managing multiple pages of the blog entries, which is similar in nature to how the gadget is able to traverse multiple feeds.

```
<table width="100%" height="100%"  border="0" cellpadding="2" >
 <tr align="center" valign="middle">

    <td width="12" id="leftarrow" class="arrow" onclick="changePage(-1);" >
    <div id="larrow" style="visibility:hidden;" title="previous 5 records">
    <b>&lsaquo;</b>
```

```
        </div>
        </td>

        <td width="44" class="sub" id="pageNum" align="center" >1/1</td>

        <td width="12" id="rightarrow" class="arrow" onclick="changePage(+1);">
        <div id="rarrow" style="visibility:hidden;" title="next 5 records">
        <b>&rsaquo;</b>
        </div>
        </td>
    </tr>
</table>
```

When the gadget loads for the first time, you have to update the pageNum element, which shows as < 16-20(22) > in Figure 7.7. Notice that the corresponding HTML code shows 1/1 as the default value of pageNum, which dynamically changes based on the value of the number of blog entries and the current page.

Initially, the pageNum is fixed to 1-5 inside the parseFeed function:

```
pageNum.innerText = "1-5 (" + rssItems.length + ")";
```

Whenever the user clicks on the Next or Previous arrow, the ChangePage function is called, which evaluates the current page and updates the pageNum label:

```
function ChangePage(offset)
{
hideFlyout();

if ((page >0)||(off>0))
{
    reset();
     myval = Math.ceil (rssItems.length/5);
      try
      {
          if (((page + off) > -1) && ((page + off) < myval))
            {
                page = page + off;
                 parseFeed(page);
            }
          else if ((page + off) === myval)
            {
                page = 0;
                parseFeed(page);
            }
          else if ((page + off) === 0)
            {
```

```
        page = myval;
        parseFeed(page);
    }

var startitems= 1 + 5 * page;
var enditems = 5 + 5 * page;
if (enditems >    rssItems.length)
{enditems = rssItems.length;}

pageNum.innerText = startitems + "-" + enditems +
                " (" + rssItems.length + ")";

}
catch(exception)
{
document.write('Error in ChangePage function');
}
}
}
```

Unobtrusive Traversing

Adding a traversing option and managing pages in the gadget adds four arrows in the gadget window, which adds complexity to the user interface and is against the guidelines of good gadget design. So, you have to add unobtrusive traversing with the page option. What this means is that you show these arrows only when user hovers the mouse over them.

The default view remains the plain and simple user interface with the additional display of the number of blog entries. The user moves the mouse over this display to see further options to traverse the feed (see Figure 7.8).

FIGURE 7.8   Unobtrusive traversing displays the page arrows only when the mouse hovers over the gadget.

This OnMouseHover function is very good design practice and is easy to implement. The obvious drawback with this approach is that the user doesn't know it exists until he moves the mouse over the page number. However, this small loss in usability is more than made up for with the efficiency of the design.

To implement mouse hover functionality, the markup must be modified:

- A <DIV> object must be added to encapsulate tables for page numbers and traversing.

- The ShowArrows and HideArrows functions must be called in the onmouseover and onmouseout events.

Implementing the <DIV> object requires the following code:

```
<div id="pagingbar" title="" onmouseover="showArrows();" onmouseout=
"hideArrows();">
<table width="100%" height="100%"  border="0" cellpadding="2" >
 <tr align="center" valign="middle">

    <td width="12" id="leftarrow" class="arrow" onclick="changePage(-1);" >
    <div id="larrow" style="visibility:hidden;" title="previous 5 records">
    <b>&lsaquo;</b>
    </div>
    </td>

    <td width="44" class="sub" id="pageNum" align="center" >1/1</td>

    <td width="12" id="rightarrow" class="arrow" onclick="changePage(+1);">
    <div id="rarrow" style="visibility:hidden;" title="next 5 records">
    <b>&rsaquo;</b>
    </div>
    </td>
 </tr>
</table>
</div>
```

Implementation of the show and hide arrows functions is fairly simple, as shown here:

```
function hideArrows()
{
document.getElementById("larrow").style.visibility="hidden";
document.getElementById("rarrow").style.visibility="hidden";
}
function showArrows()
{
document.getElementById("larrow").style.visibility="visible";
document.getElementById("rarrow").style.visibility="visible";
}
```

Traversing between multiple feeds can also be implemented in a similar manner. For title traversing, you can use the following code:

```
<div id="blogtitletable"  onmouseover="showArrowTitle();" onmouseout="
➥hideArrowTitle();">
  <table width="100%" height="20"  border="0" cellpadding="3" cellspacing="2">
    <tr align="center" valign="middle">
      <td width="4" align = right class="arrow" onclick="changeFeed(-1);
      ➥" align="right">
      <div id="larrowtitle" style="visibility:hidden;"
      title="previous blog"><b>&lsaquo;</b></div></td>
        <td class="subtitle" id="blogtitle" valign ="middle" >Vista Sidebar
        ➥ Gadget</td>
        <td width="4"  align = left class="arrow" onclick="changeFeed(+1);"
        ➥ align="left">
      <div id="rarrowtitle" style="visibility:hidden;"
      title="next blog"><b>&rsaquo;</b></div></td>
      </tr>
  </table>
</div>
function hideArrowTitle(){
document.getElementById("larrowtitle").style.visibility="hidden";
document.getElementById("rarrowtitle").style.visibility="hidden";
}

function showArrowTitle(){
document.getElementById("larrowtitle").style.visibility="visible";
document.getElementById("rarrowtitle").style.visibility="visible";
}
```

Docked, Undocked, and Mini Me Version

A docked version is the gadget's default state when it resides in the Sidebar; the undocked version comes into play when the user drags the gadget out of the Vista Sidebar and onto the desktop. This is also called the *floating state* of the gadget. The Mini Me version of a gadget is a custom option that keeps the gadget docked but reduces its height. Gadgets are all about having ready-to-use information displayed quickly, and being able to manage the information's display area to better accommodate the user's needs. This does not mean that you must provide a larger undocked version and smaller Mini Me version for each gadget. Rather, it means that you should use these options if doing so adds value to the gadget.

Although gadgets float on the desktop, most of the time they are docked to the Sidebar. The height of the Sidebar is limited and can accommodate only four or five gadgets at one particular time. This makes it necessary to create a gadget with an option to be reduced to the minimum size possible. This helps your gadget "play nicely" with other gadgets docked in the Sidebar by taking up as little Sidebar real estate as possible (see Figure 7.9).

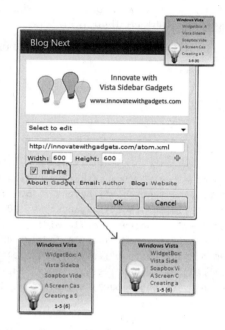

FIGURE 7.9   Mini Me option with optimum height gives users more flexibility.

You don't need any custom configuration for the undocked version, but the Mini Me version needs some custom configuration in the Settings page.

Settings Page Configuration for the Mini Me Version

The Settings page needs a check box the user can check or uncheck for the Mini Me option.

```
<input id="minime" type="checkbox" /> mini-me</div>
```

Next, add the load settings function:

```
minime.checked = System.Gadget.Settings.read("mini");
```

Finally, add in the save settings function:

```
System.Gadget.Settings.write("mini",minime.checked );
```

Gadget Window Configuration

To pass the value from the Settings page to the gadget's main window, you need an in-memory variable to store the user's choice and code in the resize function to reduce the size of the gadget, according to the user's configuration.

The gadget window needs to be resized, as follows, based on the user's selection:

```
if (System.Gadget.Settings.read("mini") ==true)
   {
      with (document.body.style)
   {
      width = 130;
      height = 100;
   }
    System.Gadget.background = "url(../images/backgroundsmall.png)";
      document.getElementById("contenttable").height = "50%";
         document.getElementById("content").style.top = "18px";
         document.getElementById("content").style.width = "72px";
         document.getElementById("content").style.left = "42px";
         document.getElementById("content").style.fontsize ="9px";
         document.getElementById("mylogo").style.top = "54px";
         document.getElementById("pagingbar").style.top = "80px";
}
```

Similarly, for the undocked version, the resize function can accommodate the style change in the following way:

```
if (System.Gadget.docked)
      {
         System.Gadget.background = "url(../images/background.png)";
            document.getElementById("contenttable").height = "90%";
              document.getElementById("content").style.top ="20px";
              document.getElementById("content").style.width = "110px";
              document.getElementById("content").style.left = "8px";
              document.getElementById("content").style.height = "100px";
              document.getElementById("content").style.fontsize ="11px";

              document.getElementById("mylogo").style.left ="2px";
              document.getElementById("mylogo").style.top ="70px";
              document.getElementById("mylogo").style.height="70px";
              document.getElementById("pagingbar").style.top = "100px";
         }
      else
      {
       System.Gadget.background = "url(../images/undocked.png)";
            document.getElementById("contenttable").height = "384px";
```

```
document.getElementById("content").style.top ="30px";
document.getElementById("content").style.width = "430px";
document.getElementById("content").style.left = "8px";
document.getElementById("content").style.height = "384px";
document.getElementById("content").style.fontsize ="11px";

document.getElementById("mylogo").style.left ="2px";
document.getElementById("mylogo").style.top ="70px";
document.getElementById("mylogo").style.height="70px";
document.getElementById("pagingbar").style.top = "400px";
}
```

NOTE

The code example has been taken from the media gadgets discussed in Chapter 11, "Radio Gadget and YouTube Gadget—Fun Gadgets."

Debugging and Deploying a Gadget

"It works on my machine." —#1 of Top 10 Excuses Made by
Programmers

—www.geek24.com

Designing and creating a gadget is only half the work in the gadget development process. After a gadget is created, the next step is to ensure its accuracy and consistency. This is done by debugging the gadget. Debugging is the process of testing, locating, and fixing the errors in the program logic. After the gadget is checked for bugs and tested properly, proper packaging is required to make the gadget distributable.

So far we have dealt only with the design and development aspects of the gadget. Debugging a gadget is the next logical step in the process and actually overlaps with its development. Put more succinctly, debugging is the iterative process of refining the gadget after it's developed. When you create a gadget you test it by installing it in the Sidebar. You test the gadget for all the features and functionality, the gadget is meant to implement. If you come across some inconsistencies, you fix them and test the gadget again.

As shown here, debugging often takes as much time as, and is an integral part of, the development process itself.

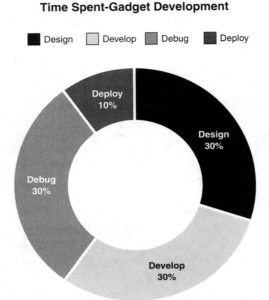

FIGURE 8.1   The four phases of gadget development are design, develop, debug, and deploy.

Debugging a Gadget

The debugging process normally involves tracing the code, and watching values and the state of the gadget during the gadget's execution. The most common scenarios are

- Finding the value of a variable at a particular point in time

- Evaluating an expression

- Branching the execution of the code based on a particular condition or value

Gadget development is based on the scripting language, and because the runtime environment of the gadget is the Sidebar itself, debugging capabilities are quite limited. Here are some of the ways to efficiently debug a gadget:

- Use additional scripts such as Windows Script Host (WScript) or Visual Basic Script (VBScript) to assist you, the developer, in tracing the gadget's behavior.

- Use additional methods in the DOM to assist in validating gadget behavior by displaying messages at specific points in the gadget's execution.

- Use debugging tools that enable you to inspect the gadget state.

The following sections look into each of these methods.

Debugging Using WScript and VBScript

The easiest way to debug a gadget is to use a message box to display the value of a variable or an expression in the gadget at different steps of debugging.

The Windows Script Host (WScript) ActiveX object and Visual Basic Script (VBScript) both provide methods to create a message box in the gadget. Windows Script Host gives pop-up functionality, whereas VBScript has a built-in `MsgBox` function.

JavaScript Alert and Confirm

JavaScript has a similar `alert` and `confirm` function, but both of these modal dialogs are suppressed for Vista gadgets. Using pop-up dialogs goes against the Windows Vista User Experience guidelines for Sidebar gadgets. More information on Windows Vista User Experience Guidelines can be found at http://msdn2.microsoft.com/en-us/library/aa511258.aspx.

Note that message box functionality is used here just for the debugging purpose. Use of message box as a feature of the Vista gadget is still not a good design.

Debugging Using WScript

The Windows Script Host is an ActiveX object provided by the Windows operating system to perform advanced system-level functionalities. It can be used in a gadget to generate a dialog box for debugging purposes.

To use the Windows Script Host pop-up dialog, like the one shown in Figure 8.2, you need to create an instance of a shell, using an ActiveX object control:

```
var WshShell = new ActiveXObject("WScript.Shell");
```

And call the popup function

```
var i = WshShell.Popup("Hello Gadget World", 7,
"Innovate With Gadgets!", 32);
```

FIGURE 8.2   Windows Script Host can be used to create a message box similar to a JavaScript alert.

You can wrap the functionality provided by the Windows Script Host into a JavaScript function that takes a message to display as a parameter. Here is sample code to create a pop-up message box, using the Windows Script Host ActiveX object wrapped inside a JavaScript function MessageJS:

```
function MessageJS(prompt)
{
var WshShell = new ActiveXObject("WScript.Shell");
var returnValue = WshShell.Popup(prompt, 7, "Innovate With Gadgets!", 32);
}
```

Imagine you have added a feed in the MyBlog Gadget but you don't see anything in the gadget window. How will you debug to find out what's happening? Follow these steps:

1. Add the MessageJS function in the gadget.js file.

2. In the ParseFeed function, add the following before the code where you put the titles to the array:

```
MessageJS(i + ":" + rssTitle);
Titles[i] = rssTitle
Descriptions[i] = rssSummary;
PublishedList[i] = rssPubDate;
```

3. Now when you run the gadget, during the loop, the gadget will show the value of rsstitle, along with the value of i for each iteration.

To make it more modular, add this function in a separate JavaScript file, debug.js, and include it in the gadget.html page:

```
<script src="code/Debug.js" type="text/javascript"></script>
```

Now look at the syntax of the Windows Script Host's popup function:

```
returnValue = WshShell.Popup(Text,[SecondsToWait],[Title],[Type])
```

The syntax of the popup function contains four parameters. Table 8.1 describes them in more detail.

TABLE 8.1   Parameters for the Windows Script Host's Pop-up Dialog

SNo	Argument	Description	Other
1	Text	String value containing the text in the pop-up message box	
2	SecondsToWait	Maximum length of time to display the pop-up message in seconds	Optional, default=infinite
3	Title	Title text string	Optional
4	Type	Type of buttons and icons (Numeric, Optional)	These determine how the message box is used.

The meaning of the button Type is determined by combining values from Tables 8.2 and 8.3.

TABLE 8.2   Button Type Values

Value	Description
0	OK button
1	OK and Cancel buttons
2	Abort, Retry, and Ignore buttons
3	Yes, No, and Cancel buttons
4	Yes and No buttons
5	Retry and Cancel buttons

TABLE 8.3   Icons Associated with Button Types

Value	Description
16	Stop icon
32	Question icon
48	Exclamation icon
64	Information icon

Possible return values, indicating which button was clicked, are listed in Table 8.4.

TABLE 8.4   Return Value of the popup Function

Value	Description
1	OK button
2	Cancel button
3	Abort button
4	Retry button
5	Ignore button
6	Yes button
7	No button

If the user does not click a button before the dialog expires (as determined by the SecondsToWait parameter), the return value is -1.

Knowledge of these parameters and return values enables the user to implement advanced conditional executions while debugging. Users can implement a conditional message box and, based on the different options, can excute different functions. This helps later in the debug process.

NOTE

More information on Windows Script Host can be found at http://msdn2.microsoft.com/en-us/library/at5ydy31.aspx.

Using Visual Basic Script

Visual Basic Script's `MsgBox` function can be used for debugging purposes. To use VBScript as a debug option from the sample code you have to do the following:

1. Add a `debug.vbs` file with the desired debug functions.

2. Include the gadget's `debug.vbs` file along with code file (`gadget.html`):

   ```
   <script src="code/Debug.vbs" type="text/vbscript"></script>
   ```

3. Call the function in the gadget's code file (`gadget.js`).

I have included, with this book's other supplemental materials, a `debug.vbs` file that can be used for this purpose. Typically the following four functions can be helpful with debugging, which of course can be extended further depending on your needs:

- `Message`, to display a value in a pop-up dialog

- `Assert`, to check the validity of an expression

- `Question`, a conditional message box; further execution depends on the user's selection

- `MessageDialog`, to display a message with customized caption text.

You can integrate these scripts into any gadget by including the `.vbs` file (`debug.vbs`) in the `gadget.html`. It works great for values of variables at different points of execution inside the gadget. Here is the code for the four functions of `debug.vbs`:

```
'/////////////////////////////////////////
' The Debug.vbs file' VBScript File
'/////////////////////////////////////////

Sub Message(alertmessage) 'For a modal dialog box to display value
    MsgBox alertmessage, 64 , "Innovate with Gadgets"
End Sub
```

This function is used to display a value in a pop-up dialog. Figure 8.3 further details how the Visual Basic `Message` function is used in the gadget.

```
Sub Assert(exp,message) 'To evaluate an expression
  if (not exp) then
    MessageDialog message,48
  end if
End Sub
```

The `Assert` function is used to evaluate an expression and check its validity.

```
Function Question(alertmessage) 'To branch execution as per users choice
    Question= MsgBox(alertmessage, 1 , "Innovate with Gadgets")
End Function
```

The `Question` function helps in creating conditional execution based on user's selection.

```
Sub MessageDialog(alertmessage, dialog)
'To display multiple debug messages with different dialog options
    MsgBox alertmessage, dialog, "Innovate with Gadgets"
End sub
```

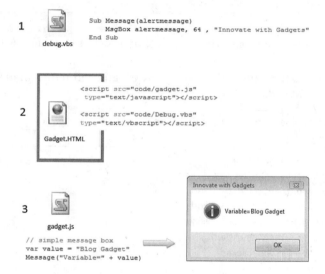

FIGURE 8.3   Using the `Message` function from `debug.vbs` to display the value of a variable.

Let's go through the detailed syntax of `MsgBox` functionality in Visual Basic Script.

```
MsgBox(prompt[,buttons][,title])
```

The three most common parameters and their descriptions are listed here:

- `prompt` (Required)—The message to show in the message box. Maximum length is 1,024 characters. You can separate the lines using a carriage return character (`Chr(13)`), a linefeed character (`Chr(10)`), or a carriage return–linefeed character combination (`Chr(13)` & `Chr(10)`) between each line.

- `buttons` (Optional)—A value or a sum of values that specifies the number and type of buttons to display, the icon style to use, the identity of the default button, and the modality of the message box. Although the default value is 0, the range of possible values is listed in Table 8.5.

TABLE 8.5   Button Values for the `MsgBox` Function

Value	Description
0	vbOKOnly—OK button only
1	vbOKCancel—OK and Cancel buttons
2	vbAbortRetryIgnore—Abort, Retry, and Ignore buttons
3	vbYesNoCancel—Yes, No, and Cancel buttons
4	vbYesNo—Yes and No buttons
5	vbRetryCancel—Retry and Cancel buttons
16	vbCritical—Critical Message icon
32	vbQuestion—Warning Query icon
48	vbExclamation—Warning Message icon
64	vbInformation—Information Message icon

- `title` (optional)—The title of the message box. Default is the application name.

The `MsgBox` function is the core of this debug process and can return one of the following values, as shown in Table 8.6.

TABLE 8.6   Return Value of the `MsgBox` Function

Value	Description
1	vbOK—OK was clicked
2	vbCancel—Cancel was clicked
3	vbAbort—Abort was clicked
4	vbRetry—Retry was clicked
5	vbIgnore—Ignore was clicked
6	vbYes—Yes was clicked
7	vbNo—No was clicked

Debugging Using JavaScript and DOM

The second option for debugging is to use JavaScript and the Document Object Model (DOM) of the HTML page to display values during testing. The elements of the Document Object Model can be used to display debug messages. This is a good option when you need a quick and easy way to trace a variable's value.

For example, `blogtitle` is one of the visible elements of the gadget whose default text is "Vista Sidebar Gadget."

```
<td class="subtitle" id="blogtitle">Vista Sidebar Gadget</td>
```

Using the DOM, the `title` property of `blogtitle` can be accessed inside the gadget code (gadget.js) in the following way:

```
document.getElementById('blogtitle').title = "currentFeed=" +
➡ System.Gadget.Settings.read("FeedURL");
```

Or in a shortcut notation simply

```
blogtitle.title= "currentFeed="+System.Gadget.Settings.read("FeedURL");
```

Figure 8.4 shows how it looks in the gadget when the mouse is over the title element.

FIGURE 8.4   Putting debug information in the tooltip is a quick and easy way to test.

This is a basic kind of debugging that can be used to display a variable's value. Any visible element in the gadget can be used to track the current value.

This is an easy and quick method to debug a particular value. There is no need to include a file or attach a debugger. Use the DOM to get to the element you want to use to display the variable value. Make sure that you comment out the debug code after you fix the error. In gadget development, there is no option to compile without debug information, which is the case with most high-level programming languages. In fact, there is no such thing as `compile` in a gadget.

Note that this method of displaying a value does not break the execution at a particular point, which means that if you want to debug a value in the loop, this method may get you only the last value in the loop. In the likely event that you miss intermediate values, a dialog box may be a better choice for debugging.

JavaScript also provides a `document.write` function, which writes the content back to the HTML page. A good scenario to implement `document.write` is in a `try-catch` block, as follows:

```
try
    {
      // my function
    }
    catch(exception)
    {
      Document.write(' Error occurred in my function');
    }
```

For advanced debugging, a proper script-debugging tool is required.

Debugging Tools

A number of script debugging tools are available; the most common among them is the Microsoft Script Debugger. However, regardless of which tool you prefer, all these debugging tools require the following:

- Script debugging enabled in Internet Explorer via the Options, Advanced tab

- In the debugger, a statement in the script where you want to halt execution

- User choice dialog box to select the debugger

Scripting Disabled in Internet Explorer

To disable scripting in Internet Explorer you need to access the Advanced tab of Internet Explorer's Options menu. As shown in Figure 8.5, both the Disable Script Debugging (Internet Explorer) and the Disable Script Debugging (Other) check boxes should be unchecked.

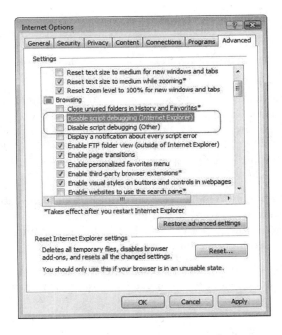

FIGURE 8.5   The Disable Script Debugging option in Internet Explorer.

Debugger Statement

A debugger statement is required in the script where you want to halt execution. The VBScript equivalent of calling the debugger is the Stop function. You can call it in either of two ways:

- As illustrated in Figure 8.6, add the following in the script to stop execution:

  ```
  debugger;
  ```

- Call a Stop function inside a VBScript file to halt execution.

This code tells Internet Explorer to pause execution and open the script debugger for further step-by-step execution. After the debugger or Stop statement is inserted in the code, as shown in Figure 8.6, a Windows dialog box appears, asking for the user to choose the script editor when the code is encountered while the gadget is running.

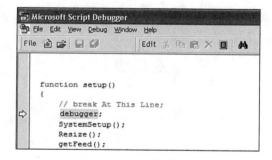

FIGURE 8.6   The execution automatically halts at the debugger statement.

Dialog Box to Select the Debugger

After the script execution reaches the line with the debugger or stop statement, it calls the System Debugger select window for the user to select the debugger and debug the code further. The user can also cancel the debugging and continue with the gadget code (see Figure 8.7).

After a debugger is selected, the code appears in the debugger, with the execution halted at the debugger or stop statement (see Figure 8.8).

You can also call a number of debug-specific functions while in debug mode to further trace variables. For example, the Debug.write or System.Debug.outputstring ("Message") functions can be used to write the output to the output window.

Microsoft Script Debugger can be downloaded from Microsoft downloads at http://www.microsoft.com/downloads. Search for "Script Debugger for Windows NT 4.0 and Later."

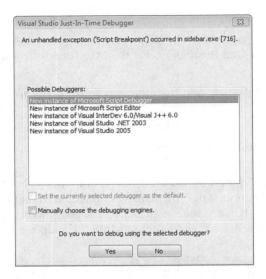

FIGURE 8.7   The debugger selection window.

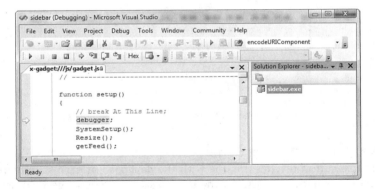

FIGURE 8.8   The code inside the Visual Studio 2005 debugger.

NOTE

Plug-ins are also available for Firefox that can be used for debugging JavaScript. More information can be found at http://www.codejacked.com/debugging-javascript-with-firefox/.

Deploying a Gadget

After the gadget is tested, the next step is to package it for distribution.

To understand the deployment process, you need to have a clear picture of

- The target folder where the gadget is deployed
- The gadget installation process
- The gadget's packaging

The gadget's packaging depends on both the target folder as well as the gadget installation process. Before going into package creation you must know where exactly these packages are deployed and what exactly happens in the installation process. This knowledge gives you a better understanding of the packages.

Gadget Installation Target

A gadget can be deployed in three different locations:

- Gadget user folders:

  %UserProfile%\AppData\Local\Microsoft\Windows Sidebar\Gadgets

  For example, if your computer username is John, USER_DATA typically translates to C:\Users\john and the full folder path is

  C:\Users\john\AppData\Local\Microsoft\Windows Sidebar\Gadgets

- Gadget system folder:

  %SystemDrive%\Program Files\Windows Sidebar\Gadgets

  If the operating system is installed in the C: drive, the full path is

  `C:\Program Files\Windows Sidebar\Gadgets`

- Gadget shared folder:

  %SystemDrive%\Program Files\Windows Sidebar\Shared Gadgets

  If the operating system is installed in the C: drive, the full path is

  C:\Program Files\Windows Sidebar\Shared Gadgets

The Vista Sidebar automatically detects the gadget as long as it resides in one of these three locations. (Let's call them **gadget folders**.)

The gadgets that come with Windows Vista reside in the gadget system folder. Whenever a user downloads and installs a gadget, it normally goes to the gadget user folder. The gadget shared folder is intended to deploy gadgets accessible to all the users of the computer.

By default the gadget is installed on the user-specific gadget folder: %UserProfile%\AppData\Local\Microsoft\Windows Sidebar\Gadgets

Gadget Installation Process

The gadget installation process is a three-step process (see Figure 8.9). Let's take the MyBlog Gadget created in Chapter 5, "Creating a Simple Gadget with RSS/Atom Feed," as an example:

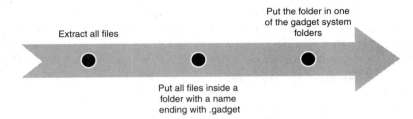

FIGURE 8.9   The standard installation process for a gadget.

1. The first step of the installation pack is to extract all files.

    - Gadget files

        - `gadget.html` and `gadget.xml`

        - `flyout.html`

        - `settings.html`

    - Code

    - Images

    - Style

2. Put all files inside a folder with a name ending with `.gadget`.

    - `GadgetName.Gadget`

3. The last step is to put the folder in one of the gadget system folders.

    - User folder

    - System folder

    - Shared folder

This is an overview of the installation process. Additional steps are required if you want to use custom ActiveX objects along with the gadget, which might be required to be registered with the computer.

Gadget Packaging

To create a deployable package for the MyBlogPack gadget, you need to create a single file that the user can double-click on to start the installation process.

The gadget can be distributed using one of the following deployment methodologies:

- Folder structure, deployed as a folder with the name MyBlogPack.gadget.

- A Zip file with the extension changed to .gadget (for example, MyBlogPack.zip to MyBlogPack.gadget).

- A cabinet (CAB) file, such as MyBlogPack.gadget. A CAB file can be code-signed to provide additional security.

- A Windows Installer (.msi file) or setup.exe.

Later in this chapter, in the section, "Deployment Using a Cabinet File," we'll examine how to deploy a gadget as a cabinet file. The next two sections detail deployment via folder structure and via a Zip file.

Folder Structure

The easiest way to deploy a gadget is by using a folder structure. This is recommended only while developing and testing the gadget in the local machine.

Figure 8.10 illustrates placing all the gadget files in a folder named GadgetName.Gadget and copying it to one of the gadget system folders.

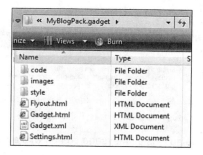

FIGURE 8.10   MyBlogPack Gadget folder.

As you see, this is the last step of the installation process, so deploying a gadget using the folder structure does work. But if you want to distribute your gadget, this is not recommended because the user might not be aware of the gadget system folders.

Using a Zip File to Distribute a Gadget

One of the most popular deployment methodologies is the Zip file. What you need to do is place all the files in the same folder and then zip them into a single Zip file, using the Windows Compressed Folder option (see Figure 8.11).

The zipped file will have the name of one of the files in the folder. For this example, it became Flyout.zip. The next step is to change the Zip filename to MyBlogPack.gadget.

The gadget is now ready to be deployed. After users double-click on the gadget or download it from a web page, they will see the dialog shown in Figure 8.12.

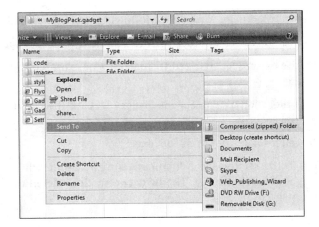

FIGURE 8.11   Zip-packaging option for a gadget.

Gadget with Publisher Name and Valid Certificate

FIGURE 8.12   The gadget's default install message comes with a security warning.

After the user clicks Install, the package goes through the standard install process: extract, create a MyBlogPack.gadget folder, and move it to the user's gadget folder, which is the default folder for gadgets.

Deployment Using a Cabinet File

Using the Windows CAB file approach enables code-signing, which ensures an extra level of security. Code signing is a method that ensures that the gadget has come from a valid gadget provider and has not been altered by anyone (see Figure 8.13).

Notice the publisher, which was "Unknown Publisher" in Figure 8.12, is now "InnovateWithGadgets.com."

A signed CAB file gadget displays the company name in the publisher portion of the security warning during the install process. A gadget, when deployed as a CAB file, can be digitally signed and transmitted along with a digital certificate. The certificate can be self signed (by the provider) or purchased by a certification authority (CA) such as VeriSign.

FIGURE 8.13   A gadget with the publisher's name and a valid certificate still shows a security warning.

CAB File Approach

This section shows you how to sign a gadget using a self-signed certificate. Creating a deployment package using the CAB file approach requires three steps:

1. Creating a CAB File

2. Creating (or purchasing) a certificate

3. Signing the CAB file with the created certificate

Creating a CAB File

Creating a CAB file needs a special tool, which can be freely downloaded from Microsoft.com at http://support.microsoft.com/kb/310618/. Just search for "Microsoft Cabinet Software Development Kit." The kit is included in Visual Studio 2005, which is used here. To create a CAB file:

1. Run Visual Studio 2005 command prompt as Administrator and change the directory to the folder that has all the files for packaging. The 2005 command prompt comes in the Visual Studio Tools section of the installation.

   For the sample gadget, you have to type the following in the command prompt:

   ```
   cd "Path of the Gadget"\MyBlogPack.gadget
   ```

2. Type

   ```
   cabarc -p -r N MyBlogPack.gadget *
   ```

8

and press Enter. The switches used in this command work as follows:

- -p option preserves the directory structure.
- -r includes files in subdirectories.
- –N creates a new CAB file.

You can see the results of running the cabarc command in Figure 8.14.

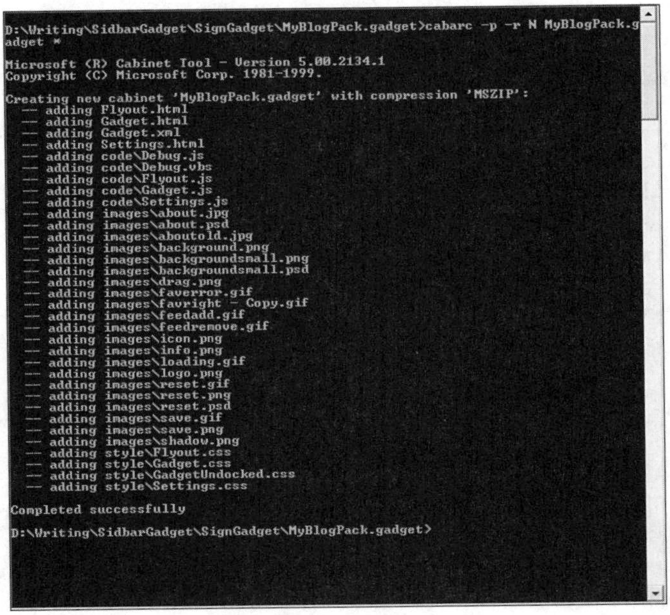

FIGURE 8.14   Generating the CAB file using Windows cabarc.

This creates a CAB file with the name MyBlogPack.gadget in the same directory.

Creating or Purchasing a Certificate

If you need to purchase a certificate you can go to www.verisign.com. An individual certificate costs around $500 per year. To create a personal certificate, in the command prompt type **makecert -sv "MyBlog.pvk" -n "CN=InnovateWithGadgets.com" MyBlog.cer**.

The switches used in this command work as follows:

- -sv creates a private key.
- -n sets the Issued To field.

Visual Studio then asks for a password, which is embedded inside the certificate and is required when you try to sign the gadget (CAB file) with this certificate (see Figure 8.15).

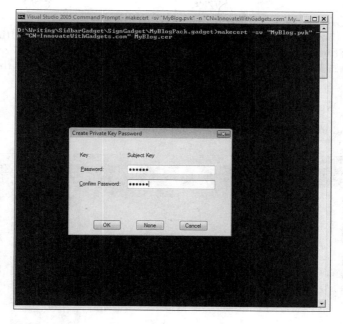

FIGURE 8.15   Entering the optional password for a certificate.

You might be required to enter the password three times, but when you are finished you will see the message Succeeded, as shown in Figure 8.16.

```
D:\Writing\SidbarGadget\SignGadget\MyBlogPack.gadget>makecert -sv "MyBlog.pvk" -
n "CN=InnovateWithGadgets.com" MyBlog.cer
Succeeded
```

FIGURE 8.16   Creating the certificate with publisher Innovatewithgadgets.com.

Figure 8.17 shows how the folder structure will look after the certificate and the CAB file are created.

FIGURE 8.17   A pair of files, MyBlog.cer and MyBlog.pvk, are created.

Signing the CAB File with the Created Certificate

The last step in the CAB file approach is to sign the CAB file, using the certificate you just created. Visual Studio 2005 also comes with a built-in Digital Signature Wizard. Just type **signtool signwizard** in the command prompt and press Enter. Then use the following steps:

1. When the Welcome page appears, click Next.

2. Browse and locate the .gadget file (see Figure 8.18). Click Next.

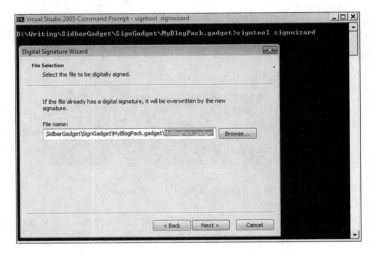

FIGURE 8.18   A Digital Signature Wizard is used to sign the gadget with the certificate just created.

3. Choose Custom Signing Options and press Next again.

4. On the Signature Certificate page shown in Figure 8.19, click Select from File, locate and open the .cer file created in step 2, and click Next.

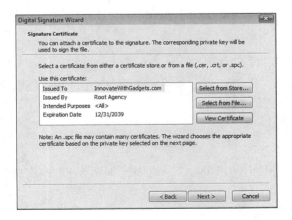

FIGURE 8.19   Using the Digital Signature Wizard.

5. The next step, shown in Figure 8.20, asks you to enter the private key created in the first step. Click Browse and select the MyBlog.pvk file. Click Next and re-enter the password just created. Choose a hash algorithm (or leave the selected one). Click Next.

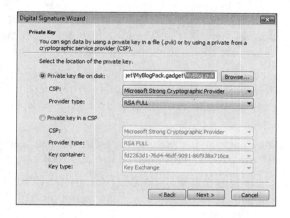

FIGURE 8.20   Adding the private key in the Digital Signature Wizard.

6. The data description page can be filled with a short description of your gadget and a web link (click Next). And the Timestamp page can be used to mark the gadget creation time (click Next).

7. You can use the Advanced option to give a higher level of security by checking the timestamp of the certificate with a publicly available dynamic link library. One of the .dll paths you can use in the timestamp page is the VeriSign public timestamp .dll (http://timestamp.verisign.com/scripts/timstamp.dll). Click Next and then Finish on the final dialog to finish signing the CAB file (see Figure 8.21).

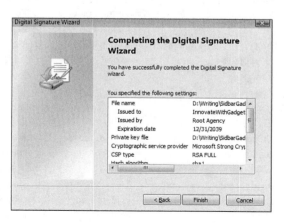

FIGURE 8.21   Completing the Digital Signature Wizard.

After the gadget is signed you can double-click the gadget to verify that the Publisher section of the security warning displays "InnovateWithGadgets.com" instead of "unknown."

A Windows Installer (`.msi` File) or `setup.exe`

Windows Installer is a software package that helps in installation, maintenance, and removal of an application on Windows. A Windows Installer packs the files in installation packages in the form of an `.msi` file or sometimes a single `setup.exe`.

Visual Studio 2005 comes with a click-once installer that can be used for this purpose. The only thing of concern is the gadget's target folder. When you create an installer you have to give the target folder path to one of the gadget folders, depending on the type of the gadget.

Using a Windows Installer package is the only way to install your gadget directly to the system folder. Otherwise the gadget is installed in the user root gadget folder.

A Windows Installer is also helpful if you want to pack an ActiveX control or a dynamic link library that needs to be registered on the client's computer. This is sometimes the case when you have a utility gadget using a library file.

Comparison of Deployment Methodologies

So far you have seen different kinds of installation mechanisms used for a gadget. The simplest of all is using the Zip file approach. Table 8.7 shows a detailed comparison of all the technologies and their advantages.

TABLE 8.7   Comparision of All the Deployment Technologies

Method	Files and Folders	Extension	Supports	Description	Advantage
Folder	One folder, MyBlog.Gadget, with all files included in it	None	User, system, and shared gadget folder installation	Copy the folder directly to the gadget folder	Ready to use; good for design, development, and debugging
Zip	One Zip file, myblog.zip, with the extension changed from .zip to .gadget, all the files compressed inside the Zip file	.gadget	User's gadget folder	One-click install for the gadget	Easy and quick, distribution over the Web
Cabinet (CAB) File	One cabinet file with a .gadget extension	.gadget	User's gadget folder	One-click install for the gadget	Ensures valid provider, more secure
Installer with .msi or setup.exe	.msi or a setup.exe; an executable with all the files compressed into it	.msi or .exe	User, system, and shared gadget folder	Custom step-by-step install wizard	Registers .dlls, advanced options

PART

Advanced Samples

IN THIS PART

Site Statistics Gadget with Ajax—An Information Gadget

"The value of an idea lies in the using of it."

— Thomas Edison

The Goal

The Site Statistics Gadget provides a concise view of counter and statistics services. The data is provided by www.sitemeter.com (see Figure 9.1). The gadget uses Ajax technology to asynchronously acquire the data from a web APIs provided by SiteMeter. The gadget also shows how to extract a part of an online web page in the flyout window and display dynamically generated graphs and statistics that the server application creates. Ajax technology, as you saw in Part II, helps acquire data from online sources in an asynchronous way.

The goals of the Site Statistics Gadget are as follows:

- Provide a subset of a service provided by the free online service www.sitemeter.com

- Show statistical data for page visits and page views

- Include an additional feature for regions, browsers, and operating system information

- Provide a shortcut link to visit the website for detail statistics
- Include the capability to add multiple websites to the Site Statistics Gadget and to easily select between websites

FIGURE 9.1   The Site Statistics Gadget from SiteMeter.

Figure 9.2 shows how the gadget appears in the Sidebar.

FIGURE 9.2   Simple view of the Site Statistics Gadget in the Vista Sidebar.

Background—www.sitemeter.com

SiteMeter is an online web service that provides comprehensive real-time website tracking and counter tools. This gives customers instant access to vital information and data regarding their websites' audiences. It provides data related to visits, page views, and referral links in an easy-to-understand manner.

SiteMeter provides a counter *widget*, a chunk of JavaScript code that can be embedded in a website and provides a visitor counter and detailed statistics of page views and visits. The information is accumulated by the www.sitemeter.com provider and is accessible as an online web service.

The following code represents the Counter Widget, which is embedded in the website http://innovatewithgadgets.com.

```
<!-- SiteMeter XHTML Strict 1.0 -->
<script type="text/javascript"
src="http://s41.sitemeter.com/js/counter.js?site=s41vistagadgets">
</script>
```

This code has a dual purpose. The first is to display the number of visitors to the website, as shown in Figure 9.3. The second is to collect all visitor information and display statistical data in a ready-to-use format.

Note the URL the Counter Widget link is http://www.sitemeter.com/stats.asp?site=s41vistagadget.

FIGURE 9.3   The Counter Widget shows the number of visits and links to sitemeter.com, which further displays the detailed visit statistics.

Here s41vistagadget is the SiteMeter–unique code to identify the website http:// innovatewithgadgets.com. This code is generated the first time you create a counter.

Site Summary Page

To display the number of visitors on the website, you can click on the counter and the code takes you to the www.sitemeter.com Site Summary page. The Site Summary page provides a view of the site usage summary (see Figure 9.4).

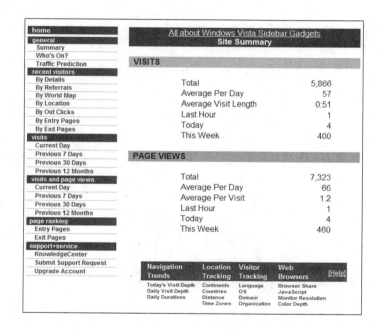

FIGURE 9.4   Site statistics for the website innovatewithgadgets.com at sitemeter.com.

In addition to the summary, the free service also provides recent visitor information, number of visits, page views, page rankings, navigation trends, location tracking, visitor tracking, browser, operating system, and so on. For the example in this book, we are going to implement the most commonly used features in the Site Statistics Gadget.

The Site Statistics Gadget uses the features provided by the free service to create a ready-to-use information gadget. More information about the services provided by SiteMeter can be found on its website at http://www.sitemeter.com.

> **NOTE**
>
> The URL for the SiteMeter Widget is http://www.sitemeter.com/stats.asp?site=s41vistagadget. s41vistagadget is the SiteMeter code that is generated the first time you create a counter for your website. This code is used to distinguish among multiple websites.

Features and Technology

The Site Statistics Gadget displays a subset of the basic online service provided by www.sitemeter.com. It uses a custom API provided by SiteMeter to pull information from the server. Features also include display of bar graphs and pie charts, such as those shown in Figure 9.5. These features are specific to the implementation of the online service and can also be customized using the data provided by SiteMeter's API.

The following technologies are used for the Site Statistics Gadget:

- Application programming interface provided by www.sitemeter.com
- Loading a portion of a web page (HTML scraping) with Ajax and DOM

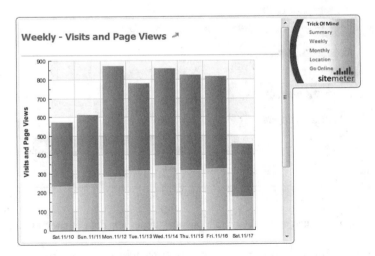

FIGURE 9.5   The Site Statistics Gadget displays a graph directly from the server.

Application Programming Interface

The first challenge is to access the data from the online API provided by
www.sitemeter.com. This is done using the following technology

- Text data using an Ajax methodology

- JavaScript and DOM to further parse and store data

The website http://www.sitemeter.com provides an API to generate the previous seven
days of page visit reports. The SiteMeter code (as discussed earlier) is the key to all the
information provided by the API, as well as the data displayed on the online web service.
This code ties the information displayed in the gadget to a specific website. The following
link displays the information of a website with the SiteMeter code `sm5sitefreestuff`:

```
tuff&p2=&p3=6&p4=0&p5=208%2E70%2E116%2E25&p6=HTML&p7=1&p8=%2E%3Fa%3Dstatistics&p9=
&rnd=47190
```

Within this URL you will find the text string p1= `sm5sitefreestuff`, which is similar to
the code string that every SiteMeter account is issued. This link, when opened in a web
browser, returns data similar to the following:

```
38,Sat.11/10¦18,Sat.11/10¦15,Sun.11/11¦10,Sun.11/11¦27,Mon.11/12¦9,Mon.
➡11/12¦17,Tue.11/13¦8,Tue.11/13¦30,Wed.11/14¦13,Wed.11/14¦27,Thu.11/15¦9,
➡Thu.11/15¦14,Fri.11/16¦7,Fri.11/16¦13,Sat.11/17¦10,Sat.11/17¦
```

The format is

```
http://sm5.sitemeter.com/rpc/v6/server.asp?
            a=GetChartData &
            n=9 &
            p1=sm5sitefreestuff &
            p2= &
            p3=6 &
            p4=0 &
            p5=208.70.116.25 &
            p6=HTML &
            p7=1 &
            p8=.?a=statistics &
            p9= &
            rnd=47190
```

The parameters passed to the SiteMeter URL are different for different accounts. The p1=
`sm5sitefreestuff` would have to be modified with the site user's code string in your
widget so that users could see their own stats.

Note that the URL http://sm5.sitemeter.com uses the same prefix (the sm[server number]
portion) as the code string. If a user has an account on server 42, this would need to

point to http://s42.sitemeter.com and, as expected, his code string would have a similar prefix, such as s42mysitecode.

The SiteMeter server-naming convention uses the following prefixes:

sm1, sm2, sm3, sm4, sm5, sm6, sm7, sm8, sm9, s10, s11 -........ s50

Keep in mind that the account must be public. If the user has an account set to private, it returns no data.

Using an Ajax Methodology with Text Data

The Ajax XMLHTTPRequest object is used to pull the text data provided by the API. XMLHTTPRequest is an object that JavaScript uses to fetch data through the Internet. The data can be in the form of XML, HTML, text, or JSON. This is the core component of Ajax (Asynchronous JavaScript and XML) that makes an information gadget work.

Use this line to create an XMLHTTPRequest object:

```
var req = new ActiveXObject("Microsoft.XMLHTTP");
```

Table 9.1 lists the most common methods of the XMLHTTPRequest object, whereas Table 9.2 lists its most common properties.

TABLE 9.1   Common Methods of the XMLHTTPRequest Object

Method	Description
abort()	Stops the current request
getAllResponseHeaders()	Returns a complete set of headers (labels and values) as a string
getResponseHeader("headerLabel")	Returns the string value of a single header label
open("method", "URL"[, asyncFlag[, "userName"[, "password"]]])	Assigns destination URL, method, and other optional attributes of a pending request
send(content)	Transmits the request, optionally with a postable string or DOM object data
setRequestHeader("label", "value")	Assigns a label/value pair to the header to be sent with a request

TABLE 9.2   Common Properties of the XMLHTTPRequest Object

Property	Description
onreadystatechange	Event handler for an event that fires at every state change
readyState	Object status integer:
	0 = uninitialized
	1 = loading
	2 = loaded
	3 = interactive
	4 = complete
responseText	String version of data returned from server process

TABLE 9.2   Continued

Property	Description
responseXML	DOM-compatible document object of the data returned from the server process
status	Numeric code returned by the server, such as 404 for "Not Found" or 200 for "OK"
statusText	String message accompanying the status code

Here is the portion of the function that pulls the information from the online API.

```
function getTextAjax()
{

    blogtitle.title = System.Gadget.Settings.read("sitemeterTitle");
    var SMC = System.Gadget.Settings.read("sitemeterCode");
    var firstthree =  Mid(SMC,0,3);
    ajaxObj = new ActiveXObject("Microsoft.XMLHTTP");
    myURL = "http://" + firstthree +
    ".sitemeter.com/rpc/v6/server.asp?a=GetChartData&n=9&p1=" + SMC +
    "&p2=&p3=6&p4=0&p5=208%2E70%2E116%2E25&p6=HTML&p7=1
    &p8=%2E%3Fa%3Dstatistics&p9=&rnd=47190";
        ajaxObj.open("GET", myURL, true);
    ajaxObj.onreadystatechange = function() {
        if (ajaxObj.readyState === 4) {
            if (ajaxObj.status === 200) {
                loading.innerText = "";
                page = 0;
                parseData(ajaxObj.responseText);
                content.style.visibility = "visible";
                loading.style.visibility = "hidden";
            } else {
                var chkConn;
                loading.innerText = "Unable to connect...";
            chkConn = setInterval(getTextAjax, 30 * 60000);
            }
        } else {
            loading.innerText = "...";
        }
    }
    ajaxObj.send(null);
}
```

This function is similar to what was used in Part II for the MyBlog Gadget. The only difference is instead of fetching XML data, as in the case of the MyBlog Gadget, here the data is in text format.

Using this code, the SiteMeter API URL is opened with the SiteMeter code as the parameter, along with the parameters requesting the site statistics. The server responds with a string that is then passed to the parseData function. Note that we are using ajaxObj.responseText instead of ajaxObj.responseXML to get this string. The reason is that the return data is in the form of plain text. responseXML is used when the return data is in XML format so that it can be further parsed.

Using JavaScript and DOM to Parse Data

The next step after retrieving the data is to parse it and display it in human-readable format. In its simplest form, the parseData function looks like the following:

```
function parseData(Data)
{
    SiteMeterDataValues = Data.split("|");

    for (i=0; i<SiteMeterDataValues.length-1; i=i+2)
    {
        PageViews[i] = SiteMeterDataValues[i];
        Visits[i] = SiteMeterDataValues[i+1];
    }


    cell0.innerHTML = '<div align="left"
    onclick="showFlyout(\'0\');">Summary</div>';
    cell1.innerHTML = '<div align="left"
    onclick="showFlyout(\'1\');">Weekly</div>';
    cell2.innerHTML = '<div align="left"
    onclick="showFlyout(\'2\');">Monthly</div>';
    cell3.innerHTML = '<div align="left"
    onclick="showFlyout(\'4\');">Location</div>';
    cell4.innerHTML = '<div align="left"
    onclick="showFlyout(\'8\');">Go Online</div>';
}
```

This function accepts the text data returned in the getTextAjax function. It splits the data in a JavaScript array, SiteMeterDataValues, and saves the corresponding values to the Pageviews and Visits arrays. The parseData function also generates the HTML data for the HTML cells to be displayed in the gadget window.

Loading a Portion of a Web Page with Ajax and DOM

Typically, you would want to display a portion of the web page in your gadget's flyout window (see Figure 9.6). This can be very useful for displaying ready-to-use information, such as if a website provides useful data in the HTML format, rather than in an XML format. In this scenario, displaying a portion of the web page directly in the gadget can be handy. The developer need not implement an extra layer to create the RSS feed and so on and use it in the gadget. This capability to load a portion of the web page directly in the gadget window provides considerable flexibility to the developer. In addition, there are the following benefits:

- No extra effort is required on the server application to extend the online service to accommodate the gadget's requirements.

- HTML data can be directly displayed in the gadget and does not need another library for loading and parsing, as it does in the case of XML data.

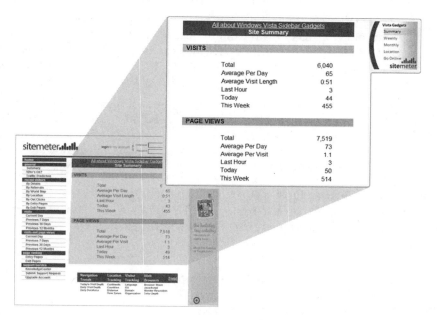

FIGURE 9.6   The Site Statistics Gadget displays a portion of the web page in the flyout window.

HTML code in a web page can have lot of nested tables and page elements, which can make traversing and parsing the data a bit tricky. The gadget should be properly tested before it is distributed.

A helpful utility is the Internet Explorer Developer Toolbar, a free Internet Explorer plug-in for quickly traversing a web page in real-time and understanding its elements and layout. It can be downloaded from http://www.microsoft.com/Downloads/details.aspx?FamilyID=e59c3964-672d-4511-bb3e-2d5e1db91038&displaylang=en.

Loading a web page feature can be divided into three parts:

- Preparing the gadget to accommodate the returned HTML

- Loading the web page, using Ajax, and inserting it into the gadget

- Extracting the HTML portion of the document for display in the flyout

Preparing the Gadget to Accommodate the HTML Data Returned

To populate the HTML data retrieved from an online page, you first have to create a hidden DIV element in the gadget main window (gadget.html). Use the following code:

```
<div id='sitesummary' style="visibility:hidden;" ></div>
```

The purpose of the DIV element is to store the HTML returned from the Ajax function getHTMLAjax in the current page. (See code for the function in the next section.)

Using a DIV element to store the HTML has a number of advantages. First, because the HTML is now part of the gadget's main window Document object, DOM Level 1 methods such as GetElementById and GetElementByTagNames can be used to search the elements. Second, the DIV element easily accommodates the HTML portion from the online web page.

Another advantage is that after you have the HTML in raw format, you can use any mechanism, such as a regular expression search, to extract and parse information from it. Many JavaScript regular expression libraries are available that can be used for this purpose. As you will see in the sample code in the next section, having a DIV element as the container of the HTML data makes HTML parsing much easier.

Loading the Web Page, Using Ajax, and Inserting It into the Gadget

The XMLHTTPRequest object is used to retrieve the HTML. Here is the function that takes a URL as the parameter and saves the returned HTML in the gadget's DIV element sitesummary.

```
function getHTMLAjax(pageURL) {
    htmlObj = new ActiveXObject("Microsoft.XMLHTTP");
    htmlObj.open("GET", pageURL, true);
    htmlObj.onreadystatechange = function() {
        if (htmlObj.readyState === 4) {
        if (htmlObj.status === 200) {
            document.getElementById('sitesummary').innerHTML
            = htmlObj.responseText;
             parseHTML()
        } else {
             chkConn = setInterval(getHTMLAjax, 30 * 60000);
        }
        }
    }
    htmlObj.send(null);
}
```

Notice the SetInterval call, which, in the case of error, calls the getHTMLAjax function after 30 minutes. Details of this function were already discussed in Chapter 5, "Creating a Simple Gadget with RSS/Atom Feed."

Note that the HTML is returned as text and is inserted directly into the DIV element previously created to hold the data. The `htmlObj.responseText` property contains the HTML of the entire page. For example, if the URL passed in the function is http://www.sitemeter.com/?a=stats&s=s41vistagadgets, the DIV element `sitesummary` will have the complete source code of the web page and become the part of the gadget window's HTML page source.

Extracting the HTML Portion of the Document for Display in the Flyout

After you have the web page's HTML, the tricky part is to extract specific information from it. As you can see in Figure 9.7, the web page contains a lot of information, but the gadget needs to display just the statistics part. You can use the Internet Explorer Developer Toolbar (mentioned earlier) to get to the HTML element (in this case it's a table) that you want to extract.

> **NOTE**
>
> The Internet Explorer Developer Toolbar can be enabled from the Internet Explorer menu bar by clicking View, Explorer bar, IE Developer Toolbar.

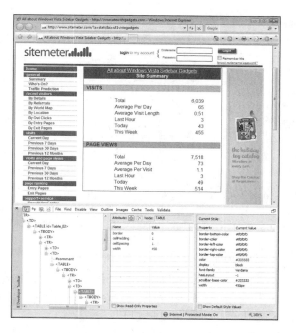

FIGURE 9.7   The figure shows the <TABLE> selected in the Explorer Toolbar (lower left). It also shows the corresponding table selected in the web page that encapsulates the site summary with the visits and page views blocks.

The Developer Toolbar also makes it easier to understand the layout and hierarchy of elements. Figure 9.7 shows the element hierarchy, which illustrates the table that has the information we want to display in the flyout window. The following function, parseHTML, parses the HTML document to acquire the table. This table is then stored in the global variable SiteMeterSummary.

```
function parseHTML()
{
try{
    tcMain = document.getElementById("Table_01");
    if (tcMain)
    {
     var TableID = tcMain.childNodes[0] ;
     var dataTable = TableID.childNodes[1].childNodes[0].childNodes[0]
      .childNodes[0].childNodes[1].childNodes[1].childNodes[1]
      .childNodes[0].childNodes[0].childNodes[1].childNodes[0];
       if (dataTable)
       {
         var str = dataTable.outerHTML
           if (str)
           {
         SiteMeterSummary = str;
       }
       }
    }
    }
    catch
    (
    document.write('Error occured in parseHTML!');
    }
}
```

There are a number of methods to traverse the DOM nodes of an HTML page. This is one of the simplest methods, but any change in the web page HTML can break this code. This method uses childNodes hierarchy, which is a W3C standard (DOM Level 1), to retrieve a collection of HTML elements. The HTML data retrieved is stored in the variable str, which is then stored in the global variable SiteMeterSummary.

More information on childNodes can be found at http://msdn2.microsoft.com/en-us/library/ms537445.aspx, and the W3C DOM Level 1 specification at http://www.w3.org/TR/2000/WD-DOM-Level-1-20000929/.

This method, parseHTML, is implementation specific and the hierarchy is applied based on the table structure of this particular page. For example, a particular web page might have table ID myuniquetable1 specified, which you want to extract. In that case you can use the getElementById function directly rather than the childNodes hierarchy.

```
function parseHTML()
{
    tcMain = document.getElementById("myuniquetable1");
    if (tcMain)
    {
        var str = tcMain.outerHTML
          if (str)
          {
        SiteMeterSummary = str;
        }
    }
}
```

Design Considerations

The Site Statistics Gadget is an information gadget, so the design needs to be simple and functional. With this goal in mind, design considerations should focus on

- Theme and images used in the gadget
- Layout of the gadget
- Usability of the gadget

The following sections take a look at these design considerations from the perspective of building the SiteMeter gadget.

Theme and Images of the Gadget

For the Site Statistics Gadget, the design starts with the theme, which is the website's logo and color scheme. Figure 9.8 shows the logo.

> **NOTE**
>
> It's important to note that the Site Statistics Gadget and the icons and logos used in the gadget are included with the permission of the website www.sitemeter.com. If you want to create a gadget for a third-party website and/or use its logos, icons, and so on, make sure that you have permission to do so.

FIGURE 9.8   The Site Statistics Gadget icon with the SiteMeter logo gives the gadget an identity.

The gadget's icon was created to match the theme. Notice how the graph in the logo is symbolic of the gadget's core functionality. Next is the gadget window (see Figure 9.9). The information gadget needs to be simple and feature rich, so a green color scheme matching the website and a simple layout is best.

FIGURE 9.9   The Site Statistics Gadget in the Sidebar mimics the www.sitemeter.com theme.

The website's logo, www.sitemeter.com, gives the gadget a sense of identity. Figure 9.10 shows some of the images used in the gadget to simulate the theme.

FIGURE 9.10   All the images used in the Site Statistics Gadget use the same color scheme.

Layout of the Gadget

The layout of the gadget is similar to the sample framework in that it utilizes the same file structure (see Figure 9.11). It needs a code file for each of the three pages—the gadget window, the flyout window, and the Settings page. The gadget framework created in Part II can be reused.

The gadget manifest is changed to accommodate information specific to the Site Statistics Gadget:

```
<?xml version="1.0" encoding="utf-8" ?>
<gadget>
<name>- Site Statistics -</name>
<namespace>Innovate.Gadgets</namespace>
```

```
<version>1.0</version>
<author name="Rajesh Lal">
<logo src="images/logo.png" />
<info url="www.innovatewithgadgets.com" />
</author>
<copyright>Copyright&#169; 2008</copyright>
<description>Counter 'n' Statistics provided by Sitemeter.com</description>
  <icons>
    <icon width="70" height="80" src="images/icon.png" />
  </icons>
  <hosts>
    <host name="sidebar">
      <base type="HTML" apiVersion="1.0.0" src="gadget.html" />
      <permissions>Full</permissions>
      <platform minPlatformVersion="1.0" />
      <defaultImage src="images/drag.png"/>
    </host>
  </hosts>
</gadget>
```

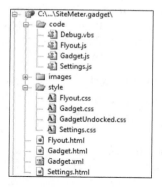

FIGURE 9.11   The file structure and layout of the Site Statistics Gadget is built upon the MyBlog Gadget framework.

As you can see in the gadget manifest, the title and description have changed but all other details are almost the same, apart from the fact that images now refer to the images specifically created for the Site Statistics Gadget.

Usability of the Gadget

The gadget's usability involves the way the gadget interacts with the user. In other words, what options does the gadget provide to the user to make it easy to traverse through different websites? In this case, the options that the gadget provides include enabling the user to specify more than one website and to easily navigate the site statistics for each website.

The standard mouseover effects display arrows in the title to traverse the different websites being monitored by the SiteMeter service. This keeps the gadget clutter free.

Figure 9.12 illustrates two instances of the Site Statistics Gadget for the sites www.innovatewithgadgets.com and www.widgets-gadgets.com.

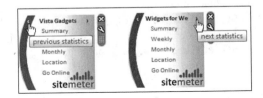

FIGURE 9.12   Unobtrusive traversing through multiple website statistics keeps the gadget interface clutter free.

Notice in Figure 9.12 how the proper use of tooltip information enhances the usability. Double-clicking on the title refreshes the site summary data.

Developing the Gadget

Using an existing framework makes creating a gadget much easier. The first part is integration, followed by refining the framework further to meet your needs. Here, we start with the gadget framework created in Chapter 7, "The MyBlog Gadget Revisited," and customize it according to our requirements.

To start, make a copy of the MyBlog Gadget project and open the folder as a website from within Visual Studio and then make changes to it. To test the gadget side by side while developing it, just copy the project source in the Users gadget folder (%UserProfile%\AppData\Local\Microsoft\Windows Sidebar\Gadgets).

In Visual Studio, go to the File menu, click Open and then the name of the submenu website, and give the location to the path of the folder. Make sure you have selected File System first. The source of the Site Statistics project and the gadget are included with this book's online supplemental materials. You can open the folder directly in Visual Studio to go through them. After you open the website you will see a file structure similar to Figure 9.11 in the Solutions Explorer.

The development of the gadget can be divided into three parts:

- Integrating the existing framework
- Retrieving data for the site summary using the API and the online web page
- Displaying graphs and pie charts based on the API and SiteMeter code

Each of these parts is detailed in the following sections.

Integrating the Existing Framework

Because the existing framework for the MyBlog Gadget is also an information gadget, you need most of the common functionality in this gadget.

The place to start is with changes in the manifest file gadget.xml and then the images for the logo, background, and so on. We then need to customize the Settings page for adding and removing items and to accommodate the title and SiteMeter code string.

A Mini Me version of the gadget option will be kept to display the gadget in a smaller window. This helps to conserve gadget real estate and provides an extra check box for added features. See Figure 9.13 for the Settings page customization. Most of these changes are done in the Settings.html and theSettings.js files.

The Added Features check box extends the basic gadget to display other statistical data related to the web browsers, operating systems, and regional information that does not show in the gadget's default simple view.

FIGURE 9.13   The Settings page for the Site Statistics gadget with added features and SiteMeter code.

By default the gadget window has the following options:

- Site summary
- Weekly statistical view
- Monthly statistical view
- Location summary
- Shortcut link to go to the website

When the Added Features option is selected, yearly summary, country view, operating system, and browser are also available (see Figure 9.14).

Added features provide the following in addition to the basic features:

- Yearly statistics

- Statistics by region

- Data on operating systems

- Types of web browsers used

FIGURE 9.14   The Site Statistics Gadget with Added Features checked shows more options.

Retrieving Data for Site Summary Using API and Online Web Page

Retrieving the data is done using functions related to two categories: the HTML data and the text data. The getHTMLAjax function parses the online web page and extracts the site summary. This HTML data is then further parsed using the parseHTML function. The getTextAjax function calls the online API and fetches the data in plain text. The parseData function then processes this information. These two function calls are wrapped inside the getData function, which is called during the first-time setup of the gadget.

Here is the code for the getData function, called inside the setup function that loads when the gadget loads the first time:

```
function setup()
{
    SystemSetup();
        Resize();
        getData();
}
function getData()
{
 getHTMLAjax("http://www.sitemeter.com/?a=stats&s=" +
 System.Gadget.Settings.read("sitemeterCode") + "&gadget=true");
 getTextAjax();
}
```

The following sections go through the HTML- and text-related functions in more detail.

The getHTMLAjax Function

The getHTMLAjax function loads the web page from which you need to fetch information—in this case, the statistics page where the summary is displayed. You need to get the summary portion of the HTML from that page and display it in the flyout window. This process is done in two parts: loading the HTML page and then extracting the HTML portion of the data.

```
function getHTMLAjax(pageURL)
{
    htmlObj = new ActiveXObject("Microsoft.XMLHTTP");
    htmlObj.open("GET", pageURL, true);
    htmlObj.onreadystatechange = function()
    {
 if (htmlObj.readyState === 4)
 {
    if (htmlObj.status === 200)
    {
    document.getElementById('sitesummary').innerHTML =
    htmlObj.responseText;
    parseHTML()
    }
    else {
    chkConn = setInterval(getHTMLAjax, 30 * 60000);
        }
 }
    }
    htmlObj.send(null);
}
```

As you can see in the function, `pageURL` is a variable that contains the SiteMeter page that has the detailed summary. The `XMLHTTP` object is used to load the page, and the HTML of the page is stored in the `sitesummary` element of the gadget window.

The `parseHTMLAjax` Function

After storing the HTML of the page in the `sitesummary` DIV element, the next step is to filter the required data; that is, the HTML table containing the Summary, Visits, and Page View portions. For this, first you need to figure out the closest table that has a unique ID in the HTML page. This is done with the IE Developer Toolbar as shown previously in Figure 9.7. In this case the ID of the table is `Table_01`, and the table that has the required HTML portion is inside the `Table_01` in the following hierarchy, as shown in the code:

```
function parseAjax()
{
    tcMain = document.getElementById("Table_01");
    if (tcMain)
    {
      var TableID = tcMain.childNodes[0] ;
      var dataTable = TableID.childNodes[1].childNodes[0].childNodes[0]
        .childNodes[0].childNodes[1].childNodes[1].childNodes[1].
        childNodes[0].childNodes[0].childNodes[1].childNodes[0];
```

```
        if (dataTable)
        {
        var str = dataTable.outerHTML
        SiteMeterSummary = str;
        }
    }
}
```

dataTable stores the HTML data of the required portion that needs to be displayed in the gadget. The outerHTML of the data table is stored in the variable SiteMeterSummary, to be displayed in the flyout window.

The getTextAjax Function

The getTextAjax function calls the online API to retrieve information from the server. This sends the SiteMeter code string as one of the parameters in the URL and retrieves the text data, which then has to be parsed.

```
function getTextAjax() {
    error.style.visibility = "hidden";
    loading.style.visibility = "visible";
    content.style.visibility = "hidden";
    loading.style.visibility = "visible";
    loading.title  = "Connecting...";

blogtitle.innerText = Mid(System.Gadget.Settings.read("sitemeterTitle"),0,14);
blogtitle.title = System.Gadget.Settings.read("sitemeterTitle");

var SMC = System.Gadget.Settings.read("sitemeterCode");
var firstthree =  Mid(SMC,0,3);

ajaxObj = new ActiveXObject("Microsoft.XMLHTTP");

myURL = "http://" + firstthree + ".sitemeter.com/rpc/v6/server.asp?a=
GetChartData&n=9&p1=" + SMC + "&p2=&p3=6&p4=0&p5=208%2E70%2E116%2E25
&p6=HTML&p7=1&p8=%2E%3Fa%3Dstatistics&p9=&rnd=47190";

ajaxObj.open("GET", myURL, true);
ajaxObj.onreadystatechange = function() {
    if (ajaxObj.readyState === 4) {
        if (ajaxObj.status === 200) {
            loading.innerText = "";
            page = 0;
            parseData(ajaxObj.responseText);
            content.style.visibility = "visible";
            loading.style.visibility = "hidden";
            } else {
```

```
              var chkConn;
              loading.innerText = "Unable to connect...";
              chkConn = setInterval(getTextAjax, 30 * 60000);
         }
      } else {
         loading.innerText = "...";
      }
   }
   ajaxObj.send(null);
}
```

In this code, myURL contains the API URL that needs to be called to get the data for the week this web address is opened, using the XMLHTTP object. The parseData function is used to parse the returned data, which takes the parameter ajaxObj.responseText.

The parseData Function

This function parses the data retrieved from the server and displays the elements in the gadget main window. This function also takes care of the Added Features option.

```
function parseData(Data)
{

    SiteMeterDataValues = Data.split("|");
    for (i=0; i<SiteMeterDataValues.length-1; i=i+2)
     {
        PageViews[i] = SiteMeterDataValues[i];
        Visits[i] = SiteMeterDataValues[i+1];
     }

  if (System.Gadget.Settings.read("completeView") ==true)
    {
    cell0.innerHTML = '<div align="left"
        onclick="showFlyout(\'0\');">Summary</div>';
    cell1.innerHTML = '<div align="left"><a
        onclick="showFlyout(\'1\');">Week</a> /<a
        onclick="showFlyout(\'2\');">Mon</a> /<a
        onclick="showFlyout(\'3\');">Year</a></div>';
    cell2.innerHTML = '<div align="left"><a
        onclick="showFlyout(\'4\');">Region</a> /<a
        onclick="showFlyout(\'5\');">Location</a></div>';
    cell3.innerHTML = '<div align="left"><a
        onclick="showFlyout(\'6\');">OS</a> /<a
        onclick="showFlyout(\'7\');">Browser</a></div>';
    cell4.innerHTML = '<div align="left" onclick="showFlyout(\'8\');">Go
        Online</div>';
    }
```

```
      else
      {
      cell0.innerHTML = '<div align="left"
          onclick="showFlyout(\'0\');">Summary</div>';
      cell1.innerHTML = '<div align="left"
          onclick="showFlyout(\'1\');">Weekly</div>';
      cell2.innerHTML = '<div align="left"
          onclick="showFlyout(\'2\');">Monthly</div>';
      cell3.innerHTML = '<div align="left"
          onclick="showFlyout(\'4\');">Location</div>';
      cell4.innerHTML = '<div align="left" onclick="showFlyout(\'8\');">Go
          Online</div>';
      }
}
```

In this code, the data is split and saved into two arrays for future use: page views and visits. The function parseData also generates the HTML for the gadget window. The variable completeView is based on the Added Features check box in the Settings page. As you can see, for each of the cells a unique number is passed in the showFlyout function. This number can vary from one to eight. The showFlyout function is discussed in more detail in the next section.

Graphs and Pie Charts Based on the API

The graphs and pie charts that make the gadget so rich and user friendly come directly from the SiteMeter website. Although these could theoretically be created from the data returned from the service, it's much easier to use the same API to display the charts that are used on the website.

It is necessary to provide different parameters to the web API when talking to the service. And, based on the parameters, different graphs are generated and displayed on the web page. This feature is implemented in the flyout window when the content is generated for display.

The showFlyout Function

The showFlyout function is called when the user clicks on the cell. The number passed to this function is used to distinguish between the cells the user has clicked. For example, if the user clicks on the last cell with the text Go Online, the parameter 8 is passed to the showFlyout function. This action triggers a new web browser with the URL as the statistics page on the SiteMeter.

In the gadget window, the showFlyout function uses the following function call for opening a browser with the SiteMeter page for that particular code:

```
System.Shell.execute(statsURL);
```

The statsURL is built based on the SiteMeter code and then passed to the shell execute function to open the web browser.

```
function showFlyout(i)
{

    if (i==System.Gadget.Settings.read("currentClickedCell"))
    {
            System.Gadget.Flyout.show = false;
            System.Gadget.Settings.write("currentClickedCell", -1);
    }
    else
    {
       flyoutType = i;
       if (i==8)
       {
     var firstthree = Mid(System.Gadget.Settings.
                read("sitemeterCode"),0,3);
     var statsURL =    "http://www.sitemeter.com/?a=stats&s=" +
                System.Gadget.Settings.read("sitemeterCode") +
                "&gadget=true"
     System.Shell.execute(statsURL);
       }
       else
       {
            System.Gadget.Settings.write("currentClickedCell", i);
          System.Gadget.Flyout.show = true;
       }
    }
}
```

The showFlyout function also stores the clicked cell index if it is other than 8 in the variable currentClickedCell, which is used when the flyout window is loaded. Table 9.3 shows the different values of the currentclicked cell passed to the showFlyout function and further stored in the flyoutType variable used in the buildMyContent function.

TABLE 9.3   Different Values of the Flyout Type Stored When the User Clicks on the Corresponding Cell

Title	CurrentClicked	Displays
Site Summary	ftype==0	Displays site summary in the flyout
Weekly - Visits	ftype==1	Displays graph of weekly visits and page view in the flyout
Monthly - Visits	ftype==2	Displays graph of monthly visits and page views in flyout
Yearly - Visits	ftype==3	Displays yearly visits and page views in flyout
Region - Continents	ftype==4	Displays region and continents in pie chart
Location - Country	ftype==5	Displays pie chart for location, countrywise
Operating System	ftype==6	Displays share of operating system in pie chart
Web Browser	ftype==7	Displays share of web browser used for accessing the website
Go Online	ftype==8	Opens the web browser with the Statistics page

The buildMyContent Function

The following shows the function buildMyContent, which is called on the page load of the flyout window.

```
function buildMyContent()
{
 var ftype = System.Gadget.document.parentWindow.flyoutType
 var flyoutSiteSummary  =
 System.Gadget.document.parentWindow.SiteMeterSummary;
 var SMC = System.Gadget.Settings.read("sitemeterCode");
 firstthree =  Mid(SMC,0,3);

     try
     {
     if ( ftype==0)
       {
         flyoutTitle ="Site Summary ";
         dataFlyout = "<center>" + flyoutSiteSummary + "</center>";
       }
     if ( ftype==1)
       {
         flyoutTitle ="Weekly - Visits and Page Views";
         ImagePath= "http://" + firstthree + ".sitemeter.com
/rpc/v6/server.php?a=GetChart&n=9&p1=" + SMC + "&p2=&p3=6&p4=0&p5=
71%2E159%2E229%2E88&p6=HTML&p7=1&p8=%2E%3Fa%3Dstatistics&p9=&rnd=59693" ;
         dataFlyout = '<br><h3><font face ="Calibiri" color="#006699">' +
 flyoutTitle + '</font>  <a title ="More details at sitemeter
statistics page" href="http://www.sitemeter.com/?a=stats&s=' + SMC + '&r=6&
gadget=true" ><img src="images/up.gif" border=0/></a></h3><hr noshade="true"
 size="1"><img src=' + ImagePath + ' border=0></font>'
       }
     if ( ftype==2)
       {
         flyoutTitle ="Monthly - Visits and Page Views";
         ImagePath= "http://" + firstthree +".sitemeter.com/rpc/v6/server.
php?a=GetChart&n=9&p1=" + SMC + "&p2=&p3=12&p4=0&p5=71%2E159%2E229%2E88&p6=
HTML&p7=1&p8=%2E%3Fa%3Dstatistics&p9=&rnd=32494" ;

         dataFlyout = '<br><h3><font face ="Calibiri" color="#006699">' +
 flyoutTitle + '</font>  <a title ="More details at sitemeter
 statistics page" href="http://www.sitemeter.com/?a=stats&s=' + SMC + '&r=
12&gadget=true" ><img src="images/up.gif" border=0/></a></h3><hr noshade=
"true" size="1"><img src=' + ImagePath + ' border=0></font>'
       }
```

```
        if ( ftype==3)
          {
            flyoutTitle ="Yearly - Visits and Page Views";
            ImagePath= "http://" + firstthree + ".sitemeter.com/rpc/v6/server
➥.php?a=GetChart&n=9&p1=" + SMC + "&p2=&p3=33&p4=0&p5=71%2E159%2E229%2E88&p6=
➥HTML&p7=1&p8=%2E%3Fa%3Dstatistics&p9=&rnd=40437" ;

            dataFlyout = '<br><h3><font face ="Calibiri" color="#006699">' +
➥ flyoutTitle + '</font>  <a title ="More details at sitemeter
➥ statistics page" href="http://www.sitemeter.com/?a=stats&s=' + SMC + '&r=
➥33&gadget=true" ><img src="images/up.gif" border=0/></a></h3><hr noshade=
➥"true" size="1"><img src=' + ImagePath + ' border=0></font>'
          }
        if (ftype==4)
          {
            flyoutTitle ="Region - Continents";
            ImagePath= "http://" + firstthree + ".sitemeter.com/rpc/v6/server.
➥php?a=GetChart&n=9&p1=" + SMC + "&p2=&p3=81&p4=0&p5=71%2E159%2E229%2E88&p6=
➥HTML&p7=1&p8=%2E%3Fa%3Dstatistics&p9=&rnd=33756" ;

            dataFlyout = '<br><h3><font face ="Calibiri" color="#006699">' +
➥ flyoutTitle + '</font>  <a title ="More details at sitemeter
➥ statistics page" href="http://www.sitemeter.com/?a=stats&s=' + SMC + '&r=
➥81&gadget=true" ><img src="images/up.gif" border=0/></a></h3><hr noshade=
➥"true" size="1"><img src=' + ImagePath + ' border=0></font>'
          }
        if (ftype==5)
          {
            flyoutTitle ="Location - Countries";
            ImagePath= "http://" + firstthree + ".sitemeter.com/rpc/v6/server.
➥php?a=GetChart&n=9&p1=" + SMC + "&p2=&p3=83&p4=0&p5=75%2E15%2E87%2E230&p6=
➥HTML&p7=1
          &p8=%2E%3Fa%3Dstatistics&p9=&rnd=74995" ;

            dataFlyout = '<br><h3><font face ="Calibiri" color="#006699">' +
➥ flyoutTitle + '</font>  <a title ="More details at sitemeter
➥statistics page" href="http://www.sitemeter.com/?a=stats&s=' + SMC + '&r=83&
➥gadget=true" ><img src="images/up.gif" border=0/></a></h3><hr noshade="true"
➥size="1"><img src=' + ImagePath + ' border=0></font>'
          }
        if (ftype==6)
          {
            flyoutTitle ="Operating System";
```

```
            ImagePath= "http://" + firstthree + ".sitemeter.com/rpc/v6/server.php
➦?a=GetChart&n=9&p1=" + SMC + "&p2=&p3=19&p4=0&p5=75%2E15%2E87%2E230&p6=HTML&p7=
➦1&p8=%2E%3Fa%3Dstatistics&p9=&rnd=48531" ;

            dataFlyout = '<br><h3><font face ="Calibiri" color="#006699">' +
➦ flyoutTitle + '</font>  <a title ="More details at sitemeter
➦ statistics page" href="http://www.sitemeter.com/?a=stats&s=' + SMC + '&r=
➦19&gadget=true" ><img src="images/up.gif" border=0/></a></h3><hr noshade=
➦"true" size="1"><img src=' + ImagePath + ' border=0></font>'
            }
            if (ftype==7)
            {
                flyoutTitle ="Web browser used";
            ImagePath= "http://" + firstthree + ".sitemeter.com/rpc/v6/server.php
➦?a=GetChart&n=9&p1=" + SMC + "&p2=&p3=13&p4=0&p5=75%2E15%2E87%2E230&p6=
➦HTML&p7=1&p8=%2E%3Fa%3Dstatistics&p9=&rnd=97912" ;

            dataFlyout = '<br><h3><font face ="Calibiri" color="#006699">' +
➦ flyoutTitle + '</font>  <a title ="More details at sitemeter
➦ statistics page" href="http://www.sitemeter.com/?a=stats&s=' + SMC + '&r=
➦13&gadget=true" ><img src="images/up.gif" border=0/></a></h3><hr noshade=
➦"true" size="1"><img src=' + ImagePath + ' border=0></font>'
            }
            document.write(dataFlyout);
        }
    catch(e)
        {
        document.write('Error occured in buildMyContent function');
        }
}
```

This function needs two values: the SiteMeter code and the variable SMC. The first three characters of the SiteMeter code distinguish the server as described earlier in this chapter, in the "Application Programming Interface" section. This is stored in the variable with the name firstthree.

As per Table 9.3, the buildMyContent function creates the HTML to be displayed in the flyout window. This function calls the online URL with different parameters to generate the image of the server statistics. The HTML is created based on the web API that generates the image to be displayed. The contents of the data flyout are finally rendered in the window using the function document.write. Figure 9.15 shows the graph view for the Monthly Visits selection by the user.

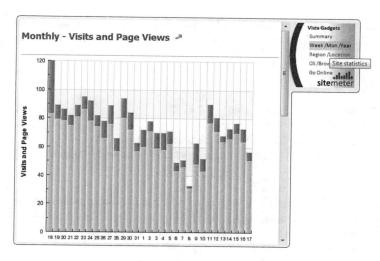

FIGURE 9.15   The flyout window generates and displays HTML based on which cell the user clicked in the gadget main window.

Let's go through an example where the flyout window type variable `ftype` value is 2. The value of 2 means that the user clicked on the monthly summary link in the gadget main window and the corresponding graph needs to be displayed in the flyout. This calls the following portion of the code:

```
if ( ftype==2)
    {
        flyoutTitle ="Monthly - Visits and Page Views";
      ImagePath= "http://" + firstthree +".sitemeter.com
➥/rpc/v6/server.php?a=GetChart&n=9&p1=" + SMC + "&p2=&p3=12&p4=0&p5=71%2E159%
➥2E229%2E88&p6=HTML&p7=1&p8=%2E%3Fa%3Dstatistics&p9=&rnd=32494" ;

    dataFlyout = '<br><h3><font face ="Calibiri" color="#006699">'
➥ + flyoutTitle + '</font>  <a title ="More details at sitemeter
➥ statistics page" href="http://www.sitemeter.com/?a=stats&s=' + SMC + '&r=
➥12&gadget=true" ><img src="images/up.gif" border=0/></a></h3><hr noshade=
➥"true" size="1"><img src=' + ImagePath + ' border=0></font>'
}
```

The code can be thought as assigning values to three variables: First is the `flyoutTitle` variable, which stores the heading of the flyout window. Next is the `imagepath` variable, which displays the actual graph or pie chart (in this case graph), based on the web API provided by www.sitemeter.com. The last variable is the `dataFlyout`, which basically encapsulates the first two variables, only in an HTML format that is written back to the flyout's HTML page.

Similarly, a value of 7 for `ftype` displays the statistics on browser usage for the website as shown in the following code (see Figure 9.16). Notice the difference in the `imagepath` variable.

```
if (ftype==7)
{
        flyoutTitle ="Web browser used";
        ImagePath= "http://" + firstthree +
".sitemeter.com/rpc/v6/server.php?a=GetChart&n=9&p1=" + SMC + "
➥&p2=&p3=13&p4=0&p5=75%2E15%2E87%2E230&p6=HTML&p7=1&p8=%2E%3Fa%3Dstatistics&
➥p9=&rnd=97912" ;

            dataFlyout = '<br><h3><font face ="Calibiri" color="#006699">' +
➥ flyoutTitle + '</font>  <a title ="More details at sitemeter
➥statistics page" href="http://www.sitemeter.com/?a=stats&s=' + SMC + '&r=
➥13&gadget=true" ><img src="images/up.gif" border=0/></a></h3><hr noshade="true"
➥ size="1"><img src=' + ImagePath + ' border=0></font>'
}
```

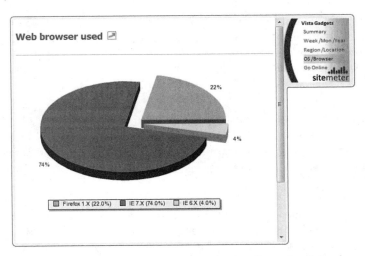

FIGURE 9.16   A flyout window showing the pie chart for the share of web browsers.

Most Recent Used .NET Projects—An Application Gadget

"Make everything as simple as possible, but not simpler."

—Albert Einstein

Recent .NET Project Gadget

A .NET Most Recently Used (MRU) .NET Projects Gadget is meant to be a quick access tool to recently used projects in Visual Studio. It displays the most recently used projects in the gadget window and when the user clicks on the link, the corresponding project is opened (see Figure 10.1). It supports three versions of Visual Studio .NET: 2003, 2005, and 2008.

Target of the Gadget

The target of the gadget is to make use of the Windows Registry and the gadget platform to give a quick and easy way to access a list of most recently used projects in the gadget. It is developed with the following goals:

- The gadget should list titles of most recently used .NET projects.

- The title should also act as a shortcut to open .NET with those projects.

- The gadget should be able to manage multiple pages of most recently used items.

Figure 10.1 shows how the gadget looks in the Sidebar.

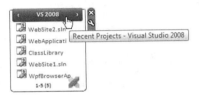

FIGURE 10.1   The gadget showing the most recently used projects in Visual Studio 2008.

> **NOTE**
>
> The chapter does not require knowledge of Visual Studio .NET. A programmer who has worked with Visual Studio will find it quite familiar, but even if you are not a .NET programmer, you can use the advanced features of the gadget, including Registry reading, Windows Management Instrumentation, and an ActiveX control in your gadget.

Background

The Recent Projects list is displayed in the Visual Studio Integrated Development Environment (IDE), as shown in Figure 10.2. The first limitation is that you have to open the IDE first and then open the desired project from the list presented by the IDE. The second limitation is the small size of the Recent Projects box, which displays only a limited number of projects/solutions information. In Figure 10.2, it shows the last five projects only.

The Most Recently Used .NET Projects gadget saves you the step of opening the Visual Studio IDE. You can click on the project you want and the IDE will open up with that project. Also, in the gadget, you have complete control of the list and count of items you want to display. With advanced management of multiple pages, you can have shortcuts to upward of 50 projects in each version of Visual Studio, all at your fingertips.

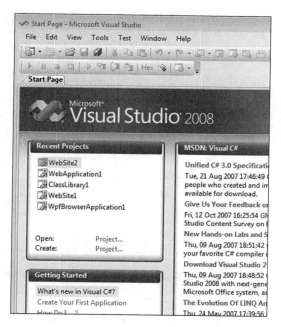

FIGURE 10.2   The Visual Studio IDE displays a limited number of most recently used items.

Features and Technology

Although the gadget looks very simple, it needs advanced features to access certain Windows features, which normally are not available from JavaScript in an HTML page.

First, the most recently used items of Visual Studio are saved in the Windows Registry as a list of records. If you open the Registry editor (click Start, Run, and type **regedit.exe**) and go to the following key node, you will see the MRU list related to Visual Studio:

```
HKEY_CURRENT_USER\Software\Microsoft\VisualStudio\8.0\ProjectMRUList
```

Figure 10.3 shows a list of projects inside `ProjectMRUList` 7. The Registry path `8.0` determines the version of Visual Studio.

If you don't have Visual Studio installed, try searching for "MRUList" in the Registry. You might find some interesting most recent used items for applications such as Windows Media Player, MSN Messenger, Microsoft Office, and so on. Most of the Microsoft applications save these settings in the Registry under `MRUList`.

The Most Recently Used .NET Projects Gadget can easily be modified to create a Microsoft Office MRU Gadget or a Media Player MRU Gadget. Even if you don't want to create an MRU Gadget, you might need to access and enumerate the Registry for other advanced functions such as retrieving the path of an application, saving and restoring the settings for a particular gadget, and so on.

10

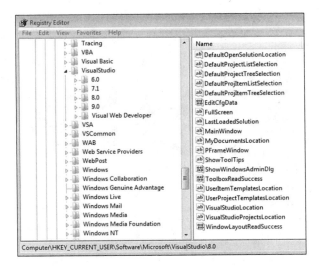

FIGURE 10.3   The most recently used items of a Visual Studio application are stored in the Windows Registry.

The first challenge is to access the Windows Registry from the Sidebar gadget. You can accomplish this by using one of the following methods:

- Using ActiveX COM technology in a gadget
- Using Windows Power Shell with Windows Management Instrumentation (WMI)

ActiveX COM Technology

ActiveX (COM) technology is the architecture that enables developers to create reusable components in the Windows environment. You can write these ActiveX components in any programming language, such as Visual C++, Visual Basic, Visual C#, .NET, and so on. They expose a set of public methods that can be called from other applications.

As illustrated in Figure 10.4, the ActiveX COM technology can be used to access all Windows APIs and advanced features, such as drivers, hardware, I/Os, and so on.

FIGURE 10.4   The ActiveX COM acts as the middle layer and gives access to advanced features and functionality not directly available to a gadget.

In this chapter we create an MRU ActiveX DLL in Microsoft Visual Basic 6.0, which is the easiest way of creating an ActiveX component and which works with the gadget.

Using an ActiveX Component

The catch with using an ActiveX component is that it needs to be registered in the user's machine. This adds an extra step in the deployment process. You cannot just zip the gadget and distribute it; you need to create a setup package that, during installation, also registers the gadget in the computer. The gadget package includes the VisualStudioMRU.dll file along with the other gadget files.

ActiveX COM Inside a Gadget

You can initialize an ActiveX COM object inside gadget code by using JavaScript, and the exposed methods of the ActiveX control can be called. Here is the sample JavaScript code that iterates through the items of the MRU list:

```
function listMRURegistry()
{
    objMRU = new ActiveXObject("VisualStudioMRU.clsMRU");
    objMRU.VisualStudioMRU_Get (8);
    for (i=1; i<objMRU.CollectionCount; i++)
    {
    document.write(objMRU.colMRUFiles.Item(i));
    }
}
```

In the development section, later in this chapter, you will see the details of the ActiveX object.

Here are the details of the code:

- In the first line you can see the creation of an object of the ActiveX component. The name of the dynamic link library is VisualStudioMRU.dll and the class file in the ActiveX object is named clsMRU.

- The second line calls the public method VisualStudioMRU_Get with the parameter 8, which represents the version of Visual Studio 2005. The parameter 7 is used to get the list for visual Studio 2003 and 9 for Visual Studio 2008. The VisualStudioMRU_Get function creates a collection of MRU items and stores it in the collection colMRUFiles.

- The third and fourth lines traverse through the collection and print all the items.

To read information from the Windows Registry, another method utilizes Windows Shell and WMI. It does not require registration of an ActiveX control and can be embedded in the JavaScript code along with the gadget code. This method is examined in the next section.

10

Windows Power Shell and Windows Management Instrumentation

To achieve Registry access and other advanced Windows features, use the Windows Power Shell and Windows Management Instrumentation. Before we go further in how to use these in the gadget, let's go through these technologies in brief.

Windows Power Shell

Windows Power Shell is an extensible command-line shell and scripting language utility that can be called directly from a gadget. It is the foundation of most of the administrative tools in the operating system and is based on .NET Framework 2.0, so it exposes a lot of features for accessing operating system functionality.

Windows Power Shell comes with Microsoft Windows Vista and can be called through the scripting language exposed by the Power Shell.

Important features of a Windows Power Shell include

- Advanced scripting language support
- Access to the file system
- Extensive set of Registry functions
- Help in system administration and accelerating automation
- Support for digital signature for scripts

Windows Management Instrumentation

Windows Management Instrumentation is an extension to the Windows driver model, and is used for managing the computer's desktop locally as well as remotely. It exposes its features through a Windows scripting language such as Visual Basic Script and Power Shell.

Features of Windows Management Instrumentation can be accessed through `WinMgmt.exe`, the executable that implements the WMI core service. WMI runs as a service in Microsoft Windows Vista.

Some of the advanced features of WMI include

- Support for C/C++ COM programming interface
- .NET management interfaces
- Remoting capabilities
- Registry access and manipulation
- The following features can be accessed through WMI with the help of `WinMgmt.exe` in a script:
  - Accounts and domains
  - Computer hardware

- Computer software

- Connecting to WMIU service

- Dates and times

- Desktop management

- Disks and file system

- Event logs

- Files and folders

- Networking

- Operating systems

- Performance monitoring

- Processes

- Printing

- Registry

- Scheduling tasks

- Services

Look for "WMI Tasks for Scripts and Applications" at msdn.microsoft.com to get complete examples of each of them. You can find details on each of the items listed here at http://msdn2.microsoft.com/en-us/library/aa394585.aspx.

With all these WMI features available through VBScript, a utility Sidebar gadget can do almost everything an operating system does, from managing the Windows desktop to providing advanced features of networking, printing, services, and so on.

> **NOTE**
>
> To use WMI script in a gadget, you need to add a VBScript file and then include it in the `gadget.html` page, using the following snippet:
>
> ```
> <script src="code/EnumMRU.vbs" type="text/vbscript"></script>
> ```
>
> Then only the function defined in the `EnumMRU` file can be called from the gadget code `Gadget.js`.

The next time you have an innovative idea for a utility Sidebar gadget, make sure to check what WMI has to offer. There is a bit of a learning curve here, but it is well worth it because WMI will save you considerable development time.

Windows Management Instrumentation for Registry Access

As you saw, WMI can be used for a variety of functionalities. Let's see how it can help you read a Registry value. Here is some sample VBScript code to access the Registry, using scripting language with WMI:

```
const HKEY_LOCAL_MACHINE = &H80000002
strComputer = "."
Set oReg=GetObject("winmgmts:{impersonationLevel=impersonate}
        !\\" & strComputer & "\root\default:StdRegProv")
strKeyPath =  "HKEY_CURRENT_USER\Software\Microsoft\VisualStudio\
        8.0\ProjectMRUList"
oReg.EnumKey HKEY_LOCAL_MACHINE, strKeyPath, arrSubKeys
```

The preceding code is used to enumerate all the values in the Registry key:

```
HKEY_CURRENT_USER\Software\Microsoft\VisualStudio\8.0\ProjectMRUList
```

Now you can look at the code line by line:

- The first line initializes the `HKEY_LOCAL_MACHINE` variable to machine-recognizable standard hexadecimal values.

- `strComputer` (line 2) represents the local host or the local computer in use and is normally referred to by a single dot; the name of the computer can also be used here.

- Line 3 assigns `oReg` to an object provided by `WinMgmt.exe` for accessing the Registry (`StdRegProv`).

- Line 4 assigns the key to the Registry path, which needs to be enumerated; in this case it is `strKeyPath`.

- Line 5 calls the `EnumKeys` method to traverse through all the items inside the key and store them in the array `arrSubKeys`.

If you find this code confusing, the good news is you don't have to worry about remembering all these details; Microsoft provides a utility for WMI that automatically generates code in VBScript for the selected functionality. The right side of Figure 10.5 shows an example of this generated code, which appears when the user selects a Registry class and property.

> **NOTE**
>
> Microsoft provides a utility for WMI for generating code in VBScript. Look for "WMI Code Creator" in msdn.microsoft.com or go to http://www.microsoft.com/downloads/details.aspx?FamilyID=2cc30a64-ea15-4661-8da4-55bbc145c30e&displaylang=en.

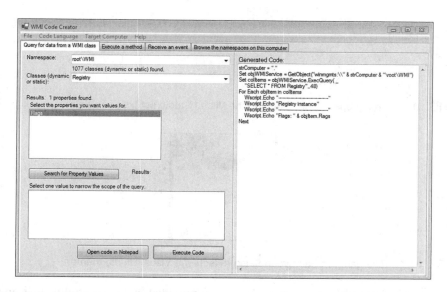

FIGURE 10.5   The WMI code generator can create chunks of code in VBScript that can be used inside a gadget.

The WMI code generator can create WMI code in C#, Visual Basic.NET, and VBScript, all of which can be used directly in the gadget.

Design Considerations

As discussed in earlier chapters, a gadget's design is a very important aspect of its creation, especially with regard to its usability. Design considerations for the sample gadget involve the following:

- The theme and images used in the gadget
- The layout of the gadget
- The usability of the gadget

Each of these considerations is detailed in the following sections as it pertains to the Visual Studio gadget.

Theme of the Gadget

For a Visual Studio MRU gadget, the design starts with a theme that is similar to that of Visual Studio itself (see Figure 10.6).

The gadget's icon has been created to match the theme of the product with which it assists the user. This theme is continued in the gadget window itself when it lists the most recently used projects (see Figure 10.7).

10

·FIGURE 10.6　The gadget's icon relates to the Visual Studio application.

FIGURE 10.7　The gadget's background also reflects the Visual Studio theme.

The intent is to look similar to the user interface provided by Visual Studio. This gives the user a familiar experience and gives the gadget an identity.

Note that if you are creating a gadget for an application that your company has developed, you can use its icons and other images to give the gadget the look and feel of the application; otherwise you need explicit permission to use the icons in the gadget.

Figure 10.8 shows some of the images used in the gadget to simulate the Visual Studio theme.

Background　　　　icons and drag image　　About Page Image

FIGURE 10.8　Images used in the MRU gadget reflect the color scheme of Visual Studio.

The icons used reflect the corresponding types of MRU projects.

Layout of the Gadget

We are going to use both methods previously discussed for Registry access so that you have two different but similar layouts for the file structure. This gives you two working gadgets, one using the WMI technology and the other with ActiveX COM technology.

The Recent Projects Gadget has the layout shown in Figure 10.9. This layout uses WMI scripts inside EnumMRU.vbs to access the Registry.

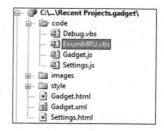

FIGURE 10.9   The VBScript file `EnumMRU` uses the WMI to enumerate and display titles from the Registry.

The Recent ProjectsX Gadget uses an ActiveX DLL developed in Visual Basic to enumerate the Registry values and has the layout shown in Figure 10.10.

FIGURE 10.10   An ActiveX component (in this case `VisualStudioMRU.dll`) can be used to enumerate the Registry values.

The Recent ProjectsX Gadget uses `VisualStudioMRU.dll` to access the Registry. Notice that there is no flyout HTML file. For this gadget, a flyout is not required; the gadget provides quick access to the most recently used projects, so in a typical scenario, the user clicks on the gadget title to open the project in Visual Studio.

Usability of the Gadget

The gadget enables the user to easily search through different versions of Visual Studio projects. The Visual Studio projects are organized with their versions under separate "pages," and the gadget enables users to easily flip through the different "version pages." This helps to keep the gadget clutter free (see Figure 10.11).

Notice how the proper use of tooltip information enhances the usability of this gadget. Also, the hand cursor on the title of the gadget and the loading image when the user double-clicks on the title both make the functionality self-explanatory. Clicking on the shortcut opens Visual Studio. Multiple pages are managed with page numbers at the bottom, which activate on mouse hover.

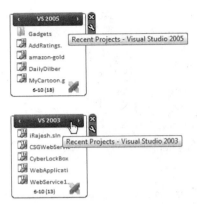

FIGURE 10.11   The gadget provides for the different versions of Visual Studio—2003, 2005, and 2008.

Developing the Gadget

After you have the plan ready and have considered all the design options, the next step is the development of the gadget. It starts with the gadget framework created earlier. This takes care of all the common options needed so that you can instead concentrate on the advanced options.

The development of the gadget can be divided into three parts:

- Integrating the existing framework
- Listing MRU items from the Registry, whether you use WMI script or Microsoft ActiveX technology
- Opening Visual Studio based on the version

Integrating the Existing Framework

From the existing framework you need to remove the files associated with the flyout and remove options from the Settings page because in this case you need a simple Settings page (see Figure 10.12).

The default height of the gadget has been set to 146 pixels to accommodate the last five most recently used projects and their respective icons. The `Gadget.html` file will hold the five DIV elements as defined in the framework. These will be used to write the titles of the MRU items. Finally, an array will be stored in the memory to manage the multiple versions of Visual Studio:

```
function defaultMRU()
{
    MRUS[0] = 7; // visual Studio 2003
```

```
    MRUS[1] = 8; // Visual Studio 2005
    MRUS[2] = 9; // Visual Studio 2008
}
```

FIGURE 10.12   The Settings page of the Recent Project Gadget displays the About screen.

The default will be Visual Studio 2005. Therefore, MRUS[1] is selected as the default. When the left- and right-arrow click events (on the title bar) fire, the changeMRU function is called. This is similar to the way the MyBlogPack Gadget works.

```
function changeMRU(val)
{
reset();
MRUCurrentID = MRUCurrentID + val;
    if (MRUCurrentID == -1)
    {      MRUCurrentID =MRUS.length -1;        }

    if (MRUCurrentID == MRUS.length)
    {      MRUCurrentID =0;        }

    System.Gadget.Settings.write("CurrentMRU",MRUS[MRUCurrentID]);
    page=0;
    ReSetup();

    if (MRUCurrentID==0)
    {document.getElementById("blogtitle").innerText ="VS 2003"      }
    if (MRUCurrentID==1)
    { document.getElementById("blogtitle").innerText ="VS 2005"       }
    if (MRUCurrentID==2)
    {   document.getElementById("blogtitle").innerText ="VS 2008"        }
}
```

10

MRUCurrentID stores the currently selected version of Visual Studio for display. The function that actually retrieves the MRU projects is the getMRU function. This function takes the page as the parameter and displays the first five MRU items for the specified page.

```
getMRU(0);
function getMRU(page)
{
reset();
var localMRU = System.Gadget.Settings.read("CurrentMRU");

   try
    {
    if (localMRU==7)
    NumberofItems = enumerateRegistry("7.1",page);
    if (localMRU==8)
    NumberofItems = enumerateRegistry("8.0",page);
    if (localMRU==9)
    NumberofItems = enumerateRegistry("9.0",page);
        if (NumberofItems>0)
         {
            loading.innerText = "";
            page = 0;
            content.style.visibility = "visible";
            loading.style.visibility = "hidden";
            error.style.visibility = "hidden";
         }
         else
         {
            var chkConn;
            content.style.visibility = "hidden";
            loading.style.visibility = "hidden";
            error.innerText = " No Settings Found!";
            error.style.visibility = "visible";
            chkConn = setInterval(getMRU(0), 5 * 60000);
         }
    }
    catch(e)
    {
            content.style.visibility = "hidden";
           loading.style.visibility = "hidden";
            error.innerText = " No Settings Found!" ;
            error.style.visibility = "visible";
    }
}
```

This function reads the `CurrentMRU` selected from gadget settings and based on that value, calls the `enumerateRegistry` function defined in `enumMRU.vbs`.

Listing MRU Items from the Registry

The most crucial part of the gadget is the enumeration of the Registry. Visual Studio stores all the `ProjectMRUList` items in the Registry under the following keys:

- `Software\Microsoft\VisualStudio\7.1\ProjectMRUList` for Visual Studio 2003

- `Software\Microsoft\VisualStudio\8.0\ProjectMRUList` for Visual Studio 2005

- `Software\Microsoft\VisualStudio\9.0\ProjectMRUList` for Visual Studio 2008

Figure 10.13 shows what it looks like if you travel down the Registry tree in `regedit.exe`.

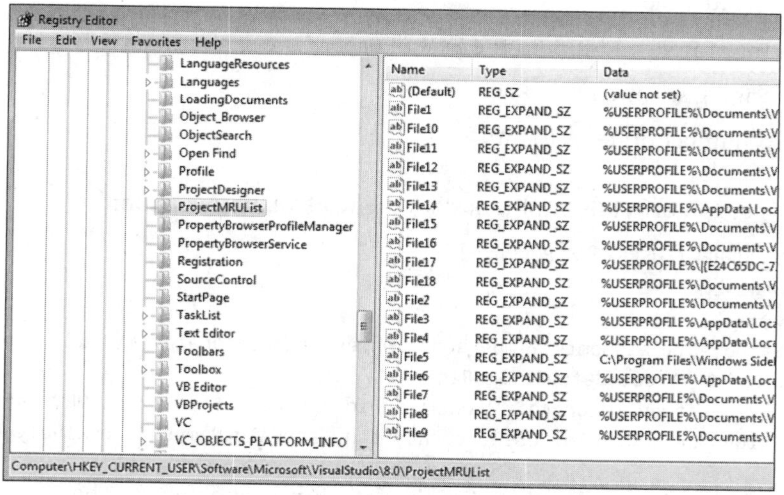

FIGURE 10.13   The Registry showing the project MRU list for Visual Studio 2005.

Notice the `ProjectMRUList` and the path in the bottom-left corner of the status bar. File1–File18 are the most recently used items for Version 8.0 (Visual Studio 2005). These values need to be translated into a path that can be linked with the title displayed in the gadget so that when users click on the gadget, they open Visual Studio with this path as a parameter to open the particular project.

Let's look at the two approaches for reading the Registry key: using both Windows Management Instrumentation script and ActiveX (COM) technology.

10

Using Windows Management Instrumentation Script

With WMI, the first step is to find out how to enumerate the `ProjectMRULists` key from the Registry. You need to create the function `enumerateRegistry`, which takes the version of Visual Studio and the page number to enumerate the Registry values.

Here is the pseudo code of the entire function:

Function `enumerateRegistry`

- Enumerate Registry WMI Script

    - Paging script starts

    - Parse each item

    - Replace %USERPROFILE% string to the user profile path

    - Create link

    - Insert item and link to the DIV in `Gadget.html`

    - Paging script ends

- Return number of items found

Here is the portion of WMI script that does the work of enumeration:

```
Const HKEY_CURRENT_USER = &H80000001
enumerateRegistry = 0
strComputer = "."
Set oReg=GetObject("winmgmts:{impersonationLevel=impersonate}!\\" &
➥ strComputer & "\root\default:StdRegProv")
strKeyPath = "Software\Microsoft\VisualStudio\" & path & "\ProjectMRUList"
oReg.EnumValues HKEY_CURRENT_USER, strKeyPath, arrValueNames, arrValueTypes
```

The path is the version of Visual Studio, the default value being `8.0`. The `oReg.EnumValues` function enumerates all the Registry values in the Registry path specified by `strKeyPath` and stores the value names and types in two arrays: `arrValueNames` and `arrValueTypes`.

Here is the complete function of `enumerateRegistry` in VBScript:

```
function enumerateRegistry(path, page)

 Const HKEY_LOCAL_MACHINE = &H80000002
 Const HKEY_CURRENT_USER = &H80000001
 Set oShell = CreateObject("Wscript.Shell")
 Set filesys = CreateObject("Scripting.FileSystemObject")
 enumerateRegistry = 0
 strComputer = "."
 Set oReg=GetObject("winmgmts:{impersonationLevel=impersonate}!\\"
     & strComputer & "\root\default:StdRegProv")
```

```
strKeyPath = "Software\Microsoft\VisualStudio\" & path & "\ProjectMRUList"
oReg.EnumValues HKEY_CURRENT_USER, strKeyPath, arrValueNames, arrValueTypes
 startpage = page * 5
 endpage = (page * 5) + 4
 For i=startpage to endpage
   document.getElementById("pageNum").innerText = startpage + 1 & "-" &
   ➥ endpage + 1 & " (" & UBound(arrValueNames)+1 & ")"

   if (i > UBound(arrValueNames)) then
   else
   iconimage = path
   oReg.GetStringValue HKEY_CURRENT_USER,strKeyPath,arrValueNames(i),strValue
   strUserProfile = oShell.ExpandEnvironmentStrings("%USERPROFILE%")
   strValue = Replace(strValue, "C:\Windows\system32\config\systemprofile",
   ➥ strUserProfile)
   finalstrValue = strValue

   if (InStr(1,strValue,"{E24C65DC-7377-472B-9ABA-BC803B73C61A}")>0)then
   strValue = Mid(strValue,1,InStr(1,strValue,"{E24C65DC-7377-472B-9ABA-
   ➥BC803B73C61A}")-3)
   iconimage="Folder"
   finalstrValue = strValue
   end if

   if (InStr(1,strValue,"{F184B08F-C81C-45F6-A57F-5ABD9991F28F}")>0)then
   strValue = Mid(strValue,1,InStr(1,strValue,"{F184B08F-C81C-45F6-A57F-
   ➥5ABD9991F28F}")-3)
   iconimage="VbProj"
   finalstrValue = strValue
   end if

   if (InStr(1,strValue,"{FAE04EC0-301F-11D3-BF4B-00C04F79EFBC}")>0)then
   strValue = Mid(strValue,1,InStr(1,strValue,"{FAE04EC0-301F-11D3-BF4B-
   ➥00C04F79EFBC}")-3)
   iconimage="CsProj"
   finalstrValue = strValue
   end if

   if (InStr(1,strValue,"{8BC9CEB8-8B4A-11D0-8D11-00A0C91BC942}")>0)then
   strValue = Mid(strValue,1,InStr(1,strValue,"{8BC9CEB8-8B4A-11D0-8D11-
   ➥00A0C91BC942}")-3)
   iconimage="VcProj"
   finalstrValue = strValue
   end if
```

10

```
    if (InStr(1,strValue,"{E6FDF86B-F3D1-11D4-8576-0002A516ECE8}")>0)then
    strValue = Mid(strValue,1,InStr(1,strValue,"{E6FDF86B-F3D1-11D4-8576-
    ➥0002A516ECE8}")-3)
    iconimage="Project"
    finalstrValue = strValue
    end if


    if (InStr(1,strValue,"{66A26720-8FB5-11D2-AA7E-00C04F688DDE}")>0)then
    strValue = Mid(strValue,1,InStr(1,strValue,"{66A26720-8FB5-11D2-AA7E-
    ➥00C04F688DDE}")-3)
    iconimage="Web"
    finalstrValue = strValue
    end if

        linkSrc = "javascript:shellOpen('"+encodeURIComponent(finalstrValue)+
        ➥"');"
        slashpos = InStrRev(strValue,"\")
        cell = i - (page * 5)

        document.getElementById("cell" & cell).innerHTML =  "<div onclick="""
➥ & linkSrc & """><img src='images/vs" & iconimage & ".png'>  " &
➥ Mid(strValue,slashpos+1,11) +"</div>"
        document.getElementById("cell" & cell).title = strValue
    end if
Next

if (UBound(arrValueNames) > 0 ) then enumerateRegistry = UBound(arrValueNames)
➥ + 1
end function
```

The code starts by enumerating the Registry value for the `ProjectMRUList` for the currently selected Visual Studio version. After all the Registry values are enumerated, the values are checked for the type of the project. Table 10.1 shows a typical list of GUID identifiers that are associated with the corresponding type of project.

Take a moment to look at sample code from the function. Here, the chunk of code checks whether the value in `strValue` contains the identifier E24C65DC-7377-472B-9ABA-BC803B73C61A (which is associated with Web Projects, as in Table 10.1) and if it does, it assigns the variable `iconimage` string to `Folder`.

```
if (InStr(1,strValue,"{E24C65DC-7377-472B-9ABA-BC803B73C61A}")>0)then
strValue = Mid(strValue,1,InStr(1,strValue,"{E24C65DC-7377-472B-9ABA-
BC803B73C61A}")-3)
iconimage="Folder"
finalstrValue = strValue
end if
```

This string later decides which icon needs to be displayed, along with the title of the project.

```
document.getElementById("cell" & cell).innerHTML =  "<div onclick=""" & linkSrc &
"""><img src='images/vs" & iconimage & ".png'>
```

TABLE 10.1   List of Project Types in Visual Studio and Their Respective GUIDs, Which Are Stored in the Registry

Project Type	Icon Used	GUID Identifier
Solution Folder	Website	{66A26720-8FB5-11D2-AA7E-00C04F688DDE}
Visual Basic	VB Project	{F184B08F-C81C-45F6-A57F-5ABD9991F28F}
Visual C#	C # Project	{FAE04EC0-301F-11D3-BF4B-00C04F79EFBC}
Visual C++	V C Project	{8BC9CEB8-8B4A-11D0-8D11-00A0C91BC942}
Visual J#	Project	{E6FDF86B-F3D1-11D4-8576-0002A516ECE8}
Web Project	Folder	{E24C65DC-7377-472b-9ABA-BC803B73C61A}

More information on identifiers for projects can be found at http://msdn2.microsoft.com/en-us/library/hb23x61k(VS.80).aspx.

Using ActiveX (COM) Technology to Read Registry Settings

In the last section you saw how to enumerate and use a WMI script to enumerate and use Registry values. This section discusses how to use an ActiveX control to achieve the same result. To do this you first need to create an ActiveX library that can enumerate the Registry and store the values in a collection object.

To create an ActiveX library in Visual Basic 6.0, you need to open a new project in Visual Basic 6.0 and choose ActiveX DLL in the New Project configuration dialog (see Figure 10.14).

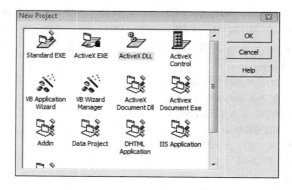

FIGURE 10.14   To create a COM library project, choose ActiveX DLL.

Change the name of the default class to clsMRU and the project to VisualStudioMRU as shown in Figure 10.15. Make sure that the instancing of clsMRU is set to GlobalMultiUse in the Properties window.

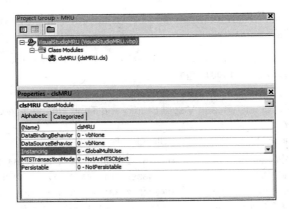

FIGURE 10.15   Visual Studio MRU project with a single class, `clsMRU`, with an instancing property of 6 `-GlobalMultiUse`.

Now that the ActiveX component is created, the next step is to add Registry functionality to it.

The ActiveX DLL has four parts:

- A reference to the Windows Registry APIs

- A collection object that stores those values and is queried by the gadget

- An enumerate Registry function that goes through each of the items

- A Registry read function that reads the value of an item

Windows Registry API   The application programming interfaces (APIs) used for Registry access are the low-level Windows APIs. Visual Basic supports numerous Windows API functions that can be used for this particular scenario. After the class is created you need Registry-related APIs, as shown in the following code:

```
'' Registry API's to Manipulate Windows
'    and Exploreres MRU's
Const HKEY_CLASSES_ROOT = &H80000000
Const HKEY_CURRENT_USER = &H80000001
Const HKEY_LOCAL_MACHINE = &H80000002
Const HKEY_USERS = &H80000003
Const HKEY_PERFORMANCE_DATA = &H80000004
Const ERROR_FILE_NOT_FOUND& = 2
Const ERROR_BADKEY& = 1010
Const REG_SZ = 1 ' Unicode nul terminated String
Private Declare Function RegCloseKey Lib "advapi32.dll" (ByVal hKey As Long) As
Long
Private Declare Function RegOpenKey Lib "advapi32" Alias "RegOpenKeyA" _(ByVal hKey
As Long, ByVal lpValueName As String, phkResult As Long) As Long
```

```
Private Declare Function RegOpenKeyEx Lib "advapi32" Alias "RegOpenKeyExA" (ByVal
hKey As Long, ByVal lpValueName As String, ByVal ulOptions As Long, ByVal
samDesired As Long, phkResult As Long) As Long
Private Declare Function RegQueryValueEx Lib "advapi32" Alias "RegQueryValueExA"
(ByVal hKey As Long, ByVal lpValueName As String, lpReserved As Long, lpType As
Long, ByVal lpData As String, lpcbData As Long) As Long
```

In Visual Basic, when you need to call a Windows API you give a reference to the low-level DLL that calls the Registry. The preceding code refers to `advapi32.dll`, which is used for Registry access.

Collection Object   A collection object is used to store all the enumerated values and standard properties to be used in the gadget. The following code shows how a public collection data structure is used to store all the MRU items:

```
Public colMRUFiles As New Collection
Public Sub AddCollection(file As String)
        colMRUFiles.Add file, UCase(file)
End Sub
' To add items in the collection

Public Sub ClearCollection()
    ' Clears all files from the list.
    Do While colMRUFiles.Count > 0
        colMRUFiles.Remove 1
    Loop
End Sub
Clear all items from the collection
Public Property Get CollectionCount() As Long
    ' Returns the number of files in the' list.
    CollectionCount = colMRUFiles.Count
End Property
```

The code shows the methods to add items to the collection, to clear the collection, and to get the number of items in the collection. The next requirement is to enumerate the Registry, as detailed in the next section.

Enumerate Registry   The enumerate Registry task is achieved by the `VisualStudioMRU_Get` function, which is based on the parameter passed. In this case, p enumerates the `ProjectMRUList` of Visual Studio 2003, 2005, or 2008 projects. Here is the code with details:

```
Public Sub VisualStudioMRU_Get(p)

    Dim buf As String
    Dim sKey As String
    Dim i As Integer
```

10

```
        If (p = 7) Then
        sKey = "Software\Microsoft\VisualStudio\7.1\ProjectMRUList"
        End If
        If (p = 8) Then
        sKey = "Software\Microsoft\VisualStudio\8.0\ProjectMRUList"
        End If
        If (p = 9) Then
        sKey = "Software\Microsoft\VisualStudio\9.0\ProjectMRUList"
        End If
            buf = RegRead(sKey, "File1", HKEY_CURRENT_USER)
          ClearCollection
            If Len(buf) Then
            For i = 1 To 50
                buf = RegRead(sKey, "File" & CStr(i), HKEY_CURRENT_USER)
                If Len(buf) Then
                    AddCollection buf
                End If
            Next
        End If
End Sub
```

This function takes the Visual Studio version as the parameter and reads the respective Registry settings. It traverses through all the values of the Registry and adds the values to the collection object. The collection object is also cleared before the items are added. Note that the function RegRead is called to retrieve the value stored for a particular file in the registry. The RegRead function is described in the next section.

RegRead Function   The last part of the enumeration is the RegRead function that is called to read the value of the key from File1 to File50 in the VisualStudioMRU_Get function:

```
Public Function RegRead(sKey As String, sValueName As String, Optional vntOption-
alHKey As Variant) As String
    ' Returns the Value found for this Key and ValueName
    '-------------------------------------
    Dim lOptionalHKey As Long
    Dim lKeyType As Long
    Dim lHKey As Long 'return handle To opened key
    Dim lpcbData As Long 'length of data In returned String
    Dim sReturnedString As String 'returned string value
    Dim sTemp As String 'temp string
    Dim lRtn As Long 'success or Not success

    If IsMissing(vntOptionalHKey) Then
        lOptionalHKey = HKEY_CURRENT_USER 'Use current user
    Else
```

```
            lOptionalHKey = vntOptionalHKey 'Use the one supplied
        End If
        lKeyType = REG_SZ 'data type is String
        lRtn = RegOpenKeyEx(lOptionalHKey, sKey, 0&, KEY_READ, lHKey)

        If lRtn = 0 Then
            lpcbData = 1024 'get this many characters
            sReturnedString = Space$(lpcbData) 'setup the buffer
            lRtn = RegQueryValueEx(lHKey, sValueName, ByVal 0&,
    lKeyType, sReturnedString, lpcbData)
            If lRtn = 0 Then
                sTemp = Left$(sReturnedString, lpcbData - 1)
            End If
            RegCloseKey lHKey
        End If
        RegRead = sTemp
End Function
```

The RegRead function extracts the value data from the string value and returns a string with the complete path.

Compiling the ActiveX DLL   After the class is created and the functionality to enumerate the Registry is taken care of, the next step is to test and then compile the ActiveX COM object. To test the functionality, add a demo project to the ActiveX project and test by directly calling the class functionality with the parameters. To do this, with the VisualStudioMRU project open in Visual Basic, go to the File menu and select Add Project. Then select a standard .exe from among the templates. A Standard Form project will be added, which can be used to test the functionality of the VisualStudioMRU.DLL.

After you have a fully tested ActiveX DLL ready to be used in the gadget, compile it as VisualStudioMRU.dll. To compile, select the VisualStudioMRU project, go to the File menu, and select Make VisualStudioMRU.dll. You are then asked for a path to store VisualStudioMRU.DLL.

After creating VisualStudioMRU.dll, go to Projects, Properties and in the Component tab select Binary Compatibility with the DLL just created (see Figure 10.16).

NOTE

Binary compatibility ensures Visual Basic will not change any of the existing class, interface, or type library IDs; however, to do so Visual Basic requires the project to specify an existing compiled version that it can compare against to ensure that existing interfaces have not been broken.

10

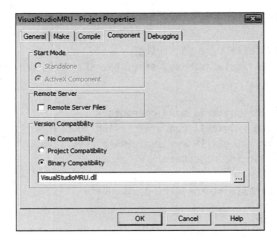

FIGURE 10.16   To compile the ActiveX DLL project, make sure that you get to Project Properties and set the binary compatibility.

After the DLL becomes binary compatible, it's ready to use. Now all you need is to put the DLL in the gadget folder and register the DLL using `regsvr32.exe`. Lets go through this process step by step.

1. If the gadget path is `%USERPROFILE%\AppData\Local\Microsoft\Windows Sidebar\ Gadgets\Recent ProjectsX.gadget`, copy the `VisualStudioMRU.dll` to this folder.

2. Type **cmd.exe** in the Start menu's Search field, right-click on the `cmd.exe` file, and select Run as Administrator in the submenu.

3. When `cmd.exe` has run in administrator mode, change the directory to `%USERPROFILE%\AppData\Local\Microsoft\Windows Sidebar\Gadgets\Recent ProjectsX.gadget`.

4. When you are at the Recent ProjectsX.gadget, type **Regsvr32 " VisualStudioMRU.dll"** to register the DLL.

After the ActiveX DLL is installed successfully, the gadget can use the ActiveX COM from the gadget code inside JavaScript.

Reading the Registry

In both scenarios for reading the Registry, you still need to open the Visual Studio project that the user selects. Do so by adding a `ShellOpen` function to the link of the DIV element, as follows:

```
linkSrc = "javascript:shellOpen('"+encodeURIComponent(finalstrValue)+"');"
```

The ShellOpen function needs to get the value from the following key to get the path of the Visual Studio executable:

```
HKEY_LOCAL_MACHINE\SOFTWARE\Microsoft\VisualStudio\8.0\InstallDir
```

The ShellOpen function also takes the path of the MRU file as a parameter and opens the solution in the corresponding Visual Studio IDE.

```
function shellOpen(value)
{
    if (MRUS[MRUCurrentID]==7)
    {
      System.Shell.execute("C:\\Program Files\\Microsoft Visual Studio .NET
➡ 2003\\Common7\\IDE\\devenv.exe ",  "\"" + decodeURIComponent(value) + "\"" );
    }
    if (MRUS[MRUCurrentID]==8)
    {
      System.Shell.execute("C:\\Program Files\\Microsoft Visual Studio 8
➡\\Common7\\IDE\\devenv.exe ",  "\"" + decodeURIComponent(value) + "\"" );
    }
    if (MRUS[MRUCurrentID]==9)
    {
      System.Shell.execute("C:\\Program Files\\Microsoft Visual Studio 9.0
➡\\Common7\\IDE\\devenv.exe ",  "\"" + decodeURIComponent(value) + "\"" );
    }
}
```

10

Radio Gadget and YouTube Video Gadget—Fun Gadgets

"People rarely succeed unless they have fun in what they are doing."

—Dale Carnegie

Media Gadgets

In this chapter, we create two gadgets that use the Windows Media Player and the Flash Player. These two technologies are used in the gadget in the form of embedded plug-ins. The Windows Media Player plug-in uses online streaming technologies to play audio in the Radio Gadget, whereas the Flash Player plug-in is used to download and play online videos, using the feed provided by YouTube.com.

The purpose of these gadgets is to implement our framework in the typical scenario of embedding media player controls inside a gadget, and of course to have some fun. The Radio Gadget embeds a Windows Media Player control and reads directly from an online streaming server. The YouTube Video Gadget opens an online feed provided by YouTube and plays the item in an embedded Flash player.

The Radio Gadget

The Radio Gadget plays a streaming radio from the Internet. In its most basic form, the Radio Gadget has Windows Media Player embedded to do most of the task of streaming audio from the server, playing the audio, and providing basic features such as volume controls, play, pause, and so on. The Radio Gadget has the following goals:

- Provide a simple implementation of Windows Media Player

- Play audio from online streaming servers

- Provide an option to increase or decrease the volume of the media player

- Support multiple streaming servers

Background—Internet Radio

Internet radio provides audio broadcasts over the Internet. Audio content from Internet radio uses streaming media technology: The audio is played and the data is received in real-time. The most popular audio streaming format is MP3.

Some of the popular Internet stations that provide streaming audio are

- **Live365**—http://www.live365.com

- **SHOUTcast**—http://www.shoutcast.com/

- **AOL Radio**—http://music.aol.com

This example focuses on SHOUTcast, which provides audio streaming in the form of playlist files that can be played directly in the Winamp player or Real Player.

If you go to Shoutcast.com and select a radio station, it asks you to save the shoutcast-playlist.pls file in your computer. If you open the PLS file in Microsoft WordPad, you will see the URLs of the streaming server and the station title. Here is how a file looks for a popular station, .977 The 80s Channel:

```
[playlist]
numberofentries=17
File1=http://scfire-dll-aa03.stream.aol.com:80/stream/1040
Title1=(#1 - 220/500) .977 The 80s Channel
Length1=-1
File2=http://another streaming server URL
Title2=(#2 - 221/500) Another channel
Length2=-1
...
Version=2
```

You can also open the playlist file in RealPlayer and view the clip information in the Properties window (see Figure 11.1). This information is important because the Radio Gadget needs the title and the radio station's URL:

Title: .977 The 80s Channel

Station URL: http://scfire-dll-aa03.stream.aol.com:80/stream/1040

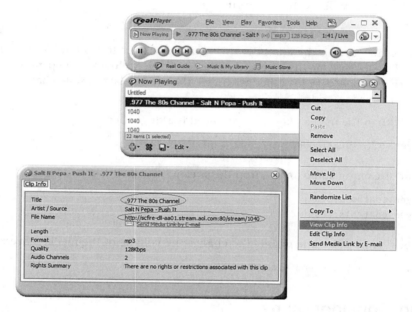

FIGURE 11.1   The playlist file can also be read in the Clip Info window of Real Player.

To download the free version of Real Player, go to http://www.real.com/player.

Features and Technology

To create a Radio Gadget based on Internet radio you need to have a media player in the gadget that can play the streaming audio directly from a URL. A number of ActiveX plug-ins, such as Windows Media Player, Divx Player, Real Player, and QuickTime, are available and can be embedded in an HTML page.

The only requirement is that the plug-in needs to have been previously installed in the user's computer. This example uses the Windows Media Player object because it is, by default, installed on Windows machines and also because it provides rich scripting support.

After you have the title and the URL of the online audio, you need to send it to the media player and execute the play command. To embed a Windows Media Player object in the gadget's main window, you need to add the following code:

```
<OBJECT id="mediaPlayer" width="0" height="0"
    style="position:absolute; left:0;top:0;"
    CLASSID="CLSID:6BF52A52-394A-11d3-B153-00C04F79FAA6"
    type="application/x-oleobject">
    <PARAM NAME="SendPlayStateChangeEvents" VALUE="True">
    <PARAM NAME="AutoStart" VALUE="False">
    <PARAM name="uiMode" value="invisible">
</OBJECT>
```

The name mediaPlayer is the identifier this example will use to work with the object in JavaScript. The CLASSID tag distinguishes different ActiveX plugins. The parameter SendPlayStateChangeEvents is called whenever the media player's state changes and is captured in the gadget code.

To set the URL to the media player, all you need is a single line:

```
mediaPlayer.url = stationURL;
```

To play the streaming audio and to stop the stream, you need just two lines:

```
mediaPlayer.controls.play();
mediaPlayer.controls.stop();
```

Finally, there's one more line required to change the volume of the media player:

```
mediaPlayer.settings.volume = currentVolume;
```

Design Considerations

The Radio Gadget is a fun gadget, so the design needs to be intuitive and simple. Design considerations involve giving the gadget a unique identity as well as an attractive look and feel. As with most gadgets, your design considerations revolve around the following:

- Themes and images used in the gadget
- Layout of the gadget
- Usability of the gadget

The following sections look into each of these in more detail with respect to the radio theme.

Theme, and Look and Feel of the Gadget

The theme of the gadget is a radio player. The image chosen is common and is used for classic physical radio. The image uniquely identifies the gadget (see Figure 11.2).

The gadget's icon was chosen to match the theme. The next thing is the gadget window (see Figure 11.3). The gadget's background image looks like a radio with three knobs.

FIGURE 11.2   A classic radio image used for the gadget's icon makes the gadget's core purpose immediately recognizable.

FIGURE 11.3   A Radio Gadget with an interface similar to a radio.

The Radio Gadget design has a simple interface: a Play button that changes to Stop when the audio is playing and Volume Up and Down buttons. There is also a Previous and Next link to move to the previous and next radio stations.

Figure 11.4 shows some of the images used in the gadget to match the radio theme.

stop.png   minus.png   play.png   plus.png

background.png   logoGadget.png   icon.png

FIGURE 11.4   The images used in the Radio Gadget all follow the same classic radio theme.

Layout of the Gadget

The layout of the gadget is similar to the framework created in Part II of this book (see Figure 11.5). Note, however, that in this case there's no need for a flyout window.

FIGURE 11.5   The Radio Gadget has a simple layout and does not have a flyout window

The gadget manifest shown here has changed to accommodate information specific to the Radio Gadget. Note the name and description have changed, but the names of the icon and the drag image remain the same. They now point to the images specific to the gadget.

```xml
<?xml version="1.0" encoding="utf-8" ?>
<gadget>
  <name>- Radio Player -</name>
  <namespace>Innovate.Gadgets</namespace>
  <version>1.0</version>
  <author name="Rajesh Lal">
    <logo src="images/logo.png" />
    <info url="www.innovatewithgadgets.com" />
  </author>
  <copyright>Copyright&#169; 2008</copyright>
  <description>Radio Gadget powered by SHOUTcast</description>
  <icons>
    <icon width="70" height="80" src="images/icon.png" />
  </icons>
  <hosts>
    <host name="sidebar">
      <base type="HTML" apiVersion="1.0.0" src="gadget.html" />
      <permissions>Full</permissions>
      <platform minPlatformVersion="1.0" />
      <defaultImage src="images/drag.png"/>
    </host>
  </hosts>
</gadget>
```

Usability of the Gadget

A marquee effect is added to the gadget when the radio is playing, so as to scroll the station name from right to left. This is a special Internet Explorer–specific effect, but because gadgets are based on Internet Explorer browser objects, you can use any of the Dynamic HTML (DHTML) effects supported by Internet Explorer.

The Play button changes to a Stop icon when the gadget is playing the audio (see Figure 11.6).

FIGURE 11.6   The Radio Gadget displays the media player's status to the user.

Notice the marquee effect in action in this figure: The status of the gadget is "Playing" and that the Play button has changed to display the Stop icon.

Developing the Gadget

Development of this gadget starts with the framework already created, but customized according to the Radio Gadget's requirements. The development can be divided into two parts:

- Integrating the existing framework
- Media Player functionality

Integrating the Existing Framework

From the existing framework, we keep the settings for adding an item and customize it to accommodate the title and URL in the Settings page. The height of the Radio Gadget is just 88 pixels, so the Mini Me option is not required. The station title and station URLs are stored in memory in an array (see Figure 11.7).

FIGURE 11.7   The Settings page for the Radio Gadget has an option to add a new radio station.

Media Player Functionality

The second part is integrating the Media Player within the gadget. To embed the Media Player in the gadget, you need to add the plug-in code to the gadget.html file, as shown here. Next is a call to the different methods of the Media Player object mediaPlayer (ID in the OBJECT code). Note that SendPlayStateChangeEvents is added as a parameter to the Media Player and the parameter uimode. Notice also that uimode's value is set to invisible to hide the media player's interface.

```
<html>
<head>
<title>Radio Player</title>
<link href="style/gadget.css" rel="stylesheet" type="text/css" />
<script language="javascript" src="code/gadget.js" type="text/javascript"></script>
```

```
<script for="mediaPlayer" event="playstatechange(newstate)">
playStateChange(newstate);</script>

</head>

<body onload="loadMain();" scroll="no">
<g:background id="bkgImage"/>
<div id="gadgetText" >
<center><div id="playbackStatus">Ready</div></center>
<div id="nowPlaying" >Radio</div>
<div id="playbackControls">
<img id="PlayImage" onclick="PlayRadio();"  src="images/play.png"/></div>
<div id="plus" >
<img id="plusImage" onclick="VolumeInc();" src="images/plus.png"/></div>
<div id="minus" >
<img id="minusImage" onclick="VolumeDec();" src="images/minus.png"/></div>
</div>
    <OBJECT id="mediaPlayer" width="0" height="0"
        style="position:absolute; left:0;top:0;"
        CLASSID="CLSID:6BF52A52-394A-11d3-B153-00C04F79FAA6"
        type="application/x-oleobject">
        <PARAM NAME="SendPlayStateChangeEvents" VALUE="True">
        <PARAM NAME="AutoStart" VALUE="False">
        <PARAM name="uiMode" value="invisible">
    </OBJECT>
</body>
</html>
```

Table 11.1 lists all the parameters that can be used to customize Windows Media Player, along with their default values and descriptions. You can also add custom parameters, such as SendPlayStateChangeEvents, in the preceding code.

TABLE 11.1   Advanced Optional Parameter List for Windows Media Player

Parameter	Default	Description
AutoStart	True	Specifies or retrieves a value indicating whether the current media item begins playing automatically.
balance	0	Specifies the current stereo balance. Values range from –100 to 100.
baseURL		Specifies the base URL used for relative path resolution with URL script commands that are embedded in media items.
captioningID	0	Specifies the name of the element displaying the captioning.
currentMarker	0	Specifies the current marker number.
currentPosition	0	Specifies the current position in the media item in seconds.
defaultFrame	-	Specifies the name of the frame used to display a URL.

TABLE 11.1   Continued

Parameter	Default	Description
enableContextMenu	True	Specifies a value indicating whether to enable the context menu, which appears when the right mouse button is clicked.
enabled	False	Specifies whether the Windows Media Player control is enabled.
fullScreen	False	Specifies whether video content is played back in full-screen mode.
InvokeURLs	True	Specifies a value indicating whether URL events should launch a web browser.
Mute	False	Specifies whether audio is muted.
PlayCount	1	Specifies the number of times a media item will play. Minimum value of 1.
Rate	1.0	Specifies the playback rate. 0.5 equates to half the normal playback speed; 2 equates to twice.
stretchToFit	False	Specifies whether video displayed by the control automatically resizes to fit the video window when the video window is larger than the dimensions of the video image.
uiMode	Full	Specifies which controls are shown in the user interface. Possible values: invisible, none, mini, full.
URL	-	Specifies the name of the media item to play. You can specify a local filename or a URL.
Volume	Last setting	Zero specifies no volume and 100 specifies full volume.
windowlessVideo	False	Specifies or retrieves a value indicating whether the Windows Media Player control renders video in windowless mode. When windowlessVideo is set to True, the Media Player control renders video directly in the client area, so you can apply special effects or layer the video with text.

We need functions that make it possible to interact with the Media Player object from the gadget window. First of all we need to know when the state of the media player changes, such as for updating the status when the player state changes from ready to playing. Also needed is functionality to play and stop the Media Player object. We need functions for the following:

- State change of the Media Player object

- Radio play and stop functions

- Functions for volume control

State Change of the Media Player Object   The SendPlayStateChangeEvents event, which was added as a parameter, updates the status to the user. If you add a custom event parameter, you need to tie it up with an actual JavaScript function. You can do this by using the following script tag in the head section of the gadget.html file:

```
<script for="mediaPlayer" event="playstatechange(newstate)">
playStateChange(newstate);</script>
```

A corresponding function in the gadget code (gadget.js) is needed to handle different status events and to change the Play button's icon between Play and Stop states. The following code shows the corresponding function in the code file:

```
function playStateChange(newstate)
{

    switch (newstate){
    case 1: // Stopped
        playbackStatus.innerHTML = "Stopped";
        PlayImage.src = PlayImage.src.replace(/stop/, "play");
        break;

    case 2: // Paused
        playbackStatus.innerHTML = "Paused";
        PlayImage.src = PlayImage.src.replace(/stop/, "play");
        break;

    case 3: // Playing
        playbackStatus.innerHTML = "Playing";
        PlayImage.src = PlayImage.src.replace(/play/, "stop");
        break;

    case 6: // Buffering
        playbackStatus.innerHTML = "Buffering";
        break;

    case 7: // Waiting
        playbackStatus.innerHTML = "Waiting";
        break;

    case 8: // Media Ended
        playbackStatus.innerHTML = "Media Ended";
        PlayImage.src = PlayImage.src.replace(/stop/, "play");
        break;

    case 9: // Transitioning
        playbackStatus.innerHTML = "Connecting";
        break;

    case 10: // Ready
        playbackStatus.innerHTML = "Ready";
        PlayImage.src = PlayImage.src.replace(/stop/, "play");
        break;
    }
}
```

The `playStateChange` parameter updates the status text in the gadget as well as the image in the gadget window to reflect the current state of the Media Player object to the user. For example, if the gadget is trying to connect to a remote radio station, the status in the gadget says "Connecting."

The PlayRadio Function   The next thing is to add the functionality that actually allows the Media Player object to play and stop, which is achieved by the `PlayRadio` function. The `PlayRadio` function also updates the station name and the station URL parameter in the Media Player object.

An element called `NowPlaying` is in the Gadget Main window:

```
<div id="nowPlaying" style="position:absolute;">Radio</div>
```

This DIV is updated in the `PlayRadio` function:

```
function PlayRadio()
{
var nowPlayingText =""
    if (PlayImage.src.indexOf("stop") > 0)
    {
        mediaPlayer.controls.stop();
        // code update the title of the radio station
        nowPlaying.innerHTML = nowPlayingText;
    }
    else
    {
        mediaPlayer.controls.play();
        nowPlayingText =
        // code to update the title of the radio station
            nowPlaying.innerHTML = nowPlayingText;
    }
}
```

> **NOTE**
>
> `mediaPlayer` (the ID given in the `gadget.html` file) is used to call the Media Player object's method directly.

Volume Functions

The last thing to add is functionality to control volume. Windows Media Player maintains the volume as a percentage from 0 (mute) to 100 (max volume). So, we set the default volume to 50% and increase and decrease the volume in 5% increments. Two knob images with plus and minus symbols call the `VolumeInc()` and `VolumeDec()` functions, respectively.

```
var currentVolume = "50";
function VolumeDec() // Decrease volume by 5
{
    intVolume = parseInt(currentVolume);
    if (intVolume > 9)
    {
    intVolume = (intVolume - 5)
    changeVolume("" + intVolume);
    currentVolume = "" + intVolume;
        minus.title = "Volume down: " + intVolume
        plus.title = "Volume up: " + intVolume
    }
}
function VolumeInc()// increase volume by 5
    {
    intVolume = parseInt(currentVolume);
    if (intVolume < 91)
    {
        intVolume = (intVolume + 5)
        changeVolume("" + intVolume);
        currentVolume = "" + intVolume;
        minus.title = "Volume down: " + intVolume
        plus.title = "Volume up: " + intVolume
    }
}
function changeVolume(value)
{
    currentVolume = "" + value + "";
    mediaPlayer.settings.volume = currentVolume;
    intVolume = parseInt(currentVolume);
}
```

The code updates the mediaPlayer.settings.volume property and also sets the tooltip text to show the user the current volume.

As you can see, the Windows Media Player object has very rich scripting support. It exposes a set of properties and methods that can be invoked directly from the script code.

> **NOTE**
>
> More information on Windows Media Player's scripting support can be found at MSDN under the title "Object Model Reference for Scripting." Here is the link: http://msdn2.microsoft.com/en-us/library/bb249259(VS.85).aspx.

The YouTube Video Gadget

This section deals with a YouTube Video Gadget. The gadget downloads RSS feeds from YouTube and plays the video links from the feed in the flyout window. The video is displayed by an embedded Flash Media Player. The YouTube Video Gadget provides the following functionality:

- Provide a simple implementation of a Flash Media Player

- Play YouTube videos, using a RSS feed provided by the website

- Display videos in the flyout window when in the docked state and in the gadget window when undocked

- Support search by keywords, using RSS feeds

Background—YouTube Video Feeds

YouTube is a popular video-sharing website that provides a number of RSS feeds for the media content. More information about the feeds can be found at http://www.youtube.com/rssls.

Some of the popular feeds provided by YouTube include

- Recently added videos at http://youtube.com/rss/global/recently_added.rss.

- Recently featured videos at http://youtube.com/rss/global/recently_featured.rss.

- Top favorites videos at http://youtube.com/rss/global/top_favorites.rss.

- Top rated videos at http://youtube.com/rss/global/top_rated.rss.

- YouTube RSS feeds also support feeds by tags. For example, use of the following URL dynamically creates a latest feed criteria for videos tagged with the keyword "Vista": http://www.youtube.com/rss/tag/vista.rss.

Let's see what an RSS feed looks like for a single item. The following shows the first item of the feed YouTube: Recently Added Videos:

```
<rss version="2.0" xmlns:media="http://search.yahoo.com/mrss/">
<channel>
    <title>YouTube :: Recently Added Videos</title>
    <link>http://youtube.com/rss/global/recently_added.rss</link>
    <image>
    <url>http://youtube.com/img/pic_youtubelogo_123x63.gif</url>
    <link>http://youtube.com</link>
    <title>YouTube</title>
    <height>63</height>
    <width>123</width>
    </image>
    <description>Recently Added Videos</description>
```

```
<item>
<author>rss@youtube.com (3awnii)</author>
<title>Retoure El jadida - Azmmour</title>
<link>http://youtube.com/?v=oZf2K82eWRM</link>
<description><![CDATA[// ...    ]]></description>
<guid isPermaLink="true">http://youtube.com/?v=oZf2K82eWRM</guid>
<pubDate>Wed, 21 Nov 2007 04:25:01 -0800</pubDate>
<media:player url="http://youtube.com/?v=oZf2K82eWRM" />
<media:thumbnail url="http://img.youtube.com/vi/oZf2K82eWRM/default.jpg" />
<media:title>Retoure El jadida - Azmmour</media:title>
<media:category label="Tags"> lmzanzen</media:category>
<media:credit>3awnii</media:credit>
<enclosure url="http://youtube.com/v/oZf2K82eWRM.swf" duration="45" type="applica-
tion/x-shockwave-flash"/>
</item>

<item>
Second item details comes here
</item>
...~
</channel>
</rss>
```

A typical feed first describes the type of the feed (in the example it's "Recently Added Videos") and then has a list of up to 20 items in a sequence. Note the details in the "item" tag, which contains the information about that single video, title, media:player url, media: thumbnail, link and description tags, which will be used in the gadget.

Features and Technology

To create a gadget to play a video, you need to embed a media player in your gadget. YouTube uses a Flash Media Player for video streaming. The advantage of the Flash Media Player is that you don't need to add any supporting code for playback functions. The Flash Media Player used by YouTube has built-in functionality for playback, so after you embed the player and take care of the URL parameter, you are finished.

The following HTML is used to embed the Flash Media Player in an HTML page:

```
<object width="425" height="355">
<param name="movie" value="http://www.youtube.com/v/_S3LR6Tu7PE&rel=1"></param>
<param name="wmode" value="transparent"></param>
<embed src="http://www.youtube.com/v/_S3LR6Tu7PE&rel=1"
type="application/x-shockwave-flash"
wmode="transparent"
width="425"
height="355">
</embed>
</object>
```

The value of the video URL is the parameter that needs to be changed for each video. In the preceding example it was set to http://www.youtube.com/v/_S3LR6Tu7PE. This HTML is used to embed the player in the flyout window when the gadget is docked and inside the gadget window when the gadget is undocked.

The following portion of code illustrates how to create the Flash Media Player in the flyout window dynamically with the URL parameter:

```
function BuildVideoObject()
{
Video_HtmlString = "<object width=\"425\" height=\"355\">
<param name=\"movie\" value=\"" + System.Gadget.Settings.read("sLink") + "
➥&rel=1\"></param>
<param name=\"wmode\" value=\"transparent\"></param>
<embed src=\""+ System.Gadget.Settings.read("sLink") +"&rel=1\" type=\
➥"application/x-shockwave-flash\" wmode=\"transparent\" width=\"425\" height=\
➥"355\"></embed>
</object>";
document.write(Video_HtmlString);
}
```

The `BuildVideoObject` function creates the HTML code to embed a Flash Media Player dynamically with the parameter `System.Gadget.Settings.read ("sLink")`. This parameter is updated every time the user clicks on a video to play.

Design Considerations

Because a YouTube Media Player gadget's look needs to be high tech and media related, I have used a TV theme for this gadget. I made the background of the gadget window a TV showing the thumbnail of the video, and I have used the flyout window to play the video.

Design considerations for this gadget involve

- Theme and images used in the gadget
- Layout of the gadget
- Usability of the gadget

Theme and Look and Feel

The theme of the gadget shown here is an LCD TV to reflect the video player functionality (see Figure 11.8). You can use any theme you want, but the idea is to have some relationship between the gadget's function and its look and feel.

The next thing to do is create is the gadget window (see Figure 11.9).

The YouTube Video Gadget enables the user to navigate to the next video and includes an option to change the feed. This is implemented with the standard multiple page management functionality, which is already a part of the existing gadget framework.

FIGURE 11.8   The icon of the YouTube Video Gadget resembles a TV.

FIGURE 11.9   The thumbnail of the video appears in the TV screen image.

Figure 11.10 shows some of the images used in the gadget to match the TV theme.

background.png   drag.png   icon.png

FIGURE 11.10   All the images used in the gadget follow the same LCD TV theme.

Layout of the Gadget

The layout of the gadget is similar to the framework (see Figure 11.11) created for the MyBlog Gadget in Part II of this book. In this case, a flyout is used for playing the video and the Settings page is used to add feeds.

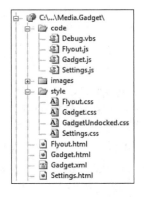

FIGURE 11.11   The standard layout from the existing framework is used for the gadget.

The gadget manifest must be modified to accommodate information specific to the media gadget. Note the change in `name` and `description`.

```xml
<?xml version="1.0" encoding="utf-8" ?>
<gadget>
  <name>- Video Gadget -</name>
  <namespace>Innovate.Gadgets</namespace>
  <version>1.0</version>
  <author name="Rajesh Lal">
    <logo src="images/logo.png" />
    <info url="www.innovatewithgadgets.com" />
  </author>
  <copyright>Copyright&#169; 2008</copyright>
  <description>YouTube Video Gadget</description>
  <icons>
    <icon width="70" height="80" src="images/icon.png" />
  </icons>
  <hosts>
    <host name="sidebar">
      <base type="HTML" apiVersion="1.0.0" src="gadget.html" />
      <permissions>Full</permissions>
      <platform minPlatformVersion="1.0" />
      <defaultImage src="images/drag.png"/>
    </host>
  </hosts>
</gadget>
```

Most of the key value pairs are similar in the gadget manifest, as they are with all the gadgets. The image names `icon.png` and `dragicon.png` remain the same, but they now refer to images specific to the gadget, as shown previously in Figure 11.10.

Usability of the Gadget

The design of the gadget also needs to ensure the gadget's usability. There are multiple video feeds, and each feed contains multiple videos. Users should be able to navigate through all the items of a single feed and also should be able to change the feed from the page level. For example, Figure 11.12 shows the second item (2/15) from the Top Rated video feed. The item number is displayed in the center bottom of the TV screen image and the feed title is displayed in the center top of the TV screen image.

A feature that makes the YouTube Video Gadget more useful and fun is its undocked behavior. When the gadget is docked the flyout window displays the video (see Figure 11.13).

The flyout window disappears as soon as the focus is out of the window; this prevents the user from playing videos when the focus is on some other window. So, we added video play functionality for the gadget when it is undocked (see Figure 11.14) to remove the restriction and make it more usable.

FIGURE 11.12   The feed title is displayed to identify the feed, and the item number (2/15) shows the current item of that particular feed.

FIGURE 11.13   The YouTube Video Gadget, when docked, shows the video in the flyout window.

FIGURE 11.14   The YouTube Video Gadget, when undocked, shows the video in the gadget window and plays the video even if the focus is on some other window.

Developing the Gadget

It's possible to use the gadget framework created in Chapter 8, "Debugging and Deploying a Gadget," and customize it according to this gadget's requirements. The gadget's development can be divided into two parts:

- Integrating the existing framework

- Adding additional features

Integrating the Existing Framework

A "Search" item, which is used to create an RSS feed by a keyword, is added to the existing framework. This is added to the array in the memory, which has all the popular RSS feeds (see Figure 11.15).

FIGURE 11.15   The Settings page enables the user to add keyword-based feeds.

This is done in two parts: the HTML code in the Settings page and the JavaScript code in the code of the Settings page.

The Code   Here is the HTML code that is added to include the search term functionality:

```
<font face = "verdana" size="2">Search term<br />
<input id="txtSearchTag"  type="text" value="Vista Gadget"/>

<img alt = "add item" id = 'additem'style="cursor:hand;" onclick="addItem();"
src ="../images/itemadd.gif" />

<img alt = "reset items to default set" id = 'resetitem' style="cursor:hand;"
onclick="resetItem();" src ="../images/reset.gif" />
```

Note that the addItem() and resetItem() functions are called by the on-click event of both the Add Item image and Reset Item image.

The corresponding JavaScript code for Add Item functionality is as follows:

```
function addItem()
{
    var Itemrepeat  = false
    for (i=0;i<System.Gadget.document.parentWindow.VideoURLs.length;i++)
    {
        var searchURL = "http://www.youtube.com/rss/tag/" +
document.getElementById("txtSearchTag").value + ".rss";

        if (System.Gadget.document.parentWindow.VideoURLs[i] == searchURL)
        {
            document.getElementById("errorid").innerText = "Item already exists!";
            Itemrepeat = true;
            break;
        }
    }

    if (Itemrepeat == false)
    {
        System.Gadget.document.parentWindow.VideoURLs.push(searchURL);
        System.Gadget.document.parentWindow.VideoURLTitles.push("Search: "
➥ + document.getElementById("txtSearchTag").value );
        document.getElementById("errorid").innerText = "Item added!";

    System.Gadget.Settings.write("VideoURL",System.Gadget.document.
    parentWindow.VideoURLs[System.Gadget.document.parentWindow.VideoURLs.
    length-1]);
        System.Gadget.Settings.write("VideoURLTitle",System.Gadget.document.
        parentWindow.VideoURLTitles[System.Gadget.document.parentWindow.
        VideoURLTitles.length-1]);

      System.Gadget.document.parentWindow.CodeCurrentId = System.Gadget.
      document.parentWindow.VideoURLTitles.length-1;
    }
}
```

This code first checks whether the RSS feed already exists. If it does, it updates the innerText of the errorid element to the Item already exists! message; otherwise it adds the following RSS feed in the array of feeds:

```
http://www.youtube.com/rss/tag/" + txtSearchTag.value + ".rss";
```

The resetItem() function in the Settings page calls the DefaultCodes function in the gadget window code page, which clears all the user-added feeds and resets the feed array to the default set of feeds.

```
function resetItem()
{
System.Gadget.document.parentWindow.DefaultCodes();
}
```

Here is what the DefaultCodes function looks like:

```
function DefaultCodes()
{
    VideoURLs.length = 0;
    VideoURLTitles.length = 0;

    VideoURLs[0] = "http://youtube.com/rss/global/top_rated.rss";
    VideoURLTitles[0] = "Top Rated";

    VideoURLs[1] = "http://youtube.com/rss/global/recently_added.rss";
    VideoURLTitles[1] = "Recently Added";

    VideoURLs[2] = "http://youtube.com/rss/global/recently_featured.rss";
    VideoURLTitles[2] = "Recently Featured";

    VideoURLs[3] = "http://youtube.com/rss/global/top_favorites.rss";
    VideoURLTitles[3] = "Top Favorites";

    // TOP VIEWED

    VideoURLs[4] = "http://youtube.com/rss/global/top_viewed_today.rss";
    VideoURLTitles[4] = "Today - Top Viewed";

    VideoURLs[5] = "http://youtube.com/rss/global/top_viewed_week.rss";
    VideoURLTitles[5] = "Week - Top Viewed";

    VideoURLs[6] = "http://youtube.com/rss/global/top_viewed_month.rss";
    VideoURLTitles[6] = "Month - Top Viewed";

    VideoURLs[7] = "http://youtube.com/rss/global/top_viewed.rss";
    VideoURLTitles[7] = "All Times - Top Viewed";

}
```

Additional Features

Apart from the standard framework function, the only function we need for making the YouTube Video Gadget is the undocked functionality. The undocked functionality is relevant for this gadget because you might need to have the gadget play video even when you are, for example, browsing a web page.

If the video play functionality is in only the Flyout window, and a new Internet Explorer session is opened while a video is playing, the flyout window collapses, instantly stopping the media. This is the basic nature of the flyout window. So, playing the video in the gadget itself makes sense. This requires additional coding to work in an undocked state.

Docked Versus Undocked   To accomodate docked and undocked modes, you first have to set the dock and undock properties of the gadget object to functions. These functions will be called whenever the gadget state changes from docked state to undocked state and vice versa.

You have to create two methods that modify the gadget's appearance, the background image, and the dimensions of the gadget in the two different states.

```
System.Gadget.onUndock = undocked;
System.Gadget.onDock = docked;
function docked()
{
    System.Gadget.background = "url('../images/docked.png')";
    with (document.body.style)
    {
        width = 130;
        height = 134;
    }
    ReSetup();
}
function undocked()
{
    System.Gadget.background = "url('../images/undocked.png')";
    with (document.body.style)
    {
        width = 442;
        height = 420;
    }
    ReSetup();
}
```

These two functions change the gadget's size and its background image and call the ReSetup function. The ReSetup function then calls the systemSetup functions, the resize function, and the getRSS function to repopulate the feeds.

Another function related to the docked versus undocked mode is the `Resize` function:

```
function Resize()
{
    if (System.Gadget.docked)
    {
        System.Gadget.background = "url(../images/background.png)";
        document.getElementById("contenttable").height = "90%";
        document.getElementById("content").style.top ="20px";
        document.getElementById("content").style.width = "110px";
        document.getElementById("content").style.left = "8px";
        document.getElementById("content").style.height = "100px";
        document.getElementById("content").style.fontsize ="11px";

        document.getElementById("mylogo").style.left ="2px";
        document.getElementById("mylogo").style.top ="70px";
        document.getElementById("mylogo").style.height="70px";
        document.getElementById("pagingbar").style.top = "100px";
    }
    else
    {
        System.Gadget.background = "url(../images/undocked.png)";
        document.getElementById("contenttable").height = "384px";
        document.getElementById("content").style.top ="30px";
        document.getElementById("content").style.width = "430px";
        document.getElementById("content").style.left = "8px";
        document.getElementById("content").style.height = "384px";
        document.getElementById("content").style.fontsize ="11px";

        document.getElementById("mylogo").style.left ="2px";
        document.getElementById("mylogo").style.top ="70px";
        document.getElementById("mylogo").style.height="70px";
        document.getElementById("pagingbar").style.top = "400px";
    }
}
```

The style of the gadget window elements is changed based on the property `System.Gadget.docked`.

The Gadget Code   The gadget window holds the thumbnail of the video in the flyout window when the gadget is docked. When the gadget is undocked, the video player is embedded into the gadget window itself:

```
if (System.Gadget.docked)
{
document.getElementById("cell" + (cell)).innerHTML = '<div onclick=
➥"showFlyout(\'' + i + '\');" ><div class="sub" title=\''+ myTitle +'\'>'+
➥ showimage +'</div></div>';
}
else
{
myVideo_HtmlString = "<object width=\"425\" height=\"355\"><param name=
➥\"movie\" value=\"" + rssLink + "&rel=1\"></param><param name=\"wmode\"
➥ value=\"transparent\"></param><embed src=\""+ rssLink +"&rel=1\" type=
➥\"application/x-shockwave-flash\" wmode=\"transparent\" width=\"425\" height=
➥\"355\"></embed></object>";
document.getElementById("cell" + (cell)).innerHTML = myVideo_HtmlString;
}
```

The source code that comes with this chapter contains both the gadgets discussed here. Most of the functionality of the YouTube Video Gadget is similar to that of the RSS Feed gadget discussed in Part II of this book.

Ajax methodology is used to download the feed, which is then parsed and displayed to the user in the gadget window. The link to the video is dynamically populated to the flyout window when a particular video item is clicked. The flyout also contains a description of the video. All the common functionalities are not detailed here and users are encouraged to open the source of the corresponding gadget in Visual Studio 2005 or Visual Studio Express, as a website, and go through the gadget's layout and source code.

Silverlight World Clock—Utility Gadget

IN THIS CHAPTER

- The Silverlight Gadget
- Design Considerations
- Developing the Gadget
- Creating a Sidebar Gadget Using Microsoft Popfly
- Where to Go from Here

"Technology is just a tool. In terms of getting the kids working together and motivating them, the teacher is the most important."

—Bill Gates

The Silverlight Gadget

The goal of this chapter is to leverage Microsoft Silverlight technology in a Sidebar gadget in the form of a world clock. A World Clock Gadget displays a clock for multiple cities. It's a simple task that enables us to concentrate more on the technology and implementation part of the job. Microsoft Silverlight is a cross-browser, cross-platform plug-in for delivering the next generation of media experiences and rich interactive applications. It supports scripting languages such as JavaScript as well as high-level programming languages such as .NET. The gadget model demonstrated in this chapter uses JavaScript to implement Silverlight.

The Silverlight World Clock uses Microsoft Silverlight 1.1 technology to create a clock gadget that not only has compelling graphics but is also feature rich. This is also a good tutorial for creating a gadget with Extensible Application Markup Language (XAML) and a Silverlight plug-in with JavaScript.

The gadget is developed with the following goals:

- Implement Microsoft Silverlight technology in the Sidebar

- Create a gadget with compelling graphics and animation

- Make a feature-rich World Clock Gadget with multiple locations

- Provide the ability to extend the gadget with new locations over time

Figure 12.1 shows how the gadget looks. The clock hand pointing down is the hour hand, the hand pointing to the left top is the minute hand, and the one pointing to the right is the second hand. Although you can't see it here, the hands are each color-coded: green, blue and red, respectively. The location, which controls the time zone, is also displayed in the top of the gadget. In this case it is *New York*. When you click on the location, the gadget time changes to the next stored locale based on its time zone.

FIGURE 12.1   A Silverlight World Clock gadget hosted in the Sidebar displays time and location.

Background—Microsoft Silverlight

Microsoft Silverlight helps create a rich interactive application (RIA). An RIA is an application that is hosted in a web browser but behaves like a desktop application.

Here are some of the popular features of Silverlight applications with respect to Sidebar gadget development:

- Includes compelling 2D vector graphics and animation

- Supports Ajax for responsive Internet applications

- Streams video/audio and scales video quality from mobile device to 720 progressive HDTV video modes

> **NOTE**
>
> To run a Silverlight application you need to install a browser plug-in of approximately 4MB. The example in this chapter uses Silverlight 1.0, which can be downloaded from http://www.microsoft.com/silverlight/downloads.aspx.

Origin of Silverlight

Silverlight, also known as WPF/E (Windows Presentation Foundation/Everywhere), is a subset of the Windows Presentation Foundation (WPF). It's a plug-in meant for web browsers. WPF is a part of the .NET Framework 3.0 application programming interface (API), as illustrated in Figure 12.2. Note that although .NET 3.0 comes pre-installed with Windows Vista, it can also be installed in Windows XP.

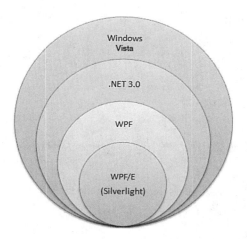

FIGURE 12.2   Overview of Silverlight and related technologies.

WPF takes advantage of advanced 3D graphics capabilities in modern machines, which are not available in Silverlight. The Aero interface provides transparent, glass-like window borders.

Figure 12.3 shows a bird's eye view of the programming model of a Silverlight application in a web page.

A Silverlight application is embedded in a web page. The embedded object takes input from an XAML file and dynamically creates the application's user interface. The XAML file contains all the information about the vector, graphics, animations, and links to audio, video, and image resources.

The core functionality of the interaction with the user and data comes from the code-behind file, which can be written in JavaScript, a .NET language such as C# or Visual Basic, or can come from an advanced programming language such as IronPython.

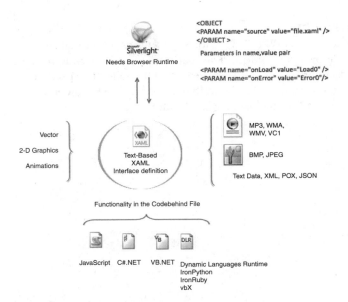

FIGURE 12.3   The Microsoft Silverlight programming model is a plug-in-based object model and supports multiple programming languages.

Features and Technology

To implement Silverlight technology in the Sidebar, it's necessary to include a number of Silverlight-specific files in the gadget. Script code is also needed to interact with the Silverlight object and the XAML file that dynamically creates the Silverlight object's interface. The World Clock Gadget displays the time for multiple locales and is based on an XAML file (see Figure 12.4).

FIGURE 12.4   A Silverlight clock displaying the time for Frankfurt, Germany.

As illustrated in Figure 12.5, the following technology is used for the gadget:

- Script for creating the Silverlight object and interaction

- Microsoft Silverlight for the gadget

- XAML file for vector graphics and animation

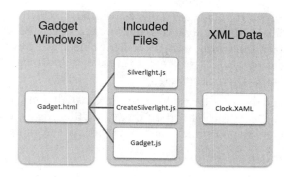

FIGURE 12.5   Embedding a Silverlight object in an HTML page requires including a bunch of Silverlight-specific JavaScript files and a core XAML file.

Let's see how these technologies are implemented in the gadget, starting with the gadget window, which holds the Silverlight object.

JavaScript for Creating the Silverlight Object

The gadget's main window includes a DIV element that embeds the Silverlight object and the `Silverlight.js CreateSilverlight.js`, and `code.js` and script files. The following shows the HTML code of the gadget window, the `gadget.html` file that embeds the Silverlight object.

```html
<html xmlns="http://www.w3.org/1999/xhtml">
<head>
    <title>Silverlight World Clock</title>
    <script type="text/javascript" src="Silverlight.js"></script>
    <script type="text/javascript" src="CreateSilverlight.js">
    </script>
    <script type="text/javascript" src="code.js"></script>
    <style type="text/css">
        .silverlightHost {
            height: 130px;
            width: 126px;
        }
    </style>
</head>
<body>
    <div id="SilverlightControlHost" class="silverlightHost">
        <script type="text/javascript">
            createSilverlight();
        </script>
    </div>
</body>
</html>
```

Note the DIV element with the ID `SilverlightControlHost`, which, as the name suggests, hosts the Silverlight object and the style class `silverlightHost`. The `silverlightHost` style class sets the height and width of the Silverlight object. The Silverlight element also includes a script function call to create `createSilverlight()`, which is defined in the included script file `CreateSilverlight.js`.

`CreateSilverlight.js` does what it says: It takes an XAML file (`Clock.XAML`) as a parameter and, based on the interface defined on the XAML file, creates a Silverlight object. Here is the `createSilverlight()` function to show the inner workings of the gadget:

```
function createSilverlight()
{
    Silverlight.createObjectEx
    (
        {
        source: "code/Silverlightclock.xaml",
        parentElement: document.getElementById("SilverlightControlHost"),
        id: "SilverlightControl",
        properties: {
                width: "130",
                height: "126",
                isWindowless: "true",
                background:'#00000000',
                version: "1.0"
        },
        events: { onLoad: handleLoad }
    }
    );
}
```

The code takes the element `SilverlightControlHost` from the parent document (`gadget.html`) and creates a `SilverlightControl` with the properties defined. Also note the event `handleLoad`, which is added to the Silverlight object that will be triggered when the `Silverlight` object is loaded.

Microsoft Silverlight

You have seen the Silverlight programming model for a web page. The programming model used for the gadget is slightly different in the way that a Sidebar gadget allows only scripting languages. Higher-level programming languages are not allowed in a Sidebar gadget.

Figure 12.6 shows a version of the Silverlight model that applies to gadget development.

The plug-in is embedded in the gadget's main window file, `gadget.html`. Three script files are used for creating and interacting with the data.

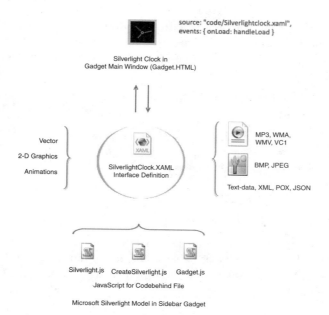

FIGURE 12.6 Using the Silverlight programming model in a Sidebar gadget is similar to embedding Silverlight in a web page, but it does not allow high-level programming languages.

The main logic resides in `Gadget.js` (as in the framework), which directly manipulates data. `Silverlight.js` is a Microsoft-supplied JavaScript file for creating an instance of the object. `CreateSilverlight.js` is where the Silverlight object is initialized with the XAML file and other required properties.

Extensible Application Markup Language

Extensible Application Markup Language is an-XML based language to describe an application's user interface. The core of Silverlight is an XAML file that is used to create compelling graphics, 2D vector images, and animations (see Figure 12.7).

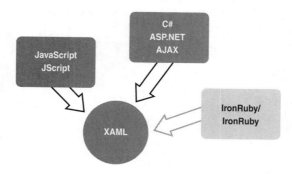

FIGURE 12.7 The XAML file is XML and can be manipulated using any supported programming language.

Programming languages that can be used with Microsoft Silverlight include JavaScript, .NET languages, and advanced dynamic languages. For the Sidebar gadget, only JavaScript is needed to create and interact with a Silverlight application. Let's see a sample XAML file.

Hello World XAML File   To create the XAML file, open Windows Notepad and type the following:

```
<Page xmlns="http://schemas.microsoft.com/winfx/2006/xaml/presentation"
➥ xmlns:sys="clr-namespace:System;assembly=mscorlib" xmlns:x=
➥"http://schemas.microsoft.com/winfx/2006/xaml" >
  <Grid>
    <TextBlock Text="Hello World" />
  </Grid>
</Page>
```

When you are finished, save the file as `HelloWorld.xaml`. While saving the file, make sure you select All Files (*.*) in the Save as Type drop-down. To view the XAML file, open the file in Internet Explorer.

> **TIP**
>
> You can also use `XAMLPAD.exe` to create and edit XAML files. XAMLPad can be downloaded from http://msdn2.microsoft.com/en-us/library/ms742398.aspx.

Microsoft Expression Studio is one of the main tools you can use to create an XAML file. You can also create the Silverlight application itself by using Microsoft Visual Studio 2008. Other tools that can be useful for creating XAML are XAMLPad and Aurora XAML Editor.

Design Considerations

The focus of the chapter is to implement the Silverlight technology. And because the gadget is a utility gadget, the design should be simple and intuitive. The design considerations involve

- Theme and images used in the gadget
- Layout of the gadget
- Usability of the gadget

Theme and Images

The theme of a World Clock Gadget needs to be simple and intuitive (see Figure 12.8). Because the animation of the clock is taken care by the XAML file, you have to create images for the background of the clock, the icon image, and the drag image.

FIGURE 12.8   The simple and intuitive clock icon for the Silverlight gadget.

Figure 12.9 shows some of the images used in the gadget to simulate the Silverlight and Clock theme.

icon.png   drag.png

background.png

FIGURE 12.9   Different images used in the gadget with the clock theme.

Layout of the Gadget

The gadget's framework is similar to our existing gadget framework. There are three new files: Silverlight.js, CreateSilverlight.js and SilverlightClock.XAML (see Figure 12.10). These files are specifically included for creating and embedding a Silverlight object. Other file structure and layout aspects of this gadget are similar to those of the existing framework.

FIGURE 12.10   The gadget's layout has additional files related to Silverlight.

The gadget manifest changes to accommodate information specific to the Silverlight World Clock Gadget. In particular, the name and description are among the changes that need to be implemented. The names of icons and the drag image, however, remain the same. The only other items that need to be changed are the actual images in the image folder.

```xml
<?xml version="1.0" encoding="utf-8" ?>
<gadget>
  <name>Silverlight Clock</name>
  <namespace>Innovate.Gadgets</namespace>
  <version>1.0</version>
  <author name="Rajesh Lal">
    <logo src="images/logo.png" />
    <info url="www.innovatewithgadgets.com" />
  </author>
  <copyright>Copyright&#169; 2007</copyright>
  <description>Shiny Silverlight Clock</description>
  <icons>
    <icon width="70" height="80" src="images/icon.png" />
  </icons>
  <hosts>
    <host name="sidebar">
      <base type="HTML" apiVersion="1.0.0" src="gadget.html" />
      <permissions>Full</permissions>
      <platform minPlatformVersion="1.0" />
      <defaultImage src="images/drag.png"/>
    </host>
  </hosts>
</gadget>
```

Usability of the Gadget

The Silverlight World Clock is meant to keep time for multiple locales. The users can add different cities with their local time shown in the Settings page. By clicking on the name of the city in the gadget, the users can traverse from one time zone location to another.

For example, Figure 12.11 shows four instances of the Silverlight World Clock Gadget for the different time zones of Frankfurt, San Diego, New York, and Mumbai.

FIGURE 12.11   The World Clock Gadget shows multiple time zones with the name of the city.

Clicking on the name of a city sets the clock to the that city, with its different time zone stored in the memory.

Developing the Gadget

So far you've seen the gadget's file structure and its layout. Its design element and usability have also been addressed. This section discusses the core functionality and the development of the gadget. It starts with the gadget framework and then customizes it according to its unique requirements.

The development of the gadget can be divided into three parts:

- Integrating the existing framework

- Creating the XAML file

- Integrating the Silverlight clock logic

Integrating the Existing Framework

In the existing framework, two options have been added: a text box for adding a new time and location and buttons to add a new city and reset to defaults (see Figure 12.12).

FIGURE 12.12   The Settings page of the gadget accommodates the addition of a new city and its time.

When a new location is added, the time difference of the new location is saved with respect to the current time of the computer. This difference is used to calculate the current time of that location in the future.

Four arrays store the values in the main gadget:

```
var ClockLocations= new Array();
var ClockValuesHourDiff= new Array();
var ClockValuesMinDiff= new Array();
var ClockValuesSecDiff= new Array();
```

When the user adds a new locale, the current time parameters are subtracted from the new time and stored in the array. Here is the code for adding a new locale with new time parameters:

```
var now = new Date();
var clockhours = now.getHours();
var clockminutes = now.getMinutes()
var clockseconds = now.getSeconds();

var hourPart= Mid(document.getElementById("txtTimeValue").value,0,2);
var minutePart= Mid(document.getElementById("txtTimeValue").value,3,2);
var secondPart= Mid(document.getElementById("txtTimeValue").value,6,2);

ClockLocations.push(timeLocation);
ClockValuesHourDiff.push(hourPart-clockhours);
ClockValuesMinDiff.push(minutePart-clockminutes);
ClockValuesSecDiff.push(secondPart-clockseconds);
```

When the user resets items in the Settings page, the DefaultTime function is called from the Settings page, and it resets the array to only one location, MyHome, -as illustrated here:

```
System.Gadget.document.parentWindow.DefaultTimes();
Function DefaultTimes() {
ClockLocations.length=0;
ClockValuesHourDiff.length=0;
ClockValuesMinDiff.length=0;
ClockValuesSecDiff.length=0;

var now = new Date();
    ClockLocations[0] = "My Home";
    ClockValuesHourDiff[0] = now.getHours();
    ClockValuesMinDiff[0] = now.getMinutes() ;
    ClockValuesSecDiff[0] = now.getSeconds();
}
```

As you can see in the code, the MyHome location will always have the current time from the computer. The next thing to tackle is the creation of the XAML file.

The XAML File

The XAML file, SilverlightClock.XAML, is the core of the user interface. It has a root element, Canvas, which hosts all the vector graphics and animation of the elements in the application. Figure 12.13 shows an overview of the XAML file that is used in the World Clock Gadget.

```
<Canvas
  xmlns="http://schemas.microsoft.com/winfx/2006/xaml/presentation"
  xmlns:x="http://schemas.microsoft.com/winfx/2006/xaml"
  Width="130" Height="126"  Background="transparent" >
    <!-- Canvas Properties ( brush, colors etc) -->
  <Canvas.OpacityMask>...>
    <!-- Interaction of elements (rotation of clock hands) -->
  <Canvas.Triggers>...>
    <!-- Element (Central Clock Circle /dot) -->
  <Ellipse ...>
    <!-- Element (Text block for Location "My Home") -->
  <TextBlock ...>
    <!-- Element (Hours hand)-->
  <Path ...>
    <!-- Element (Minutes hand)-->
  <Path ...>
    <!-- Element (Seconds hand)-->
  <Path ...>
</Canvas>
```

FIGURE 12.13   An XAML file is a formatted XML file.

Elements of the SilverlightClock.XAML File

The XAML file for the World Clock Gadget includes some elements for the clock's hands and code for their animation. Note that there are no images in the XAML file. The complete clock animation is a vector image created dynamically based on the coordinates supplied in the XAML file.

Canvas.Triggers contains the elements that are animated. Ellipse, TextBlock, Path, and other items are elements of the user interface. The Path elements are used for the clock hands, which are animated. There are three clock hands with the names hourAnimation, minuteAnimation, and secondAnimation, as shown in the next section. The next section discusses the XAML code for the animation.

The Animation

The clock has animation for three hands. The rotation of the clock hands requires defining the element and setting up the environment for the animation. The following code shows the definition of the hours hand element:

```
<!-- Element (Hours hand)-->
  <Path x:Name="HourHand" Stretch="Fill" Stroke="#FF008000"
    StrokeThickness="3" Width="33.413" Height="21.259"
        Canvas.Left="23.721"
        Canvas.Top="70.121"
        Data="M252,242 L298,183"
        RenderTransformOrigin="1.287,-0.266" >
    <Path.RenderTransform>
      <RotateTransform Angle="180" x:Name="hourHandTransform"/>
    </Path.RenderTransform>
  </Path>
```

The hours hand element is defined as a <Path> with name HourHand. You will also notice the attributes such as width and height of the hour hand, stroke for color, and

Canvas.Left and Canvas.Top for the location of the hand. Other attributes are used to render the hand on the Silverlight object. The tag Path.RenderTransform identifies the name of the actual animation hourHandTransform, which is defined in the Canvas.Triggers portion as shown next.

The animation of the elements in the XAML file is handled by the Canvas.Trigger element in the XAML file:

```
<Canvas.Triggers>
    <EventTrigger RoutedEvent="Canvas.Loaded">
      <BeginStoryboard>
        <Storyboard>
          <!-- This animation targets the hour hand transform -->
          <DoubleAnimation x:Name="hourAnimation"
            Storyboard.TargetName="hourHandTransform"
            Storyboard.TargetProperty="Angle" From="180" To="540"
            Duration="12:0:0" RepeatBehavior="Forever"/>
          <!-- This animation targets the minute hand transform -->
          <DoubleAnimation x:Name="minuteAnimation"
            Storyboard.TargetName="minuteHandTransform"
            Storyboard.TargetProperty="Angle" From="180" To="540"
            Duration="1:0:0" RepeatBehavior="Forever"/>
          <!-- This animation targets the second hand transform  -->
          <DoubleAnimation x:Name="secondAnimation"
            Storyboard.TargetName="secondHandTransform"
            Storyboard.TargetProperty="Angle" From="180" To="540"
            Duration="0:1:0" RepeatBehavior="Forever"/>
        </Storyboard>
      </BeginStoryboard>
    </EventTrigger>
  </Canvas.Triggers>
```

The first part of the Triggers code defines the animation for the hour hand, which is defined as hourAnimation. It has the TargetName property set to hourHandTransform. The angle property has a value from 180 to 540, which signifies a full 360° rotation in a clockwise direction.

As you might have noticed, the animation code needs to be inside the storyboard element in a XAML file. This is by design.

The second part of the code is the duration of the animation for the hour hand, Duration="12:0:0", which signifies that in 12 hours the hour hand will make a complete rotation from 180° to 540°. Similarly, the minute hand duration is Duration="1:0:0", which means the minute hand will complete a rotation in one hour. And for the Seconds hand we have Duration="0:1:0", which means the rotation has to be completed every minute.

Silverlight Clock Logic

The clock logic of the gadget can be described in the following parts:

- The XAML file creates an animated clock.

- The gadget code sets the hour, minute, and second hands to specific angles based on the selected local time.

- Gadget settings enable the user to add multiple locations and times, which are stored in an array in memory.

- When the user clicks on the location, the next array item is displayed and the clock is adjusted to the time for that local region

XAML File Creates the Clock

In Figure 12.14, the left side shows the clock with animation that is created by the XAML file; the right side is a transparent image that becomes the background of the gadget and the host window of the clock.

FIGURE 12.14   The clock hands are created dynamically by the XAML file (left) and the background image (right) of the clock.

The XAML file contains the image in the vector file along with the animation information. Note that the XAML file does not contain any logic that allows it to interact with the outside world. Without the code file, the XAML file would have the three clock hands rotating forever, based on the values in the animation.

Next we implement the hour, minute, and second hands:

```
<!-- Element (Hours hand)-->
<Path x:Name="HourHand" Stretch="Fill" Stroke="#FF008000"
        StrokeThickness="3" Width="33.413" Height="21.259"
        Canvas.Left="23.721" Canvas.Top="70.121"
        Data="M252,242 L298,183"
        RenderTransformOrigin="1.287,-0.266" >
    <Path.RenderTransform>
      <RotateTransform Angle="180" x:Name="hourHandTransform"/>
    </Path.RenderTransform>
</Path>
```

```
<!-- Element (Minutes hand)-->
<Path x:Name="MinuteHand" Stretch="Fill" Stroke="#FF1B4AEE"
        StrokeThickness="2" Width="30.042" Height="25.321"
          Canvas.Left="28.2" Canvas.Top="72.352"
        Data="M252,242 L298,183"
        RenderTransformOrigin="1.287,-0.266" >
    <Path.RenderTransform>
      <RotateTransform Angle="180" x:Name="minuteHandTransform"/>
    </Path.RenderTransform>
</Path>

<!-- Element (Seconds hand)-->
<Path x:Name="SecondHand" Stretch="Fill" Stroke="#FFFF0000"
        StrokeThickness="1" Width="27.339" Height="22.207"
        Canvas.Left="31.445" Canvas.Top="71.415"
        Data="M252,242 L298,183"
        RenderTransformOrigin="1.287,-0.266">
    <Path.RenderTransform>
      <RotateTransform Angle="180" x:Name="secondHandTransform"/>
    </Path.RenderTransform>
</Path>
```

The code generates the vector images for the hour, minute, and second hands. Note that each hand is related to a transformation that is defined in the Canvas.Triggers section. When the gadget is loaded, the XAML file reads the defining information (width, height, top, left, data, and so on) and creates the clock for the first time. Note that these attributes merely define the user interface and the animation of the clock. The XAML file does not include the logic to set the time for a particular region. This logic is added in the script that is called when the gadget is loaded for the first time.

Gadget Code Sets the Time

The gadget, when first loaded, calls the onload event (handleLoad) of the Silverlight object, which is defined in the CreateSilverlight code file:

```
function createSilverlight()
{
    Silverlight.createObjectEx
    (
        {
        source: "code/Silverlightclock.xaml",
        parentElement: document.getElementById("SilverlightControlHost"),
        id: "SilverlightControl",
        properties: {
                width: "130",
                height: "126",
                isWindowless: "true",
```

```
                           background:'#00000000',
                   version: "1.0"
               },
               events: { onLoad: handleLoad }
           }
       );
   }
```

The HandleLoad Function   When the Silverlight object is loaded, it calls the handleLoad function in the gadget code:

```
function handleLoad(control, userContext, rootElement)
{
    SilverlightControl = control;
    theTextBlock = SilverlightControl.content.findName("location");
    theTextBlock.addEventListener("MouseLeftButtonDown", "txtLClicked");
    setClock(0);
}
```

The handleLoad function does two things:

- Adds an event to capture mouse clicks in the location text area
- Sets the clock for the current system time

The SetClock Function   Here is the part of the SetClock function to set the clock hands to the current time:

```
function setClock(clockValue) {
var now = new Date();
var hourAnimation = SilverlightControl.content.findName("hourAnimation");
var minuteAnimation = SilverlightControl.content.findName("minuteAnimation");
var secondAnimation = SilverlightControl.content.findName("secondAnimation");

// now is the current time in JavaScript
clockhours = now.getHours();
clockminutes = now.getMinutes();
clockseconds = now.getSeconds();
// Find the appropriate angle (in degrees) for the hour hand
// based on the current time.
if (hourAnimation)
        {
            angle = (clockhours/12)*360 + clockminutes/2
            angle += 116.5;
          hourAnimation.from = angle.toString();
            hourAnimation.to = (angle + 360).toString();
        }
```

```
if (minuteAnimation)
            {
                angle = (clockminutes / 60) * 360;
                angle += 127;
                minuteAnimation.from = angle.toString();
                minuteAnimation.to = (angle + 360).toString();
            }
if (secondAnimation)
            {
                angle = (clockseconds / 60) * 360;
                angle += 127;
                secondAnimation.from = angle.toString();
                secondAnimation.to = (angle + 360).toString();
            }
}
```

The function sets the time, based on the current time and the existing value of the hour, minute, and second hands. The values 116.5, 127, and 127 are added to the current hour, minute, and second settings to calculate the current time. This uses the JavaScript built-in Date function to get the current time.

```
var now = new Date();
// now is the current time in JavaScript
clockhours = now.getHours();
clockminutes = now.getMinutes();
clockseconds = now.getSeconds();
```

Based on the values, the angle is calculated and then the hour, minute, and second hands are set to the corresponding angles.

Multiple Locales

The gadget uses an array to save multiple locales along with the time difference of the locales with respect to the system time. Here is how it is managed in the background (using the sample data):

```
function DefaultTimesAdd()
{
ClockLocations.length=0;
ClockValuesHourDiff.length=0;
ClockValuesMinDiff.length=0;
ClockValuesSecDiff.length=0;

var now = new Date();
    var GMTminus8 = 0;
    // I have taken GMT - 8 as the current home
    // If your location is GMT minus 6   initialze the value of
    // GMTminus8   in the the above line as 2
```

```
// the new value will be "var GMTminus8 = 2";
ClockLocations[0] = "San Diego";
ClockValuesHourDiff[0] = GMTminus8;
ClockValuesMinDiff[0] = 0 ;
ClockValuesSecDiff[0] = 0;
ClockLocations[1] = "New York";
ClockValuesHourDiff[1] = GMTminus8 + 3 ;
ClockValuesMinDiff[1] = 0;
ClockValuesSecDiff[1] = 0;

ClockLocations[2] = "Mumbai";
ClockValuesHourDiff[2] = GMTminus8 -1;
ClockValuesMinDiff[2] = 30;
ClockValuesSecDiff[2] = 0;

ClockLocations[3] = "Frankfurt";
ClockValuesHourDiff[3] = GMTminus8-3;
ClockValuesMinDiff[3] = 2;
ClockValuesSecDiff[3] = 0;
}
```

This is based on sample data. If you want to add a time and location, add the hour, minute, and second difference from the current time in the array. If the current time is for San Diego, the time difference for New York will be hour 3, minutes 0, seconds 0.

User Clicks on the Next Locale

The mouse click event is added in the following text block:

```
theTextBlock.addEventListener("MouseLeftButtonDown", "txtLClicked");
```

The txtLClicked method changes the text to the next locale:

```
function txtLClicked(sender, args)
{
    changeLocation(1);
    theTextBlock.Text = ClockLocations[ClockCurrentId];
}
```

You can implement the changeLocation function as follows:

```
function changeLocation(val)
{
    ClockCurrentId = ClockCurrentId + val;
    if (ClockCurrentId == -1)
    {
```

```
ClockCurrentId =ClockLocations.length -1;
}

if (ClockCurrentId == ClockLocations.length)
{
ClockCurrentId = 0;
}
setClock(1)
}
```

The setClock function updates the clock time, depending on whether the current system time can be used or the system time needs to be adjusted for the locale time.

```
if (clockValue==0)          // 0 = take the value of the system clock
 {                           // now is the current time in JavaScript
        clockhours = now.getHours();
        clockminutes = now.getMinutes();
        clockseconds = now.getSeconds();
 }
 else
 {
   clockhours = now.getHours() + ClockValuesHourDiff[ClockCurrentId];
   clockminutes =now.getMinutes() +ClockValuesMinDiff[ClockCurrentId];
   clockseconds  = now.getSeconds() + ClockValuesSecDiff[ClockCurrentId];
 }
```

Creating a Sidebar Gadget Using Microsoft Popfly

Microsoft Popfly is a website that allows users to create online mashups, web pages, widgets, and even Vista Sidebar gadgets using Microsoft Silverlight and the set of online tools provided.

> **NOTE**
>
> *Mashups* are web modules that combine the functionality of two or more websites or services.

It provides interactive tools to drag and drop services provided by multiple vendors and web applications, and creates innovative web modules. Popfly requires users to log in with their Windows Live ID.

Website Comparison Gadget

This section shows the step-by-step process of creating a gadget for website comparison using Microsoft Popfly. Imagine you want to know the popularity of three websites in

Windows Live Search. The criteria is based on the number of search results in which each of the following websites appears in Live Search (www.Live.com):

- www.innovatewithgadgets.com

- www.widgets-gadgets.com

- www.trickofmind.com

- www.csharptricks.com

For example if you search for "www.innovatewithgadgets.com" and get 14 results for it, as well as 15 for www.widgets-gadgets.com, 11 for www.trickofmind.com, and 19 for www.csharptricks.com, you will assume that csharptricks.com is the most popular of all. The second part is the display of the gadget in the form of a bar graph that appears after you get the values of the numbers of search results for each of the websites (see Figure 12.15).

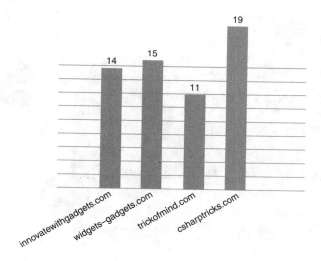

FIGURE 12.15   The bar graph reflects the number of results in Live Search for each website.

Creating a Mashup Using Microsoft Popfly

This section looks at how you can use Microsoft Popfly to create a mashup. Microsoft Popfly has multiple modules, also called *blocks*, which can be used to create mashups and then convert them into Sidebar gadgets. In this case the mashup being built is one that uses Live.com and bar graph modules.

The process is twofold, first creating the mashup and then porting it to the Vista Sidebar. For this scenario the following are needed:

- Four Live.com search modules, one for each website

- One bar graph module, which takes the output of the search modules and displays it all in a graph

After you log in to Microsoft Popfly, follow the step-by-step process:

1. Find the item labeled Live Search in the list on the left under the Tools category.

2. Drag the Live Search block into the middle of the screen, which is also called as the *design surface*. Click on the wrench beside the block to zoom in. Change the operations to `totalNumberOfResults` and the query value to the first website, www.innovatewithgadgets.com, as shown in Figure 12.16.

FIGURE 12.16   The Live Search module for the website www.innovatewithgadgets.com.

3. Click on the wrench to get back to the design surface.

4. Repeat step 1 through step 3 for each of the three remaining websites, www.widgets-gadgets.com, www.trickofmind.com, and www.csharptricks.com.

5. Find the item labeled Bar Graph in the list on the left, under the Display category.

6. Drag the Bar Graph block into the middle of the screen.

7. Click on one of the Search blocks and then click the Bar Graph block. This joins the Search block with the Bar Graph block. Do this for each of the Search blocks. The updated design surface should look like Figure 12.17.

FIGURE 12.17   Three Live Search blocks connected with the Bar Graph block.

8. Click on the wrench beside the Bar Graph block to zoom in and then click the Switch to an Advanced View button. Replace the JavaScript code in the editor with the following text:

```
barGraph.__reserved.pendingCalls = 1;
var result = barGraph.addBar(data["Live Search"], "blue", "http://www.
➥innovatewithgadgets.com", "innovatewithgadgets.com");
var result2 = barGraph.addBar(data["Live Search (2)"], "Red", "http://www.
➥widgets-gadgets.com", "widgets-gadgets.com");
var result3 = barGraph.addBar(data["Live Search (3)"], "Green", "http://www.
➥trickofmind.com", "trickofmind.com");
var result4 = barGraph.addBar(data["Live Search (4)"], "Yellow", "http://www.
➥csharptricks.com", "csharptricks.com");
```

The code tells the Bar Graph block to take the input from each of the Live Search blocks and create a bar for them.

9. Click on the wrench to zoom out.

10. Click on the Preview link to see the mashup in action. You will see an image similar to Figure 12.15, shown earlier in this chapter.

Porting a Mashup to Vista Sidebar as a Gadget

After you are satisfied with the mashup, click on the Save link at the top-right corner to save it to My Projects. In My Projects, you will see an option to share the mashup with others. A shared mashup has an option to be added as a Sidebar gadget (see Figure 12.18).

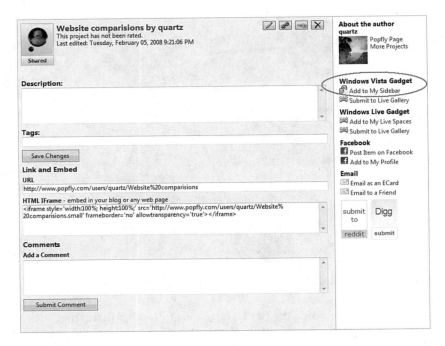

FIGURE 12.18   To port a mashup to the Vista Sidebar, first share the gadget.

Feel free to experiment with different websites in this mashup, even creating mashups using different available blocks. Figure 12.19 shows the Sidebar gadget just created with Microsoft Popfly.

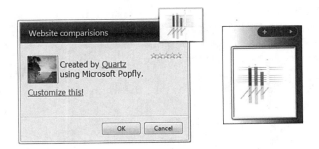

FIGURE 12.19   Microsoft Popfly can be used to create innovative Sidebar gadgets in minutes.

Where to Go from Here

This chapter showed you how to use Silverlight to create a gadget from scratch as well as how to use online tools such as Microsoft Popfly to create gadgets in minutes. The important point is not the tool, but the innovation platform that Sidebar gadgets provide. With a Website Comparison Sidebar Gadget I can track the popularity of four websites without even typing a word and see instant results.

Looking back to previous chapters, if I need to watch the top video in YouTube, the Media Gadget can make life much easier, and if you work on Visual Studio, the Recent Project Gadget is an indispensable tool. Finally, the MyBlog Gadget can consolidate all the feeds I subscribe to in a ready-to-read format.

As you go forward in creating your own gadgets, use the gadget examples found in this book as a base. These are not the only way to create gadgets, to be sure, but they do provide a starting point as useful tools for your future gadget development.

12

PART IV

Appendixes

IN THIS PART

Tips and Tricks

"These are much deeper waters than I had thought."

—Sherlock Holmes ("The Reigate Puzzle")

Automatic Update and User Tracking

One critical, post-deployment piece of functionality that virtually all gadgets need is the capability to automatically update the gadget. What is required is the capability to make sure that the user is notified and updated when a new or updated version of the gadget is available. This functionality is not available in the Gadget API, so we have to create our own methodology for updating a gadget.

Gadgets don't collect user emails, you can't send a newsletter to notify all a gadget's users, nor do they have a help section that might provide an easier path for users to check for updates. And very often, gadgets don't have a full-fledged website where a user can come back to check for the latest version. To avoid having multiple versions of the gadget floating around, it's important to add this functionality in the gadget itself. The gadget should contain the code necessary for it to check for updates at regular intervals.

Checking for a New Version of the Gadget

There are three considerations with regard to gadget updates:

- Putting the gadget version information online

- Adding the code in the gadget to check the current version against any available newer version of the gadget

- Notify the user if a new version is available

Putting the Gadget Version Information Online

Remember that the gadget.xml file contains the gadget's version information; one way to retrieve the newer version of the gadget is to host this file online. If you have updated your gadget, you would like to update the version field in the gadget's manifest file. The original gadget.xml, which is on the user's machine, might have the gadget version as 1.0 as shown here:

```
<version>1.0</version>
```

The newer gadget, instead, contains the version information as 1.1 as well as a new info url, www.innovatewithgadgets.com/newgadget, which is the download URL for the newer gadget. The updated gadget.xml file follows. Please note the version and the info url.

```
<?xml version="1.0" encoding="utf-8" ?>
<gadget>
  <name>- Innovate -</name>
  <namespace>Innovate.Gadgets</namespace>
  <version>1.1</version>
  <author name="Rajesh Lal">
    <logo src="images/logo.png" />
    <info url="www.innovatewithgadgets.com/newgadget" />
  </author>
  <copyright>Copyright&#169; 2007-2008</copyright>
  <description>Sidebar Gadget description</description>
  <icons>
    <icon width="70" height="80" src="images/icon.png" />
  </icons>
  <hosts>
    <host name="sidebar">
      <base type="HTML" apiVersion="1.0.0" src="gadget.html" />
      <permissions>Full</permissions>
      <platform minPlatformVersion="1.0" />
      <defaultImage src="images/drag.png"/>
    </host>
  </hosts>
</gadget>
```

You then have to host the updated `gadget.xml` file online so that it can be compared in the gadget code against the existing version. The path of the newer gadget is stored in the `info url` field in `gadget.xml`. This URL, as you will see later, is retrieved to notify the user about the new gadget location.

Inserting Code to Check the Version

The next step is to add the functionality in the gadget to compare the existing gadget version with the newer version available online. A function, `checkForUpdate()`, to do so is added in the `utility.js` file included with this book. You can access the functions by adding the following to the `gadget.html` file:

```
<script src="code/utility.js" type="text/javascript"></script>
```

In the `utility.js` file, you can find four global variables to help with update management:

```
// for updating the gadget
var updateAvailable =false;
var globalUpdateMessage ="Go to gadget website";
var globalUpdateURL ="http://innovatewithgadgets.com";
var globalUpdateGadgetXML ="http://mywebsite.com/Gadget.xml";
// Change mywebsite.com value in globalUpdateGadgetXML variable to the
// gadget.xml file in your website
```

The `updateAvailable` variable is set to a value of `true` if the version of the gadget online is newer than the version of the existing gadget. The variable, `globalUpdateURL`, stores the URL where the user can go to download the new gadget. This variable is updated from the newer version of the `gadget.xml` file from the `info url` field. Finally, the `globalUpdateGadgetXML` variable holds the path of the newest version of the `gadget.xml` file.

Note that the `globalUpdateGadgetXML` variable is declared in the gadget's `utility.js` file and is packed with the first version of the gadget, so when you come up with a new version of the gadget, your existing user base already has a gadget with an `update url` pointing to this fixed location (http://mywebsite.com/gadget.xml in the earlier code). Because the URL is coded into the gadget, you won't be able to change it and you have to make sure to upload the new `gadget.xml` file in that location only.

Now it's time to implement the `checkForUpdate` function:

```
// for updating the gadget
// include Utility.js in gadget.html
function checkForUpdate()
{
    var xmlDoc = new ActiveXObject("Microsoft.XMLDOM");
    xmlDoc.async = false;
    xmlDoc.load(globalUpdateGadgetXML);
    var gadget = xmlDoc.selectNodes("gadget");
    var Results = gadget[0].childNodes[2].text;
```

```
var InfoURL = gadget[0].childNodes[3].childNodes[1].getAttribute("url");
xmlDoc=null;
 if (Results > System.Gadget.version)
 {
   if (InfoURL.indexOf("http://")==-1)
   {
    InfoURL = "http://" + InfoURL;
    // InfoURL must contain http://
   }
   globalUpdateURL=InfoURL;
   globalUpdateMessage = "An update is available,";
   globalUpdateMessage += " visit" + globalUpdateURL;\
   updateAvailable=true;
   UpdateBackground();
 }
 else
 {
  globalUpdateMessage = "Go to gadget website";
 }
}
```

The function `checkForUpdate()` uses XMLDOM to load the online `gadget.xml` file. It then parses the version and URL information:

```
var Results = gadget[0].childNodes[2].text;
```

`Results` contains the version and `InfoURL` is the update URL:

```
var InfoURL = gadget[0].childNodes[3].childNodes[1].getAttribute("url");
```

> **NOTE**
>
> Note that this approach assumes that your `gadget.xml` file is similar to the `gadget.xml` file that comes with the samples. The parent-child relations shown here gadget[0].childNodes[3]. childNodes[1].getAttribute("url"); are relative to the nodes in the `gadget.xml` file. This implementation can be further improved using advanced XML parsing methods such as XPath and so on.

The result is then compared with `System.Gadget.version`, and if it is greater, the `updateAvailable` flag is set to `true` and the `UpdateBackground` function is called. The `UpdateBackground` function, as discussed in the next section, notifies the user about the update.

Notifying the User That a Newer Version Exists

After a newer version is detected, the user needs to be notified that a newer version of the gadget exists and that the gadget can be updated. This can be done in different ways.

A visual clue such as an information icon can be used; a message can be displayed, and so forth. The important part is to convey the information to the user that a new version of the gadget is available.

One unobtrusive way to communicate that information is to change only the background image, as shown in Figure A.1.

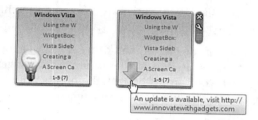

FIGURE A.1   The image on the left shows the gadget in its usual state. The image on the right shows the gadget with the background changed to display a download arrow, indicating that an update is available.

Here is the code used in this gadget for changing the background:

```
function UpdateBackground()
{
  if (System.Gadget.Settings.read("mini") ==true)
  {
    if (updateAvailable)
    {
     System.Gadget.background =
     "url(../images/UpdateAvailableSmall.png)";
     document.getElementById("mylogo").title =globalUpdateMessage;
     document.getElementById("infourl").href = globalUpdateURL;
    }
  }
  else
  {
    if (updateAvailable)
    {
    System.Gadget.background = "url(../images/UpdateAvailable.png)";
    document.getElementById("mylogo").title =globalUpdateMessage;
    document.getElementById("infourl").href = globalUpdateURL;
   }
  }
}
```

This code assumes that the UpdateAvailable.png file exists. Notice that the function also updates the tooltip and the link to the new URL.

Tracking Your Users

The next tip I am going to share with you is how to track users. By tracking I don't mean tracking user's personal information, but statistical data like how many people are using the gadget, or how users are grouped by different patterns such as demographic, usage, and so on. Before writing this book I created two gadgets and was updating them regularly. In one of the updates, I started tracking the users. I was surprised to discover that one of the gadgets had more than 10,000 users and the other one had fewer than 10. It was obvious which gadget I would concentrate on and continue supporting.

Tracking the number of users of the gadget, and other statistics about users, provides a lot of useful information that can be used to further improve the gadget. If you are displaying a web page in the gadget, you can easily track the number of visitors to the web page by using tools and widgets like the ones from sitemeter.com.

You can do two things with gadgets to track users:

- Add a tracking code in the links
- Track the XML feed used by the gadget

Using Tracking Codes

The first option is to put a tracking code in all the links to your website that the gadget makes. For example, if the gadget links to the website www.innovatewithgadgets.com, change the link to www.innovatewithgadgets.com?gadget=true. With this URL, web traffic analysis software collects information specific to that URL. You can then use that information to determine the number of visitors coming to your website through the gadget.

For gadgets that use online feeds, the best way to track users is with the use of a feed distribution network such as www.feedburner.com.

Feed Tracking with FeedBurner

FeedBurner provides an easy way to distribute your RSS/Atom feed and provides a multitude of statistics (see Figure A.2). All you need is a free account and the URL of your RSS/Atom feed. FeedBurner "burns" the feed and provides you with a new address for your RSS/Atom feed; for example, http://feeds.feedburner.com/trickofmind.

After it is set up, you can use FeedBurner's feed address in the Sidebar gadget and monitor your site statistics with FeedBurner's analysis tools.

One thing you need to consider while using FeedBurner's feed is using Microsoft XML DOM instead of AJAX (XMLHTTPRequest object) for retrieving the feed. FeedBurner uses a number of secure and nonsecure servers, which sometimes cause issues when using AJAX calls. The following section gives you more details on the two methodologies.

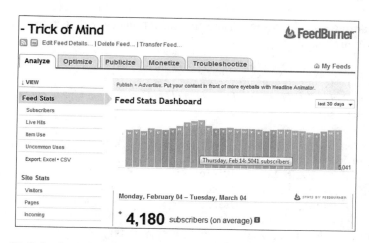

FIGURE A.2   Statistics for last 30 days of the feed for Trickofmind gadgets.

Reading XML, XHTML, RSS/Atom, HTML, Text, and JSON Data

Sidebar gadgets often need to get data from online resources. The data is often in multiple formats, such as XML, XHTML, RSS/Atom, HTML, or even just plain text. Over the course of this book I have discussed using AJAX along with the XMLHTTPRequest object to retrieve data. The XMLHTTPRequest object fits the bill most of time, but there are cases where you need additional robustness or flexibility.

Using Microsoft XML DOM is much more robust than an AJAX call. If you have hosted your feed in a content distribution network like FeedBurner, using the AJAX method can be inconsistent. For additional flexibility for manipulating feeds, consider using the Windows RSS platform. Here are the options for reading data from an online resource:

- XMLHTTPRequest object (AJAX method) for reading data in XML, XHTML, RSS/Atom, text, HTML and JSON (JavaScript Object Notation) formats

- Microsoft XMLDOM object for XML, XHTML and RSS/Atom data formats

- Windows RSS platform and Microsoft Feed Manager, specifically for RSS/Atom data

I compare each of these methods in the following sections.

The XMLHTTPRequest Object

The XMLHttpRequest (XHR) object is an API that the scripting language can use to retrieve XML and other text data from a web server. This communication can be made asynchronous and can be used for retrieving almost all kinds of data, namely XML, HTML, text, JSON, and so forth.

Here is an example of data retrieval using the XMLHTTPRequest object, which you will find in the gadget template Innovate.gadget:

```
//////////////////////////////////////////////////////////////////////////
// XML Functions TO GET  feed
//////////////////////////////////////////////////////////////////////////
function GetFeed() {
 try
 {
   error.style.visibility = "hidden";
      loading.style.visibility = "visible";
      content.style.visibility = "hidden";
    loading.style.visibility = "visible";
    loading.title  = "Connecting...";
    var rssObj  = new ActiveXObject("Microsoft.XMLHTTP");
    rssObj.open("GET", System.Gadget.Settings.read("FeedURL") + "?"
            + Math.random()*1 ,true);
    rssObj.onreadystatechange = function() {
        if (rssObj.readyState === 4) {
            if (rssObj.status === 200) {
                loading.innerText = "";
                rssXML = rssObj.responseXML;
                page = 0;
                ParseFeed();
                content.style.visibility = "visible";
                loading.style.visibility = "hidden";
                if (chkConn) { clearInterval(chkConn); }
            } else {
              var chkConn;
              content.style.visibility = "hidden";
              loading.style.visibility = "hidden";
              error.innerText = " Service not available ";
              error.style.visibility = "visible";
              chkConn = setInterval(GetFeed, 30 * 60000);
            }
        } else {
            loading.style.visibility = "visible";
            loading.title = "Connecting...";
        }
    }
    rssObj.send(null);
    }
    catch(e)
    {
            content.style.visibility = "hidden";
            loading.style.visibility = "hidden";
```

```
        error.innerText = " Service not available" ;
        error.style.visibility = "visible";
  }
}
```

This is also the best approach when you are trying to read text, HTML, or JSON data from an online resource asynchronously.

For more information on XMLHTTPRequest object, see http://msdn2.microsoft.com/en-us/library/ms535874(VS.85).aspx.

Microsoft XML DOM

The XML DOM (Document Object Model) is a standard object model for manipulating XML via an API. It is useful for accessing and manipulating XML documents, its elements, attributes, and text.

Here is an example of using XML DOM to retrieve data:

```
//////////////////////////////////////////////////////////////////////////////
// Using Microsoft.XMLDOM Functions TO GET  feed
//////////////////////////////////////////////////////////////////////////////
function getFeedXMLDOM() {
 try
 {
     error.style.visibility = "hidden";
   loading.style.visibility = "visible";
   content.style.visibility = "hidden";
   loading.style.visibility = "visible";
   loading.title  = "Connecting...";

   var xmlDocument = new ActiveXObject('Microsoft.XMLDOM');
   xmlDocument.onreadystatechange = function () {
     if (xmlDocument.readyState == 4) {
       loading.innerText = "";
          rssXML = xmlDocument;
          page = 0;
          ParseFeed();
          content.style.visibility = "visible";
          loading.style.visibility = "hidden";
        }
      else
      {
          loading.style.visibility = "visible";
          loading.title = "Connecting...";
      }
    };
```

```
  xmlDocument.load(System.Gadget.Settings.read("FeedURL"));
  }
  catch(e)
  {
      content.style.visibility = "hidden";
      loading.style.visibility = "hidden";
      error.innerText = " Service not available" ;
      error.style.visibility = "visible";
  }
}
```

The major difference is in the ActiveX object used. In the AJAX method it was
`Microsoft.XMLHTTP`, and in the preceding method it's `Microsoft.XMLDOM`. Once you
retrieve the XML data, you can then parse it the same way in both the methods.

> **NOTE**
>
> `Microsoft.XMLDOM` is only meant for XML data and cannot be used for text or HTML data.

Here is an example from my personal experience. For one of my gadgets I was using the
`XMLHTTPRequest` object with XML data distributed by FeedBurner. FeedBurner has multiple
servers to manage the bandwidth. Both secure and nonsecure servers are used and the
feed is distributed over the network. This caused inconsistency in the AJAX method.
When the user count for the gadget increased to more than 10,000, I started getting
complaints from users. On numerous occasions, users were getting unspecified errors. I
changed the `XMLHTTPRequest` object to `XMLDOM` and since then, I've never had any problems. Right now the same gadget has more than 25,000 users.

For more information and a beginner's guide on XML DOM visit
http://msdn2.microsoft.com/en-us/library/aa468547.aspx

Windows RSS Platform & Microsoft Feed Manager

One of the great additions in Windows Vista and IE 7 is the improvement in the
Windows RSS platform. The Windows RSS platform enables applications to access and
manipulate RSS feeds. It exposes several ActiveX objects and APIs that can be used in a
gadget. Here is the list of objects that can be used to retrieve online feeds:

- The `Feed` object manipulates a single RSS feed.

- The `FeedFolder` object exposes methods to manipulate the Common Feed List
  folder hierarchy and properties of a feed folder.

- The `FeedItem` object has methods and properties for a single item in an RSS feed.

- The `FeedManager` object provides methods to access the Common Feed List, which
  is a hierarchy of RSS feeds to which the user is subscribed.

These objects can be used together for advanced feed manipulations; for example, to subscribe to new feeds, enumerate existing subscriptions, access feed properties, manage feeds into folders, normalize the XML source of a feed, and so forth. It works for all kinds of feeds and channels. The ActiveX object can be instantiated with

```
FeedManager = new ActiveXObject(Microsoft.FeedsManager);
```

If you are going to create a gadget specific for feed management, I would suggest looking through the script files of the existing `RSSFeeds.Gadget` sample that comes with Windows Vista.

For more information on feed objects visit http://msdn2.microsoft.com/en-us/library/ms684749(VS.85).aspx

Globalization and Localization

Globalization enables an application to work in different countries. There are two aspects of globalization:

- **Internationalization**—Enabling the application to be used without language or culture barriers; that is, language and culture information comes from a resource rather than having been hard-coded in the application.

- **Localization**—Translating and enabling the product for a specific locale by using the resource file to provide translations of the application text into a specific language and culture.

Let's see how gadgets support localization.

First take a look at the universal directory structure. If the file structure is in the common root as shown in Figure A.3, it can serve multiple locales without any change.

FIGURE A.3   The gadget works for all the locales but displays the same information, data, and images in each. The gadget is not tailored to specific locales.

The gadget in this figure shows only the language and culture used when the gadget was created. If you want to support the gadget for different locales, you need multiple folders inside the gadget package—one for each locale, each of them containing localized HTML, JavaScript, and image files. You can also have common files that work regardless of locale. This works because the Sidebar automatically retrieves the HTML files in the appropriate directory that is associated with the current locale setting.

Let's look at how the Sidebar checks for files inside the gadget folder.

If the current locale is fr-FR for French-France, the Sidebar looks for files and images in folders in this order until a match is found:

1. `GlobalDemo.gadget/fr-FR`

2. `GlobalDemo.gadget/fr`

3. `GlobalDemo.gadget`

So, nonlocale files and images can be put in the `GlobalDemo.gadget` folder and can be used across the gadget. Figure A.4 shows a gadget with three locales: en-US for American English, es-ES for Spanish in Spain, and fe-FR for French in France.

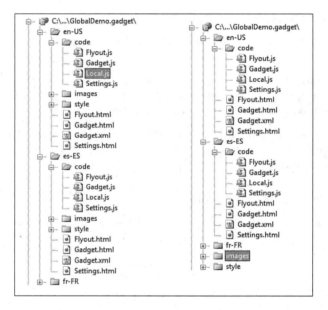

FIGURE A.4   Note the folder structure on the right side shows common images and the style folder in a non–culture-specific, root folder.

You can pack your gadget with all the locale folders, or, if you know your user's locale, you can have multiple `.gadget` packages, one for each locale. For example, on your website you may ask users what their locale is and provide them a link to the appropriate package to download.

Localized Gadget Example

Among the downloads for this book you will find a `GlobalDemo.gadget` with a structure similar to that found in Figure A.4. Using a `local.js` file is a standard way of storing locale-specific text. Here is how the `local.js` file looks for the sample gadget inside the en-US/code folder:

`local.js` for en-US locale:

```
// en-US Locale specific "sample" text
var globalTitle ="Globalization Sample";
var globalWelcomeMessage = "Welcome";
var globalDecription ="I hope you like it !";
```

Similarly, `local.js` for other locales is as follows:

es-ES `local.js` file:

```
// es-ES Locale specific "sample" text
var globalTitle ="Muestra del Globalization";
var globalWelcomeMessage = "Recepción";
var globalDecription ="¡Espero que tengas gusto de él!";
```

fr-FR `local.js` file:

```
// fr-FR-ES Locale specific "sample" text
var globalTitle ="Échantillon de globalisation";
var globalWelcomeMessage = "Bienvenue";
var globalSettingsDecription ="J'espère que vous l'aimez !";
```

This is just to show you a standard way of doing this; of course a real gadget will have a lot more data then these three global variables. The idea behind this is that wherever these variables are used, include the `local.js` file and the gadget then automatically displays locale-specific text. You can find the code to include the `.js` file in `gadget.html`:

```
<script src="code/local.js" type="text/javascript"></script>
```

Here is the gadget in action for the en-US locale:

FIGURE A.5   The `GlobalDemo.gadget` with a background image specific to the current locale: en-US.

And here is the function `SetGlobalText` that sets the text dynamically and is called during setup:

```
function Setup()
{
  SystemSetup();
```

```
  Resize();
  SetGlobalText();
}
function SetGlobalText()
{
gadgetTitle.innerText=globalTitle;
helloglobal.innerText = globalWelcomeMessage;
globaldescription.innerText = globalDecription;
}
```

The sample gadget `GlobalDemo.gadget` uses common style information while at the same time specifying different images for each locale. You can use this gadget as a starting point for your own locale-specific gadget. The next section gives a list of locale and country codes that are required for the purpose.

Locales with Country Codes

To see a list of country codes for all the locales that can be used inside a gadget, visit the "Language Codes" section of MSDN at http://msdn2.microsoft.com/en-us/library/ms533052(VS.85).aspx.

Graphic Design

We discussed in Chapter 3, "An Approach to Design," how to make the gadget look elegant and match the Windows Vista theme. You saw how a gadget background image with alpha transparency and shadow enhances the presentation. In this section, we will go a bit further and look at how to achieve those effects for an image used in a gadget. There are two ways of doing this:

- Use gadget protocols on standard PNG images for advanced photo effects such as applying transparency, shadow, thumbnail generation, icon extraction, and so on.

- Create a PNG image with alpha transparency and shadow effect using a photo-editing tool such as Adobe Photoshop or Paint.NET.

This section looks at both these techniques. Microsoft provides a set of protocols to work efficiently on images. These protocols are simple HTML tags that can be applied to elements. These protocols can add effects to images without the use of any photo-editing software.

Gadget Protocols for Image and Text

There are four gadget-specific protocols that add effects to the user interface. All these protocols start with the letter *g* and have special properties and methods that modify the gadget's appearance. They are applied in the gadget along with other HTML elements. Here is the list:

- g:background

- g:text

- g:image

- gimage

As you will see later, gimage and g:image are two separate protocols and are used for different purposes. The gimage protocol was developed later to address advanced functionalities not available in g:image.

g:background

The g:background protocol is used to define the background of the gadget. It can also contain multiple g:text and g:image elements. The methods of this protocol are listed in Table A.1.

TABLE A.1   Methods of the g:background Protocol

Method	Description
addGlow	Adds a glow effect
addImageObject	Adds a g:image element to the g:background element
addShadow	Adds a shadow effect to the g:background image
addTextObject	Adds a g:text element to the g:background element
removeObjects	Removes all g:text and g:image elements

The sample gadget (GraphicDemo.gadget) which comes with the chapter uses these methods. Here is a typical implementation of g:background in an HTML page:

```
<g:background id="imgBackground" src="images\background.png" />
```

g:text and g:image

g:text and g:image are the two gadget-specific elements used to modify text and images. They also expose methods and properties that modify the gadget's appearance and are used similar to the g:background protocol in an HTML page. The methods of the g:text and g:image elements are listed in Table A.2.

```
<g:text id="txtDemo">Demo Text</g:text>
<g:image src="..\gDemo.png" id="imgDemo" />
```

TABLE A.2   Methods of g:text and g:image

Method	Description
addGlow	Adds a glow effect
addShadow	Adds a shadow effect

gimage

The `gimage` protocol is also used to display images from a user's computer. The advantage of using `gimage` is you can provide a path to any file (not just images) and the `gimage` protocol extracts the icon of the file and displays it. This protocol is also very useful for enhanced thumbnail handling and image sizing. You can specify the image height and width as a `querystring` appended to the source path as shown in the sample code. Note that the implementation of this protocol is slightly different from other protocols, which can be used as HTML elements.

Here's an example that shows the source of the `gimage` as a JavaScript file.

```
<img id="myGImage"
src="gimage:///C:\Users\user\AppData\Local\Microsoft\Windows Sidebar\
➥Gadgets\GraphicDemo.gadget\code\Gadget.js" />
```

The following example shows the dynamic thumbnail generation for the image. Note that it passes the height width as `querystrings` :

```
var requiredHeightWidth= "?width=15&height=15";
var gImage = document.createElement("img");
gImage.src = "gimage:///" + System.Gadget.path +
            "\\images\\gdemo.png" + requiredHeightWidth;
```

Sample Gadget g:Demo

The download file set for this chapter contains the gadget `GraphicDemo.gadget` (see Figure A.6). I suggest that you play around with it to see examples of the protocols discussed in the previous sections.

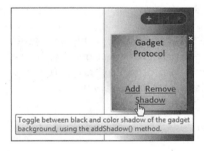

FIGURE A.6   The Gadget Protocol Demo uses g:background and the addShadow() method for a shadow effect in the gadget background.

The following is the HTML code for this gadget:

```
<body onload="Setup()">
    <g:background id="imgBackground" src="images\background.png">
    <div>
    <div id="blogtitletable">
```

```
      <table width="100%" height="20"  border="0">
          <tr align="center" valign="middle">
            <td width="1"align="right"></td>
            <td class="subtitle" id="gadgetTitle" valign ="middle" >
            Gadget Protocol</td>
            <td width="1"align="right"></td>
          </tr>
        </table>
      </div>
      <fieldset id="GDemoImage">
      </fieldset>
          <div id="protocolbar" title="">
<table width="100%" height="20"  border="0">
<tr valign="middle">
<td><a onclick="addImage()">Add</a></td>
<td><a onclick="removeElements()">Remove</a></td></tr>
<tr valign="middle">
<td><a onclick="setBackgroundShadow()">Shadow</a></td></tr></table>
      </div>
      </div>
      </g:background>
</body>
</html>
```

Note that the g:background protocol is used to specify the gadget's background image.

Here's the JavaScript code:

```
function Setup()
{
 setBackgroundShadow();
}
function setBackgroundShadow()
{
 if(backGroundShadow=="black")
 {
    imgBackground.opacity = 100;
    imgBackground.addShadow("black", 50, 50, 0, 0);
    backGroundShadow="color"
 }
  else
  {
    imgBackground.opacity = 100;
    imgBackground.addShadow("Color(255, 255, 0, 0)", 50, 25, 0, 0);
    backGroundShadow="black"
 }
}
```

The `setBackgroundShadow` method uses the opacity and the `addShadow` method of the protocol to add the shadow effect:

```
function addImage()
{
    var file= System.Gadget.path + "\\images\\gdemo.png";
    var oDemoRect = GDemoImage.getBoundingClientRect();
    var img = new Image();
    img.src = file;

    var imgDemo= imgBackground.addImageObject
    (file, oDemoRect.right - img.width - 10, oBoundingRect.top);

    imgDemo.opacity = 50;
    imgDemo.addGlow("Color(255, 255, 0, 0)",50,25);
}
```

The `addImage()` method uses the `addImageObject()` method of the `g:background` protocol to add an image dynamically:

```
// Remove all image and text elements added to the background since load.
function removeElements()
{
    imgBackground.removeObjects();
}
```

The `removeElements` method uses the `removeObjects` method of the `g:background` protocol.

More in information on these graphic protocols can be found at http://msdn2.microsoft.com/en-us/library/bb508512(VS.85).aspx

---

CAUTION

When you are using Visual Studio to create HTML pages, by default Visual Studio adds the `DOCTYPE` and `xmlns` attributes in the `<HTML>` element. Make sure to remove those before testing for gadget protocols. Your HTML code should look like the following:

```
<html><head> <title>My Gadget </title></head>...
```

Contrast this with the default HTML page as generated by Visual Studio:

```
<!DOCTYPE html PUBLIC "-//W3C//DTD XHTML 1.0 Transitional//EN"
"http://www.w3.org/TR/xhtml1/DTD/xhtml1-transitional.dtd">
<html xmlns="http://www.w3.org/1999/xhtml" >
<head> <title> My Gadget </title></head>...
```

The next section shows you how to create a transparent PNG file in Adobe Photoshop.

Creating a Transparent PNG File in Photoshop

Because all the images used in a gadget are typically transparent PNG images, let's create one in Adobe Photoshop, specifically an `icon.png` for the gadget which is used in Chapter 5.

1. Open Photoshop and click on File, New, and configure it according to the specifications shown in Figure A.7.

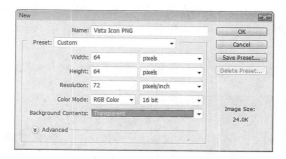

FIGURE A.7   The settings shown here create a 64×64–pixel transparent image.

2. Zoom the image to 400% and then select the Rounded Rectangle tool shown in Figure A.8.

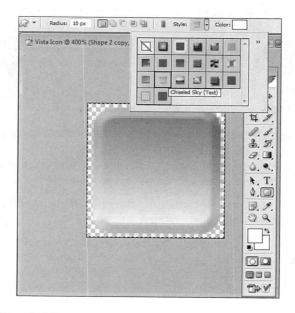

FIGURE A.8   The Rounded Rectangle tool, which created the oval rectangle, is selected in the toolbar. The chiseled sky pattern gives a sky color; play around with other combinations and shades.

3. Your background of the icon is ready; now open the image that you want as a foreground of the icon in a separate window. Make sure that the image's width and
   height are each less than 64 pixels.

4. Make a copy of the image layer by pressing Ctrl+A to select the entire image. Now
   go to File, New Image, and click on Ctrl+C to copy there. Now you should see the
   image in two layers. The background layer is blank and the foreground layer is the
   image.

5. In the foreground image, use the Polygonal Lasso tool to select the capture edges of
   the image.

6. Right-click on the selection and click on Select Inverse (see Figure A.9).

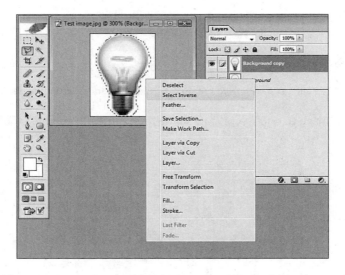

FIGURE A.9   After cropping the image using the Lasso tool, make the background invisible.

7. Press the Delete key and make sure that the background layer is invisible by clicking
   the eye icon in the Layers tab beside the background layer.

8. Drag the layer to the window containing the original shape and save it as a Vista
   icon, using the .png format (see Figure A.10).

Now that you've seen one way of creating a transparent icon or a PNG image with Adobe
Photoshop, the next thing to learn is how to create the shadow/outer edge for the gadget
background image.

FIGURE A.10   Here you have a transparent icon to use for a gadget.

Creating Outer Edges/Shadow Effects in Photoshop

The gadget background image supports translucent edges or what is called a *shadow effect*. This gives the gadget a rich and sophisticated look. This can be achieved with the gadget protocol (refer to the section "Sample Gadget g:Demo," where you added shadow effects using the addShadow method with the g:background protocol), but for those who want to get their hands dirty, here is one way of doing it in Photoshop.

You can achieve this effect in Photoshop by using the Layer style, as shown in the following steps. Note that the maximum width of the docked image needs to be 130 pixels, so you need to account for the shadow, which should be 2 pixels wide on the left and 3 pixels wide on the right. Let's begin.

1. Take an image with width equal to 130 pixels minus 5 pixels—that is, 125 pixels. Open it in Photoshop. This example uses the default image, without shadow, for the Currency gadget (see Figure A.11).

FIGURE A.11   Here is how a docked gadget looks with shadow (left) and without shadow (right).

2. Go to the Image menu and select Canvas Size. Increase the canvas size width and height by 5 pixels, as shown in Figure A.12.

3. Go to the Layer menu and select Layer Style. Click on Drop Shadow. The configuration, shown in Figure A.13, creates a shadow of 3 pixels along the right side of the image and a similar shadow effect at the bottom.

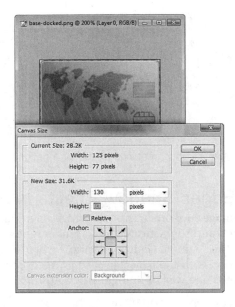

FIGURE A.12   Increasing the canvas size by five pixels accommodates the shadow.

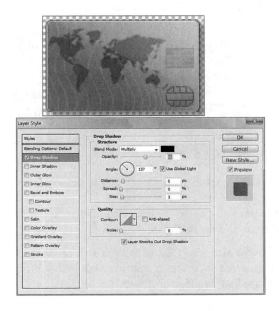

FIGURE A.13   This creates a 3-pixel shadow on the right and bottom side of the gadget background image.

4. Select Outer Glow for 2 pixels of shadow on the left and top, as shown in Figure A.14.

FIGURE A.14   To create a shadow on the left and top, use the Outer Glow effect, with the size set to 2 pixels.

5. Save the file as a PNG format and you are finished. You can see the results in Figure A.15.

FIGURE A.15   The background PNG image has now both a 3-pixel shadow in the right and 2-pixel shadow in the left.

Note that the gadget design specification needs a limit to the width of its shadow to the right and left. However, to give a proper shadow effect to the gadget background, top and bottom also uses two and three pixels shadows, respectively.

This is one way of creating shadows; if you don't have Photoshop; try downloading Paint.NET, which gives similar options to create a shadow. Visit http://www.getpaint.net/ for a free download.

Security and Other Resources

Gadget security is a big concern in the community because many gadgets can easily be written to introduce vulnerabilities to the user's computer. A gadget can contain a script that executes locally and that can access local files and folders. Gadgets run in Explorer's Local Machine Zone. This zone does not appear in Internet Explorer's security tab but does exist as a fifth security zone. Administrators can edit the settings of this zone by modifying the Registry.

Security settings for all users on the machine are in the Registry at the following location:

HKEY_LOCAL_MACHINE\Software\Microsoft\Windows\CurrentVersion\Internet Settings\Zones\0

By default, scripts in the Local Machine Zone can create instances of local ActiveX controls and download data across domains. Gadgets can do this also but with one limitation: Gadgets cannot download and install *new* ActiveX controls. The User Account Control (UAC) in Windows Vista prevents gadgets from running with administrative privileges.

For more information on Vista Security, visit Windows Vista Sidebar Security at http://msdn2.microsoft.com/en-us/library/aa965881.aspx.

To avoid these security concerns keep the following in mind:

- **Avoid using ActiveX controls**   in your gadget. The end user may not be comfortable if your gadget uses or installs an ActiveX control. If your gadget needs to access the local machine's resources, use the Windows Management and Instrumentation (WMI) API to query and access information. WMI is very powerful and can return detailed information about hardware devices and software processes. This was discussed in Chapter 2, "The Architecture." As well as used extensively in Chapter 10, "Most Recently Used .NET Projects—An Application Gadget."

  Keep in mind, however, that with Vista's User Account Control, a gadget lacks administrative access and might not be able to use the full capability of the WMI API. See "User Account Control and WMI" at http://msdn2.microsoft.com/en-gb/library/aa826699.aspx and "Inspect Your Gadget" at http://msdn2.microsoft.com/en-us/library/bb498012.aspx for a list of guidelines.

- **Use signed certificates**   to ensure that the gadget is coming from the right source. You saw in Chapter 8, in the section "CAB File Approach," how a certificate can be used to digitally sign a gadget. Remember, though, that this assures 100% authenticity only if the certificate is from a trusted authority such as Thawte or VeriSign.

- **Use Windows Live Gallery**   for gadget deployment. After the gadget is ready for distribution, consider hosting it with Windows Live Gallery at http://gallery.live.com. Windows Live Gallery regularly monitors gadgets hosted by the website and checks for security issues. This has two benefits: First, the gadget is exposed to millions of users; second, the user relies on the website and has greater confidence in the Live Gallery website than in an independent gadget provider.

Protecting Your Code

Gadgets are HTML, CSS, and JavaScript files, along with some images, all zipped together. So, the source of the gadget goes with the gadget. You may therefore be concerned about the intellectual property of the code in the gadget.

The best way to secure your intellectual property is to protect the code—that is, the JavaScript file.

Here are two of the methods you can use for that:

- **JavaScript Compressors**—These are algorithms that typically reduce the JavaScript file size by half by removing all the whitespace and comments. Some algorithms can obfuscate the function names to reduce the size of the file and the readability of the script. The algorithm is not meant for true obfuscation, but the process makes the code look messy and, in a way, makes it difficult for an outsider to understand.

  One such compressor, made by Douglas Crockford, is JsMin, which you can find at http://fmarcia.info/jsmin/test.html. There is another that comes with the DOJO toolkit. This one can be found at http://www.dev411.com/dojo/javascript_compressor/.

- **JavaScript Obfuscators**—These are algorithms that convert scripts into a highly mangled and obfuscated form. This makes them extremely difficult to study, analyze, reuse, and rework while retaining the functionality of the original code. They also hide the structure (control flow, division into subroutines and classes) of the script completely.

The disadvantage of a JavaScript obfuscator algorithm is that it might not be completely accurate, so test the obfuscated code or use a commercial obfuscator. Personally, I find the JavaScript compressor JSMin good enough for the purpose.

Gadgets in an Enterprise (Accessing SQL Server)

Gadgets can also be effectively used as supplements to enterprise-level applications. You saw in Chapter 9, "Site Statistics Gadget with AJAX—An Information Gadget," how gadgets can be used to access web services. Let's see how a gadget can access a local or remote SQL Server database.

Note that the database connection object `adodb.connection` is an ActiveX control that needs to be already installed in the client machine. Here is sample code for accessing a table in a local or remote database:

```
Function AccessSQLServer(databaseSource, databaseName, username, passWord)
{
var gadgetSqlConnection = new ActiveXObject("adodb.connection");
gadgetSqlConnection.open("Provider=sqloledb;Data Source="
       + databaseSource+ ";Initial Catalog="+databaseName+";User
       Id="+userName+";Password="+passWord+";");
var gQuery ="select * from TableName";
var gadgetRecordSet = gadgetSqlConnection SqlConnection.Execute(gQuery);var result
➥= "";
 while (gadgetRecordSet.eof == false)
   {
```

```
        result = result + gadgetRecordSet (1) + "<br>";
        gadgetRecordSet.moveNext();
    }
  gadgetContent.innerHTML = result;
}
```

The function takes databaseSource, databaseName, and the username and password as parameters, creates an instance of the database connection, and opens it with the parameters provided. The gadgetgRecordset object then queries the database with the query provided in the gadgetgQuery variable.

Here is another example of a gadget that access Microsoft Dynamics, http://www.codeproject.com/KB/gadgets/DynamicsCRMGadget.aspx.

Resources and References

For more resources and information, you can visit http://www.innovatewithgadgets.com/Extra/Gadget-Links-Used.htm. There you will find all the links and references used in this book.

Extras

"Now this is not the end. It is not even the beginning of the end. But it is, perhaps, the end of the beginning."

Sir Winston Churchill

Reusable Framework for Creating Gadgets

The Web-based companion materials for this book located at www.innovatewithgadgets.com include a gadget framework that has all the required files to get you started on your first gadget. The project template, `Innovate.Gadget`, can be used in two different ways:

- Use the Source Innovate.gadget folder as your gadget directory.

- Add `Innovate.gadget.zip` to the Project Template folder of Visual Studio.

To add the file `Innovate.gadget.zip` as one of the project templates, copy it to C:\Users\[*username*]\Documents\ Visual Studio 2005\Templates\ProjectTemplates. This assumes that Visual Studio is installed in your C: drive; otherwise use, the installation drive. If you are using Visual Studio Express or Visual Studio 2008, look for the Project Template folder and copy the zip file there. After it is added, you can see the project template while creating a new website, as shown in Figure B.1.

Among the files you'll find at this book's website are individual image files and assets that you can use in your gadgets, as shown in Figure B.2.

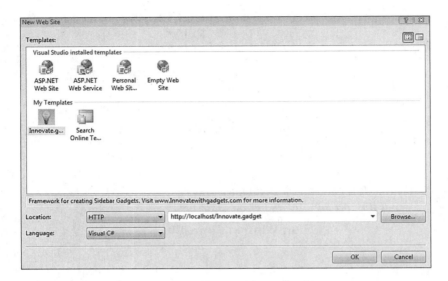

FIGURE B.1   The gadget template as it appears in the New Web Site dialog box in Visual Studio 2005.

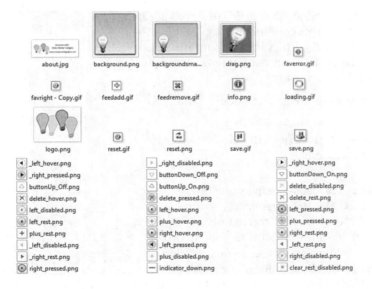

FIGURE B.2   Additional images for creating gadgets.

I have also added the certificate InnovateWithGadgets.cer that can be used to sign your gadgets. More details about signing your gadgets can be found in Chapter 8, "Debugging and Deploying a Gadget."

Sample Gadgets Based on the Framework

When I first created the gadget framework used throughout this book, I was surprised how easily I was able to create a gadget with almost any idea. As an example, I have included these three fun gadgets:

- Widget-Box Gadget

- Comic-Strip Gadget

- Trick-of-Mind Gadget

> **NOTE**
>
> These gadgets are provided for educational purposes only.

These three gadgets are each detailed in the following sections, including screenshots to give you a glimpse of what they look like. As with the rest of this book's online contents, you can find more information at www.innovatewithgadgets.com.

The Widget-Box Gadget

The Widget-Box Gadget displays feeds from the website http://widget-box.blogspot.com/. You can select from numerous web widgets, games, and videos designed to be accessible live on web pages, blogs, and even your Vista Sidebar. Figure B.3 shows the Widget-Box Sidebar Gadget hosting a SpringWidget.

FIGURE B.3   The Widget-Box Gadget, displaying a SpringWidget.

Here is a list of web widgets supported by the Widget-Box Gadget:

- Google gadgets for your web page

- Flickr Slideshow badge

- Yahoo! web widgets

- Yourminis web widgets

- SpringWidget

- Ebay "To Go" widget

- Amazon widget

- Soapbox/YouTube videos

- And more

To share a widget with everyone, go to www.blogger.com and log in, using the following information:

> Username: widgetboxgadget@gmail.com
>
> Password: SidebarGadget

Create a new post and add the widget as shown in Figure B.4.

FIGURE B.4   Add the widget code in the description and check Preview; the figure shows the eBay "To Go" Widget in preview mode with dimension.

After it has been added, the widget automatically shows up in the gadget. The dimension at the end of the widget title is used exclusively by the Sidebar gadget, so add the dimension in the format you want displayed (WxH). In Figure B.4, it is 355×300.

To create a personalized version of the gadget, create a blog at www.blogger.com with posts for widgets you want to add and change the widget feed in the Settings page from http://feeds.feedburner.com/Widget-Box to your own feed. Don't forget to share the gadget with everyone at www.innovatewithgadgets.com.

The Comic-Strip Gadget

The second gadget I created was based on multiple feeds for comic strips (see Figure B.5). It's a fun gadget that's well worth trying out.

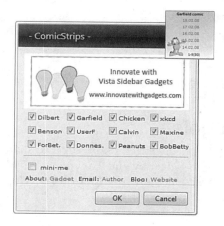

FIGURE B.5   Setting the Comic-Strip feed options.

The Trick-of-Mind Gadget

Finally, there is the gadget I created for my personal website, www.trickofmind.com. Figure B.6 shows the Trick-of-Mind Gadget in action.

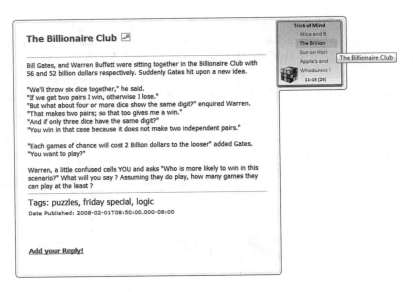

The Billionaire Club 🖼

Bill Gates, and Warren Buffett were sitting together in the Billionaire Club with 56 and 52 billion dollars respectively. Suddenly Gates hit upon a new idea.

"We'll throw six dice together," he said.
"If we get two pairs I win, otherwise I lose."
"But what about four or more dice show the same digit?" enquired Warren.
"That makes two pairs; so that too gives me a win."
"And if only three dice have the same digit?"
"You win in that case because it does not make two independent pairs."

"Each games of chance will cost 2 Billion dollars to the looser" added Gates.
"You want to play?"

Warren, a little confused calls YOU and asks "Who is more likely to win in this scenario?" What will you say ? Assuming they do play, how many games they can play at the least ?

Tags: puzzles, friday special, logic
Date Published: 2008-02-01T08:50:00.000-08:00

Add your Reply!

Trick of Mind
Alice and B
The Billion
Sun on Hori
Apple's and
Whodunnit !
11-15 (25)

The Billionaire Club

FIGURE B.6   Trick-of-Mind gadget in action.

Share Your Gadgets

If you use the framework to create a gadget, don't forget to share it with us. I would be delighted to see it. Send me the gadget by email at connectrajesh@hotmail.com. I will post it at www.innovatewithgadget.com/extras for other developers to use, review, rate, and comment on.

Now, go innovate!

Index

G

J - K - L

How can we make this index more useful? Email us at indexes@samspublishing.com

How can we make this index more useful? Email us at indexes@samspublishing.com

How can we make this index more useful? Email us at indexes@samspublishing.com

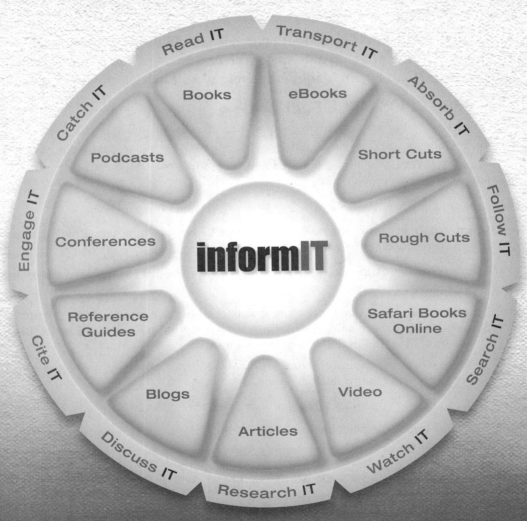

LearnIT at InformIT

Go Beyond the Book

11 WAYS TO LEARN IT at **www.informIT.com/learn**

The digital network for the publishing imprints of Pearson Education